bell hooks's Radical Pedagogy

Also Available from Bloomsbury

Pedagogy, Politics and Philosophy of Peace,
edited by Carmel Borg and Michael Grech
Critical Education in International Perspective, Peter Mayo and Paolo Vittoria
Transnational Feminist Politics, Education, and Social Justice,
edited by Silvia Edling and Sheila Macrine
Capitalism, Pedagogy, and the Politics of Being, Noah De Lissovoy
Critical Human Rights, Citizenship, and Democracy Education,
edited by Michalinos Zembylas and André Keet
Education, Equality and Justice in the New Normal,
edited by Inny Accioly and Donaldo Macedo
A Pedagogy of Faith, Irwin Leopando
Wonder and Education, Anders Schinkel

bell hooks's Radical Pedagogy

New Visions of Feminism, Justice, Love, and Resistance in the Classroom

Edited by Megan Feifer, Maia L. Butler,
and Joanna Davis-McElligatt

BLOOMSBURY ACADEMIC
LONDON • NEW YORK • OXFORD • NEW DELHI • SYDNEY

BLOOMSBURY ACADEMIC
Bloomsbury Publishing Plc, 50 Bedford Square, London, WC1B 3DP, UK
Bloomsbury Publishing Inc, 1359 Broadway, New York, NY 10018, USA
Bloomsbury Publishing Ireland, 29 Earlsfort Terrace, Dublin 2, D02 AY28, Ireland

BLOOMSBURY, BLOOMSBURY ACADEMIC and the Diana logo
are trademarks of Bloomsbury Publishing Plc

First published in Great Britain 2025

Cover design by Grace Ridge
Cover photographs by Gloria Watkins, Copyright © Gloria Watkins. Reprinted by
permission of The Estate of Gloria Watkins, aka bell hooks. All Rights Reserved.
Other cover images: dmilovanovic, Tolga TEZCAN and alubalish via Getty Images

A catalogue record for this book is available from the British Library.

A catalog record for this book is available from the Library of Congress.

ISBN: HB: 978-1-3504-4158-3
         PB: 978-1-3504-4159-0
         ePDF: 978-1-3504-4161-3
         eBook: 978-1-3504-4160-6

Typeset by Integra Software Services Pvt. Ltd.

For product safety related questions contact productsafety@bloomsbury.com.

To find out more about our authors and books visit www.bloomsbury.com
and sign up for our newsletters.

to bell

and to each and every one of us who read and teach and struggle with and practice her pedagogies in our daily lives and classrooms and communities

may we continue your work of imagining that another world is possible, and remember that we can be transformational—each and every one of us—in its becoming

Contents

Figures

Table

Contributors

Hazel T. Biana is Professor of Philosophy at De La Salle University, Manila, Philippines, where she teaches Women in Philosophy, Feminist Philosophy, and Ethics courses. She is also Research Fellow at the Southeast Asia Research Center and Hub, and the previous Vice President of the Philosophical Association of the Philippines. Aside from engaging with bell hooks's works, she is also interested in the philosophy of place.

Kosha D. Bramesfeld is Associate Professor, Teaching Stream, in the Department of Psychology at the University of Toronto Scarborough (UTSC). She directs the UTSC Authentic Learning Lab (ALL) where she works in partnership with undergraduate students and community leaders to advance authentic teaching and research practices. She teaches courses in social and community psychology, the psychology of prejudice and oppression, and research methods. She was a 2021 recipient of UTSC Assistant Professor Teaching Award.

Maia L. Butler is Associate Professor of African American Literature at the University of North Carolina Wilmington, where she is also Affiliate Faculty in Women's and Gender Studies and Africana Studies. She is a literary geographer researching and teaching in African American/Diasporic, Anglophone Postcolonial, and American (broadly conceived) studies, with an emphasis on Black women's literature and feminist theories. She is co-editor of a volume titled *Narrating History, Home, and Dyaspora: Critical Essays on Edwidge Danticat* (University Press of Mississippi 2022), and has chapters in *Bloomsbury Handbook to Edwidge Danticat* (Bloomsbury 2021), *Approaches to Teaching the Work of Edwidge Danticat* (Routledge 2019), and *Revisiting the Elegy in the Black Lives Matter Era* (Routledge 2019). She has collaborative work in a colloquium section of *Frontiers: A Journal of Women's Studies* called "Sowing the Seeds: Decolonial Practices and Pedagogies" (September 2020) and an article in *College Literature*: "Blogging Race, Blogging Nation: Digital Diaspora as Home in Chimamanda Ngozi Adichie's *Americanah*" (2022). She is Co-founding Vice President of the Edwidge Danticat Society.

María Heysha Carrillo Carrasquillo is a doctoral candidate in the Department of Teacher Education and Learning Sciences at North Carolina State University. Her research interests incorporate critical and decolonial pedagogies in community spaces, multilingual education, and educator preparation. María Heysha was a graduate researcher in the Literacy and Community Initiative at the Friday Institute for Educational Innovation. In this role, she worked closely with historically marginalized youth, informing and adapting tools so they could amplify their voices by writing and publishing their stories and testimonios.

Crystal Chen Lee is Associate Professor of English Language Arts at North Carolina State University. Her research lies at the nexus of teacher education, literacy, community engagement, and marginalized youth. Crystal is the founder and director of The Literacy and Community Initiative, a university community partnership that amplifies student voices through student publication, advocacy, and leadership. She received her Ed.D. from Teachers College, Columbia University. She recently co-authored a book entitled *Amplifying Youth Voices through Critical Literacy and Positive Youth Development: The Potential of University-Community Partnerships*.

Dr. Rev. Natalie Coe has taught for nearly twenty years at Green Mountain College in Poultney, VT. As a professor she has created a variety of highly engaging courses in biology, chemistry, psychology, and religion and regularly developed and delivered courses within the institution's environmental liberal arts core. Natalie has also worked at the Long Trail School, an International Baccalaureate high school in Dorset, VT, as a chemistry teacher and as the social justice academic curriculum coordinator. She was ordained as an interfaith minister by One Spirit Learning Alliance in NYC in 2017 and appointed Associate Minister of the First Congregational Church of Fair Haven, VT, in 2021. She received her Ph.D. in Biochemistry from the University of Minnesota (1999) and her BS in Chemistry from the University of Vermont (1991). Her scientific articles, creative nonfiction, and poems have appeared in a variety of journals including *Forests, Conservation Genetics, Writing for Education, Her Words*, and in books/collections, such as *Nature and Culture in the Northern Forest* and *the Encyclopedia of Life Sciences*. She is now an MFA candidate at the University of North Carolina in creative writing.

Nicole Crevar is Visiting Assistant Professor of Multiethnic Literatures at Miami University of Ohio. Her research interests include contemporary multiethnic American literature, madwomen and mad studies, trauma theory, and neoliberalism. She served as the Graduate Co-Director of Wildcat Writers, a college-pathway, community-engagement program that partners Title I high school students with University of Arizona writing students. She has a co-edited collection titled *The Madwoman in Social Justice Movements, Literatures, and Art* (Vernon Press).

Jade Da Costa is a sociologist, community organizer, creative writer, and educator across Central Southern Ontario. Da Costa has a Ph.D. in sociology from York University and is currently working as Banting Postdoctoral Fellow at the University of Guelph, in affiliation with Re•Vision: The Centre for Art and Social Justice. Their research, organizing, art, and teaching all converge on topics of social justice movements; anti-racism, decolonization, and intersectionality; qualitative, digital, and arts-based methods; and critical and engaged pedagogy. To learn more about Da Costa's work, please visit www.jadecrimson.com.

Joanna Davis-McElligatt is Assistant Professor of Black Literary and Cultural Studies at the University of North Texas, where she is Affiliate Faculty in Women's and Gender Studies, and LGBTQ Studies. Her first monograph, entitled Black Aliens: Kinship in the Cosmic Diaspora, is forthcoming from The Ohio State University Press. She is the co-editor of three volumes: *Narratives of Marginalized Identities in Higher Education: Inside and Outside the Academy* (Routledge 2019), *Narrating History, Home, and Dyaspora: Critical Essays on Edwidge Danticat* (University Press of Mississippi 2022), and *BOOM! Splat!: Comics and Violence* (University Press of Mississippi 2024). Her scholarly work appears or is forthcoming in *south: a scholarly journal, Mississippi Quarterly, The Cambridge Companion to New Faulkner Studies* (Cambridge University Press 2022), *The Cambridge Companion to the American Graphic Novel* (forthcoming, Cambridge University Press), *A History of the Literature of the U.S. South* (Cambridge University Press 2021), *Routledge Companion to Literature of the U.S. South* (Routledge 2022), and *Small Screen Souths: Region, Identity, and the Cultural Politics of Television* (LSU Press, 2017), among other places. Her work on comics has appeared in *The Comics Journal, Snapshots: Teaching Love and Rockets* (forthcoming 2023), *Graphic Novels for Children and Young Adults* (University of Mississippi Press, 2017), and *The Comics of Chris Ware: Drawing Is a Way of Thinking* (University of Mississippi Press 2010). She is the illustrator for *Educating for Social Justice: Field Notes from Rural Communities* (Brill/Sense 2020). Her areas of teaching and research include Africana studies, critical race and ethnic studies, literary theory, women's, gender, and sexuality studies, comics studies, southern studies, and twentieth- and twenty-first-century US literary studies. She is currently serving as Member at Large for the William Faulkner Society, and is the Immediate Past President of the Comics Studies Society.

Caitlin M. Donovan is Assistant Director of and Faculty in the Master of Arts in Teaching Program at Duke University. She earned her doctorate in Teacher Education and Learning Sciences at North Carolina State University, where she worked in community-based organizations and with pre-service teachers to develop critical literacy practices. Her research interests center on critical digital literacies, critical memetics, writing communities, and teacher preparation. You can find her work in *English Education, Critical Memetic Literacies in English Education, Better Practices: Experts Explain How They Teach Writing Online*, and *Genders, Cultures & Literacies: Understanding Intersecting Identities* and in public scholarship venues.

Patti Duncan is Professor of Women, Gender, and Sexuality Studies at Oregon State University, where she specializes in women of color feminisms, transnational feminisms, and queer studies. She is the author of *Tell This Silence: Asian American Women Writers and the Politics of Speech*; co-editor of *Mothering in East Asian Communities: Politics and Practices*; co-editor of *Women's Lives around the World: A Global Encyclopedia*, and co-editor of *Women Worldwide: Transnational Feminist Perspectives* (2nd ed.). Her work has appeared in *Women's Studies Quarterly; Frontiers: A Journal of Women's Studies; Qualitative Inquiry; Atlantis: Critical Studies in Gender, Culture, & Social Justice; The Journal of the Motherhood Initiative for Research and Community Involvement*, and many book collections. Since 2016, she has served as the editor of *Feminist Formations*.

Megan Feifer is Assistant Professor of African American Literature at Berea College. Her research and teaching interests focus on the counter-narratives and counter-archives contemporary African American/Diasporic writers produce in response to what Anne McClintock terms the "official ghosting," or inability/ unwillingness of nations to confront and account for the "past." She is the author of the article "The Remembering of Bones: Working through Trauma and the Counter-Archive in Edwidge Danticat's *The Farming of Bones*" and co-editor of *Narrating, History, Home, and Dyaspora: Critical Essays on Edwidge Danticat*, University Press of Mississippi (2022). She also has work in *The Bloomsbury Handbook to Edwidge Danticat* (2021) and *Revisiting the Elegy in the Black Lives Matter Era* (2019). She is Co-Founder of the Edwidge Danticat Society and co-creator of the bell hooks digital archive project, a digital repository of select artifacts from the bell hooks papers currently housed in the Special Collections and Archives of Berea College.

Alyssa Garcia, a first-generation Dominican-Cuban Latinx scholar, received her PhD in Anthropology from the University of Illinois, Urbana-Champaign. She currently serves as a Weinberg College Adviser and Assistant Professor of Instruction in Gender & Sexuality Studies Program at Northwestern University. Her teaching and research interests include Latin American & Caribbean Studies, Ethnic-Latinx Studies, Intersectionality, Critical Race Theory, Feminist Ethnography, Feminist Pedagogy, African Diaspora Studies, and Applied Anthropology. Dr. Garcia's research examines the intersections of race, gender, and sexuality in Cuba through an analysis of discourses of sex-work and the body. Her current project is a historically grounded ethnography that traces chronologically the public supervision and state regulation of Black female bodies in Cuba. Her selected publications include "Federada Testimonios On the Ground: Revealing the Gendered Limits in Operationalizing the Cuban Revolution's Campaign Against Prostitution" *Meridians* (2020); "Continuous Moral Economies: The State Regulation of Bodies and Sex-Work in Cuba," *Sexualities* (2010); "Situating Race, Navigating Belonging: Mapping Afro-Cuban Identities in the U.S.," *Latina/o Research Review* (2009); and "Counter-Stories of Race and Gender: Situating the Experiences of Latinas in the Academy," *Latino Studies Journal* (2005).

Savannah Geidel is Writing Lecturer at North Carolina State University. In her courses, she often employs place-based pedagogies to help students bridge the gap between their public and private lives. As an educator, her goal is to make writing and reading relevant, accessible, and meaningful for students by connecting academia to students' lived experiences. Savannah's current research focuses on connections to and perceptions of place.

Judelysse Gomez was born and raised in the Washington Heights neighborhood of NYC and is the daughter of immigrant parents from the Dominican Republic. The philosophy informing Dr. Gomez's work centers on the understanding that individuals' experiences are influenced by the contexts in which they are embedded. Her experiences both personal and professional have informed her passion for antiracist social justice, empowerment, and liberation. This cuts across her clinical, research, and consultation work, as well as her mentoring and teaching. Dr. Gomez has recently transitioned out of the tenure-track assistant professoriate and is focused on pursuing her passion for clinical, research, and community-based practices that are trauma informed and liberation focused.

Beverly Guy-Sheftall is Founding Director of the Women's Research and Resource Center (1981) and Anna Julia Cooper Professor of Women's Studies at Spelman College. For many years, she was Visiting Professor at Emory University's Institute for Women's Studies where she taught graduate courses in women's studies. At the age of sixteen, she entered Spelman College where she majored in English and minored in secondary education. After graduating with honors, she attended Wellesley College for a fifth year of study in English. In 1968, she entered Atlanta to pursue a master's degree in English; her thesis was entitled, "Faulkner's Treatment of Women in His Major Novels." A year later she began her first teaching job in the Department of English at Alabama State University in Montgomery, Alabama. In 1971, she returned to her alma mater Spelman College and joined the English Department. She has published a number of texts within African American and women's studies which have been noted as seminal works by other scholars, including the first anthology on Black women's literature, *Sturdy Black Bridges: Visions of Black Women in Literature* (Doubleday, 1980), which she co-edited with Roseann P. Bell and Bettye Parker Smith; her dissertation, *Daughters of Sorrow: Attitudes toward Black Women, 1880–1920* (Carlson, 1991); *Words of Fire: An Anthology of African American Feminist Thought* (New Press, 1995); an anthology she co-edited with Rudolph Byrd entitled *Traps: African American Men on Gender and Sexuality* (Indiana University Press, 2001); a book coauthored with Johnnetta Betsch Cole, *Gender Talk: The Struggle for Women's Equality in African American Communities* (Random House, 2003); an anthology, *I Am Your Sister: Collected and Unpublished Writings of Audre Lorde*, co-edited with Rudolph P. Bryd, Johnnetta B. Cole, and Guy-Sheftall (Oxford University Press, 2009); an anthology, *Still Brave: The Evolution of Black Women's Studies* (Feminist Press, 2010), with Stanlie James and Frances Smith Foster. Her most recent publication (SUNY Press, 2010) is an anthology co-edited with Johnnetta B. Cole, *Who Should Be First: Feminists Speak out on the 2008 Presidential Campaign*. In 1983, she became founding co-editor of *Sage: A Scholarly Journal of Black Women*, which was devoted exclusively to the experiences of women of African descent. She is Past President of the National Women's Studies Association (NWSA) and was elected to the American Academy of Arts and Sciences in 2017.

Erin Hipple is a white, queer, nonbinary, disabled, and neurodivergent person who is also an educator, healer, and qualitative researcher. Their background is in social work, psychology, music, theater, and writing. Erin's interests include exploring resilience in LGBTQIA+ identities and alternative sexuality communities, the power of storytelling, radical embodiment, and exploring (individual + collective) healing through liberation-based frames. Their teaching, therapy, and research are informed (as much as is possible within the constraints of the systems in which they are required to operate) by intersectionality, mad praxis, disability justice, and transformative justice. Erin seeks to cultivate therapeutic and educational spaces that center action through an ethic of care, the inclusion of all bodies, creativity, and (somatic + emotional) self-reflection in the collective pursuit of sustainable futures.

Charisse S. Iglesias received her Ph.D. in Rhetoric, Composition, and the Teaching of English at the University of Arizona. Prior to graduate school, she was a Peace Corps Volunteer in Indonesia where she collaborated with Indonesian schools, universities, and organizations to manage community-funded career development and youth leadership events. Dr. Iglesias continued her commitment to community-engaged practice in her doctoral studies with her research on critical service-learning, practitioner training, and organizational structures. In practice, she co-directed the University of Arizona college-pathway community writing program, Wildcat Writers, that partners Title I high school classrooms with the University of Arizona writing classrooms to collaborate on community-responsive writing projects. Her dissertation research provides a structural model that triangulates community engagement through a reciprocity lens by looking at three different domains—administration, training, and teaching—and is informed by accountability. Currently, Dr. Iglesias is Training and Resource Director with public health nonprofit, Community-Campus Partnerships for Health to create, adapt, and facilitate training workshops for international and US-based researchers and community partners on community engagement issues.

Maxwell Irving has been instructing social sciences courses on the college level since 2003, is a full-time teacher at Tucson High Magnet School, and part-time instructor at Pima Community College. He specialized in cultural anthropology when receiving his M.A. in Religious Studies from the University of Colorado at Boulder in 2006. He is keenly aware that there is an inherent need for culturally relevant and responsive education at every academic level in our current historical moment. He promotes respectful and civil dialogue as him and his students expand their identities and come to an understanding of each others'.

Meika Loe is Professor of Sociology, Women's Studies and LGBTQ Studies at Colgate University in New York, where she teaches courses on Gender and Medicine, Death, Dying, and Grief, and Sociology of the Life Course. She recently coordinated a session for NWSA with Laury Oaks on the feminist pedagogies of bell hooks and Becky Thompson.

Jennifer C. Mann is a Research Scientist in the Center for Child and Family Policy at Duke University. She is focused on designing and testing a professional learning program for teachers that utilizes culturally relevant pedagogies and integrates community cultural wealth into the use of high-impact instructional strategies with multilingual learners. Additionally, Dr. Mann is Adjunct for Duke's Program in Education, where she teaches Instructional Methods for Teaching Multilingual Learners for Master of Arts in Teaching candidates. Dr. Mann has been an educator/teacher educator for seventeen years, having taught high school English, elementary and adult English as a Second Language (ESL), and undergraduate and graduate pre-service teachers. In 2023, she received her Ph.D. in Teacher Education and Learning Sciences from North Carolina State University, where she specialized in Literacy and English Language Arts. Dr. Mann's research interests include multilingual learners, culturally sustaining critical pedagogies, and equity-centered, participatory qualitative methodologies.

Marlaina H. Martin joined the University of Vermont's Department of Anthropology as a Henderson-Harris Postdoctoral Fellow in Fall 2024. Long interested in generative overlaps between identity and cultural production, she explores how Black women and nonbinary media-makers go about envisioning, creating, and sharing projects that challenge, if not wholly reimagine, normalized production models that cast Hollywood—and its promoted economic, cultural, and social structures—as not just standard but ideal. To do so, Martin intentionally looks to spaces and communities of independent media production—particularly photography, film, video, and social media content creation—to center the voices, experiences, and aspirations of these often-marginalized people in the contexts they have chosen to enter, if not build themselves. Martin's mixed-methods approach combines participant observation, content analysis, formal and semi-formal interviewing, archival research, and cyberethnography. Through research flexible in its theoretical and methodological pathways, Martin asks: "How does education in and access to media technologies enable different Black feminist (re)imaginings of self, social circle, and larger (even future) worlds?" Martin earned her Ph.D. in Anthropology in 2019 and her M.A. in 2015 from Rutgers University, New Brunswick. She also completed a Women's and Gender Studies graduate certificate. She double majored in Anthropology (honors) and American Studies for her B.A. degrees at Brown University in 2011. She has had various fellowships, including the Public Anthropology Postdoctoral Fellowship at *SAPIENS Anthropology Magazine*, a joint Visual Culture Postdoctoral Fellowship with the Phillips Collection art museum and the University of Maryland, College Park's Anthropology Department, and a two-year President's Postdoctoral Fellowship at the University of Maryland, College Park. Finally, Martin has also been published by *Transforming Anthropology, Routledge, The Feminist Wire, OMERTAA, Current Anthropology, Society for Cultural Anthropology*, and PBS.

Bunny McFadden is a Chicana mother who tinkers with words for a living. She's the winner of the 2021 Golden Ox and is published widely in everything from horror and sci-fi anthologies to travel websites like Fodor's. She is a writer, independent education and equity consultant, and language arts educator. Her dissertation focuses on decolonizing pedagogy through autoethnography. As a consultant, she has been published in *SIETAR* and the *Journal of Sustainability Education*. Bunny has been invited to speak at the Leadership in Diversity Conference at the University of Connecticut; the Royal Centre School of Speech and Drama at the University of London; the Assembly for the Teaching of English Grammar; and Women with Resolve Conservation Advocacy's partnership with UNICEF. She has an upcoming chapter in the book *It Takes a Village: Academic Mothers* (2023), as well as a chapter in *Gifted(ish)*, edited by Kaitlin Phillips. Her website is www.docbunny.com.

Charles McMartin is Assistant Professor of English specializing in Composition at Utah State University Tooele. He earned his Ph.D. in Rhetoric, Composition, and the Teaching of English from the University of Arizona. His research focuses on culturally sustaining pedagogies, community writing, student activism, and NextGen faculty and staff leaders. As a former high school English teacher, he advocates for turning the focus of universities toward their local schools and empowering students to become leaders in their communities and professions.

Michelle Mendez is a counseling student and graduate researcher at Arcadia University. She identifies as a Latine/x, disabled, cis-gender female. She is a first-generation college graduate, an older sister, daughter, and friend. Prior to graduate school, Michelle obtained her BS in Psychology with a concentration in neuroscience from the Pennsylvania State University. Throughout her undergraduate career, she assisted in conducting research for the Psychology Department where she observed sexual differences in visual perception. As a graduate researcher for Arcadia's Counseling Department, she assists in conducting research related to multiculturalism, intersectionality, and educational curriculums. In the future, Michelle hopes to integrate collective care with mindfulness and preventative care treatment modalities.

Margarita Raya Mojica is a proud daughter of Mexican immigrants and the first generation in her family to graduate from university. Her undergraduate and graduate degrees are from Western Illinois University. She has taught middle school students in the East Moline School District 37 since 1996, working with English language learners including newly arrived immigrants and refugees. In 2020 she was named as one of ten middle school teachers honored as a Golden Apple Fellow in the state of Illinois. As an Illinois Golden Apple Fellow she was afforded the opportunity to take courses from Northwestern University in the spring of 2021, including Latinx Feminisms. It was her final project for the Latinx Feminisms course that led to the formation of Latinx Workshop at Glenview Middle School in East Moline, Illinois. This year-long, project-based program centers the Latina voice, culture, strength, and untold history. Members of Latinx Workshop are seventh and eighth graders who have given back to their community in numerous ways, including The Dignity Project that has provided discreet pouches with pads in every Glenview Middle School classroom and office for student use and the purchase of over 400 pairs of women's underwear donated to the school for girls who happen to bleed through their underwear at school. They have worked to end the stigma of menstruation for girls!

Nancy Morales is an Indigequeer (Zapotec) feminist scholar-activist, whose research examines Indigenous women and queer youth's self-determination practices to build Indigenous Latinx communities. She is also a co-founder and former advisor of Collective of Pueblos Originarios in Diaspora (CPOD), a student campus organization that heightens the visibility of Indigenous students (Maya, Mixtec and Zapotec) in diaspora at the University of California, Santa Barbara. Her goal is to pursue various forms of scholar activism. For more see https://nancy-morales.com.

Oluwanifemi Olugbemiga was born in Nigeria and raised in the city of Chicago. She completed her B.A. in Africana studies and psychology from Connecticut College and her M.A. in social work from Howard University. Oluwanifemi currently works in the nonprofit space as a youth development director at So What Else Inc. Her direct practice experience in behavioral mental health has influenced her research focus on how the arts continue to be an individual and community healing tool throughout the African diaspora, as well as how the introduction to the arts at an early age can be a tool of teaching social and emotional regulation and help student develop coping skills in the midst of living in inner cities across the DMV. In her personal work, Oluwanifemi is a singer/songwriter based in the District of Columbia, who explores vulnerability and self-awareness through the mediums of contemporary R&B and neo soul genres.

Rachel Panton is Assistant Professor of Writing in the Department of Communication, Media, and the Arts in the Halmos College of Arts and Sciences at Nova Southeastern University. As a writing instructor for more than twenty years, her courses and interests primarily focus on women's narratives of wellness and transformation. Most recently, Dr. Panton served as a guest editor for the University of California, Berkeley's *Race and Yoga Journal*, where she led the publication for "Sassin' through Sadhana," a special volume dedicated to the stories of Black women yoga instructors, inspired by her dissertation research. This work is now becoming a book in her forthcoming edited anthology, *Black Girl's Om Too: Black Women's Bodies & Resistance to the Visual and Narrative Rhetoric of Yoga* (University Press of Mississippi). As a writing coach and editor, Dr. Panton also serves aspiring women authors in Black and Brown communities to write and publish their own stories. Her most recent scholarly work has appeared in *Black Women's Mental Health: Balancing Strength and Vulnerability* (SUNY, 2017) and *New Directions in Teaching and Learning* (Jossey-Bass, 2016). Dr. Panton's latest projects include *Ancestors, Orishas, and Ocean Conservation: The Rhetoric of (Mami) Wata in Afro Diasporic Environmentalist Education in Florida* (co-authored with Dr. Charlene Desir, forthcoming) as well as a co-edited anthology with Funlayo Woods-Menzies entitled, *Calling of the Crowns: Black American Priestess Narratives of Awakening to the Divine Feminine, Divination, Healing, and Spiritual Modalities of Service in African Diasporic Religions* (forthcoming).

Katie B. Peachey is a doctoral candidate in the Literacy and English Language Arts program at North Carolina State University. She previously taught middle school and high school English in central Pennsylvania. Katie currently works as the Literacy and Community Initiative (LCI) site coordinator at CORRAL Riding Academy, a community-based organization that provides holistic equine therapy and educational support to adolescent girls. Her current research interests include humanizing writing instruction, critical literacy, and writing feedback.

Lauren Reid is a biracial/Black and Jewish mother of two littles, stepmother, and wife. She is Associate Professor of Counseling and Director of the Graduate Program in Counseling at Arcadia University. Dr. Reid earned her B.A. in psychology from Loyola University in Maryland, Ed.M. and M.A. in Psychological Counseling from Teachers College, Columbia University, and Ph.D. in Counseling Psychology from the University of Miami. Her research focuses on multicultural training as well as the lived experiences and mental health of Black and biracial people. Dr. Reid is a licensed psychologist; her practice specializes in working with biracial/multiracial people and mothers. In all aspects of her work, Dr. Reid is justice oriented, liberation focused, and anti-oppressive.

Laiba Rizwan is a second year master's student in the neuroscience program at Western University, Canada. As part of her master's thesis, she is currently attempting to examine reliable techniques of quantifying neuromelanin—a proxy marker of dopamine metabolism using MRI scans. She completed her Honours B.Sc. with high distinction in Psychology at the University of Toronto, where she investigated the role of educational games in reducing discrimination. Having worked as a public relations director for a nonprofit organization for people with disabilities, Laiba found herself particularly invested in devising disability awareness tools. To this end, she employed a participatory research design and leaned on voices of lived experience to determine what comprises an effective disability awareness training paradigm. Laiba currently serves as Graduate Teaching Assistant at Western University where she places a huge emphasis on skill-building, critical thinking, and student empowerment. The idea of mentorship—empowering people to think critically and supporting them on their pursuit for self-actualization—appeals to her due to its impact on her academic and personal lives. Laiba credits much of her academic success to her mentors, whose thoughtful mentorship and kind guidance paved the way for her successes and self-growth. In the spirit of paying it forward, she is actively involved in activities related to teaching and learning. In addition, she has participated in various training programs aiming to promote student-centered learning experiences. She also serves as a mentor with the Women in Science Mentorship Program at Western University. Her long-term professional goal is to obtain a research and teaching position in the field of clinical neuroscience and psychology. Laiba is proud to identify as a first-generation Canadian. She is also the first and only female in her family to have traveled internationally for higher education.

Jasjit Sangha is an educational developer in antiracist pedagogies at the University of Toronto. In her current role she brings comprehensive experience to her work with faculty through her background in student development, adult learning, mindfulness, and equity and inclusion. Her knowledge of teaching and learning is also informed by her work as an instructor at the undergraduate and graduate levels, teaching courses in Sociology, and Education. She has also studied the neuroscience of mindfulness and self-compassion, trained with the Search Inside Yourself Leadership Institute, and is completing a two-year Mindfulness Meditation Teacher Certification Program. She brings this lens to her equity work on campus. She has published two books, contributed to edited collections related to teaching diverse classroom and presented at national conferences. She completed her Ph.D. in Adult Education through Ontario Institute for Studies in Education at University of Toronto. She is passionate about cultivating spaces for transformative adult learning and holding spaces for deep dialog about challenges we are facing in education while also cultivating hope and possibility about action and change.

Desireé T. Self is a Black queer writer, performer, and doctoral candidate in Women's, Gender, and Sexuality Studies at Stony Brook University. Desi's general research interests include Black queer studies, Black feminist theory, critical surveillance studies, radical pedagogy, affect, poetry, and embodied research methodology. Currently, Desi is diligently working to build an upper-level undergraduate Black Queer Feminist Methods course which engages key Black feminist and queer Black thinkers in an effort to actively seek to respond to the following singular question throughout: what constitutes a liberatory method? Ultimately, Desi aspires to engage folks on relationships between surveillance, education, and activism that emphasize queer of color critique, Black feminist interventions, and collective organizing however that manifests.

Nicole A. Spigner is Assistant Professor in Black Studies and English at Northwestern University. She has held fellowships with the Alice Kaplan Humanities Center and Woodrow Wilson Institute (now called the Institute for Citizens & Scholars) and completed her Ph.D. at Vanderbilt University. Her manuscript in development, tentatively entitled *Niobe en Noire: Black New Women and Ovidian Transformation*, examines through a Black feminist lens transformation in the figures of the mother, mermaid, and echo in the works of Black New Women classicists. Spigner serves on the boards of *Issues in Critical Investigation* and the *A-Line Journal*. You may find her work in *Flesh of the Matter*, Brill's *Companion to Classical Reception in the Early Americas*, the *A-Line Journal*, and Public Books and is forthcoming in *Race and the Classics* (2025). At Northwestern, she teaches courses on Black feminism, Black classicism, nineteenth-century African American and American literature, the Black Gothic and speculative fiction, and more broadly, women's literature of the African diaspora.

Melanie Taddeo is a passionate advocate for disability rights and inclusion who, at the age of twenty-one, suffered a massive stroke that left her completely paralyzed on her left side and legally blind. After years of therapy, she was able to regain her independence and went on to become the first legally blind teacher to graduate in Ontario. She is a certified special education teacher with over twenty years of experience in program development, fundraising, community outreach, volunteer management, and public speaking. Melanie founded Connect 4 Life and Voices 4 Ability; V4A Radio is based on her personal experience of the lack of programs that promote independence for people with disabilities. She has made it her goal to help empower others to achieve their dreams despite the challenges they face. Melanie has assisted hundreds of people through Connect 4 Life's programs such as the first broadcast training program for individuals with disabilities: "An Accessible voice in Broadcasting," life skills training program, and public speaking. Melanie's passion is evident in everything she does to ensure that each client sees their abilities and not only their disabilities. She has been a Toastmaster for eight years achieving her Distinguished Toastmaster (DTM), was the recipient of Member Making a Difference award (MMAD) in 2020, and is now using her speaking to inspire others across the globe as a champion of inclusion. In addition, she published her first book in

2019, *My Unforeseen Journey Losing Sight Gaining Vision*. Melanie empowers entrepreneurs, professionals, and community leaders to embrace challenges and to overcome unforeseen change with dignity, and ease. Most recently, she has created a company called Gaining Vision, to help promote inclusion across the world, ensuring that every person feels heard, seen, and valued just as they are. Her story is proof that despite adversity success is possible with hard work and perseverance.

Jack Wolcott is an MSW student and researcher at West Chester University of Pennsylvania. Before social work school, Jack got their B.A. in art and psychology at the University of California, Santa Cruz, and worked in the California public school system as an AVID mentor and an after-school art teacher. Their direct service experience includes a peer specialist certification, residential case management, and mobile psychiatric rehabilitation work. Currently, they work as a student intern at Jefferson Hospital in Philadelphia providing DBT therapy, and as a research graduate assistant. In their personal and professional life, Jack aspires for liberation from capitalism and all forms of oppression and envisions a move toward liberatory practices of community care. They hope for a future where they can support social workers in unionizing!

Foreword, by Beverly Guy-Sheftall

[...] dissidents are anchored to revolutionary possibilities that demand both intellectual discipline and irrepressible courage to speak the unspeakable, to stand alone if necessary, and to accept the material and emotional consequences of tramping over hegemony's "holy" ground.

—Antonia Darder[1]

[The] learning process comes easiest to those of us who teach who also believe that there is an aspect of our vocation that is sacred; who believe that our work is not merely to share information but to share in the intellectual and spiritual growth of our students. To teach in a manner that respects and cares for the souls of our students is essential if we are to provide the necessary conditions where learning can most deeply and intimately begin.

—bell hooks[2]

While reading both Antonia Darder's riveting anthology *A Dissident Voice: Essays in Culture, Pedagogy & Power*, and bell hooks's *Radical Pedagogy: New Visions of Feminism, Justice, Love, and Resistance in the Classroom*, I am reminded of teachers, scholars, activists, feminists, colleagues—**dissidents**—who emerged from marginalized/racialized communities in the United States and impacted our intellectual lives in significant ways. None has been more so than bell hooks, with whom I shared a forty-year friendship. It is important, which the co-editors do here, to embrace the dissident women among us, so often maligned and misunderstood. For four decades, bell hooks's dissenting voice, in her writing and teaching, has been loud and unrelenting, beginning with the publication of her first book, *Ain't I a Woman: Black Women and Feminism* (1981) followed by, to name a few, *Feminist Theory: From Margin to Center* (1984), *The Will to Change: Men, Masculinity, and Love* (2004), and *Teaching to Transgress: Education as the Practice of Freedom* (1994). In her May 2014 Commencement speech at Berea College, where she spent the final years of her life, she reminded her audience that "for many years, I ran away from Kentucky. Convinced that there was no place for a radical, wild woman like me to belong here."[3] One of the most prolific and radical contemporary Black feminist scholars/critics, bell hooks's *Talking Back: Thinking Feminist, Thinking Black* (1989) provides a portrait of a dissident Black intellectual whose untimely death at 69 in December 2021 generated perhaps the most commentary that I recall ever having read when a Black woman writer departs. *bell hooks's Radical Pedagogy* is the most compelling, insightful, moving, loving retrospective on her extraordinary pedagogical genius to have emerged among this robust outpouring of praise-songs to bell.

My friendship with Gloria Watkins (she was not yet the now-legendary bell hooks) began at the 1981 National Women's Studies Association (NWSA) conference in Storrs, Connecticut; Audre Lorde delivered a groundbreaking, hard-hitting keynote speech, "The Uses of Anger: Women Responding to Racism," during which she spoke about the racism of white women. This was the same year that the Women's Research & Resource Center at Spelman College was founded. Gloria was promoting her first book, *Ain't I A Woman: Black Women and Feminism.* We shared a dormitory room, talked all night the first day we met—about the whiteness of the women's liberation movement in the United States and NWSA—and continued to talk until her untimely death. I did not realize then why we spent all night that first night talking and why we would continue talking for the next four decades. Later, I came to realize it was our memories of dissident women in our families and our passionate connection to feminist politics. Among the many memories of bell hooks I shared with friends over the past several years, this is my favorite, which I shared with Professor Barbara Ransby.

Loving my feminist friend/comrade for forty years—unconditionally and deeply—enriched my life in ways that I am only now grasping.[4] We gathered at Spelman, Oberlin, the New School and of course Berea College. We talked about books, politics, teaching, shopping, partners, the lives we crafted, the friends we shared, and our dreams and disappointments. When I saw her at her home in Berea on November 25, a few weeks before she died, I thought it might be the last time. I told her I would always love her and her writings.

What I came to cherish about the embrace of my own dissident feminist identity, like the essayists in this powerful anthology, I learned from reading and talking endlessly to Gloria/bell which began that night at NWSA. Like another dissident scholar/activist Angela Davis and the architects of the Combahee River Collective statement, bell hooks emerges from a robust African American Left tradition which is anti-capitalist, anti-imperialist, and critical of patriarchy, wherever it rears its head. Near the beginning of *Talking Back*, bell acknowledges Davis's impact on her as a young, evolving dissident: "'When I was a young soldier for the revolution.' Angela Davis spoke these words. They moved me. I say them here and hope to say them in many places. This is how deeply they touched me—evoking memories of innocence, of initial passionate commitment to political struggle.""[5]

bell hooks's transgressive writings would have a significant impact on my evolving scholarship and pedagogy, as was the case with the extraordinary, diverse community of contributors here. In her first monograph on Black women and feminism, she makes the surprising point that nineteenth-century white female reformers harbored more intense racist attitudes toward Black women than they did toward Black men, which is ironic in light of the "bonds of womanhood" thesis which many other white feminist historians advanced in their attempts to explain alliances between Black and white women in various reform movements. hooks argues that it was fear of contamination and sexual competition that caused white women to resist cooperation with Black women, including in women's mobilizations during the so-called first wave of the women's movement:

> Black men were more accepted in white reform circles than black women. Negative attitudes toward black women were the result of prevailing racist-sexist stereotypes that portrayed black women as morally impure. Many white women felt that their status as ladies would be undermined were they to associate with black women. No such moral stigma was attached to black men. Black male leaders like Frederick Douglass, James Forten […] and others were occasionally welcome in white and social circles […] Given […] the history of white male sexual lust for black females we cannot rule out the possibility that white women were reluctant to acknowledge black women socially for fear of sexual competition […] White women saw black women as a direct threat to their social standing—for how could they be idealized as virtuous, goddess-like creatures if they associated with black women who were seen by the white public as licentious and immoral?[6]

In her second book, *Feminist Theory: From Margin to Center* (1984), now widely used in women's studies classes, there is a hard-hitting analysis of the insensitivity of women's studies programs in the early years to race, class, and ethnicity and a biting critique of racist writings by white feminists: "White women who dominate feminist discourse, who for the most part make and articulate feminist theory, have little or no understanding of white supremacy as a racial politic, of the psychological impact of class, of their political status within a racist, sexist, capitalist state." The publication of this collection of essays could not have emerged at a more critical time, as the excellent introduction underscores, as well. It is clear to me and the progressive scholars and teachers here that Black feminist discourse is the most radical and threatening work that has emerged since the 1970s within the context of African American studies because of its anticapitalist, antiimperialist, anticolonialist, antiheterosexist, antipatriarchal, and antiracist truth-telling with respect to what ails the United States and too many classrooms. I am reminded again of the Combahee River Collective's 1977 "A Black Feminist Statement" in which there is this powerful assertion: "If black women were free, it would mean that everyone else would have to be free since our freedom would necessitate the destruction of all the systems of oppression."

Despite the disturbing and widespread book-banning season in our schools and libraries, it makes sense that Black women's writing, especially Black feminist texts, are under attack, including the feminist work of Kimberlé Crenshaw, Angela Davis, Cathy Cohen, Alice Walker, and bell hooks, to name a few. In the words of African American Policy Forum's (AAPF) "Freedom to Learn" statements in their Open Letter:

> Promoters of this racially extremist agenda have banded together with others across the political spectrum to wage a war against their own invented grievance that they have labeled as "wokeism." They have attacked librarians, surveilled and harassed teachers, canceled classes, banned books, and weaponized the law to forbid ideas, frameworks, and viewpoints in the nation's schools, colleges, and workplaces [...] they broadened their attacks to discredit frameworks that Black women and queer people have produced in order to explain, describe, and transform the conditions of their lives.[7]

Freedom-loving people are certainly indebted to the decades-old work of Black feminist writers and teachers such as bell hooks. This multidimensional collection of reflections on her radical pedagogy is without parallel, and illuminates in different ways the backlash that Black feminist work inside and outside the classroom is facing. This anthology certainly makes visible why radical Black feminists remain the targets of white supremacist advocates because of Black feminists's unrelenting demands for revolutionary action and a new world— messages that are at the center of hooks's pedagogical praxis and discourse.

If I could speak to Gloria one more time, I would tell her what it meant to share a long friendship with a "dissident." Observing her in many classrooms and reading her feminist books, I found it easier to resist stifling gender norms in both my personal and professional lives as they related to appropriate behavior for "good," "lady-like" women. I journeyed to distant and unfamiliar places, wore the clothes I wanted to wear, wrote the books I wanted to write, studied the transgressive Black women I wanted to be like (Lorraine, Alice, Angela,

Audre), took unpopular stances, refused to be quiet in public, risked being misunderstood, chose the friendships and partnerships I desired, and advocated loudly for my passions. Fears I might have harbored about being too aggressive or even the stereotypical "angry Black woman" or gender nonconforming had to be abandoned. I am fortunate to have joined the professoriate and embraced the radical pedagogies she promoted. Like the contributors of this groundbreaking anthology, I am grateful for her example.

Notes

1 Antonia Darder, *A Dissident Voice: Essays on Essays on Culture, Pedagogy, and Power*, new edition (New York: Peter Lang Inc., International Academic Publishers, July 22, 2011).
2 bell hooks, *Teaching to Transgress: Education as the Practice of Freedom* (New York: Routledge, 1994).
3 bell hooks, "bell hooks Where I'm From," Appalachian Women Writers Symposium, Berea, Kentucky, September 9, 2015, 1:02:39, https://berea.access.preservica.com/uncategorized/IO_a5bff444-7799-451a-be54-ac1b0f18076e/.
4 Personal correspondence with Barbara Ransby.
5 bell hooks, *Talking Back: Thinking Feminist, Thinking Black* (Boston, MA: South End Press, 1999), 3.
6 bell hooks, *Ain't I a Woman: Black Women and Feminism* (Boston, MA: South End Press, 1981), 130–1.
7 The African American Policy Forum, "Freedom to Learn," *The African American Policy Forum*, 2023, https://www.aapf.org/freedomtolearn.

Introduction

Megan Feifer, Maia L. Butler, and Joanna Davis-McElligatt

Over the course of her extraordinary life, bell hooks—visionary feminist thinker, cultural critic, and professor—authored an expansive and wide-reaching body of work, including scholarly articles, critical essays, nonfiction, poetry, manifestoes, public scholarship, and literature for children and young adults. Across her *oeuvre*, hooks critiqued what she defined as the imperialist, white-supremacist, capitalist, cis-hetero patriarchy, or those interlocking systems of oppression in opposition to which she framed her analysis of media, literature, art, pedagogy, politics, and culture. In each of hooks's book-length texts—from *Ain't I A Woman: Black Women and Feminism* (1981) to *Uncut Funk: A Contemplative Dialogue* (2018)—she grounded her investigation of transnational feminisms in an engaged pedagogical praxis, and in systems of transformative justice, love, and resistance to antiblackness and toxic masculinities. Both militant and vigilant in her analysis of the power dynamics at play in educational spaces, hooks remained critically hopeful of our collective ability to (re)imagine and (re)create radical spaces of pedagogical, social, and political possibility. It is here where we, following hooks, must also consider what it means to be "radical," to find ourselves working within oppressive systems while simultaneously moving against them, tearing them down, and beginning something new. hooks herself was no stranger to the complexities of and tensions inherent in radical pedagogy—in her life, she moved intentionally between classrooms on Ivy League and community college campuses, public spaces, prisons, high schools, kitchen tables, and living rooms, and consistently discovered ways to do emancipatory work. hooks defined radical pedagogy as the work of "expanding beyond boundaries," essential intellectual, social, and emotional labor that "has made it possible for me to imagine and enact pedagogical practices that engage directly both the concern for interrogating biases in curricula that reinscribe systems of domination (such as racism and sexism) while simultaneously providing new ways to teach diverse groups of students."[1] For that reason, we understand hooks's radical pedagogy to mean a (re)visioning of pedagogical praxis, a working inside and remaining outside, a deliberate moving toward a critical horizon where systems of oppression and harm no longer exist. We are also mindful that the work of radical pedagogy takes place within the teacher-scholar as much as without. hooks calls for teachers to (re)vision the self, to do the work of self-actualization, to respect the bodymindspirit, and to treat education as a sacred, holistic vocation; indeed, as hooks argues, "any radical pedagogy must insist that everyone's presence is acknowledged"—teachers, students, and their communities.[2]

Since hooks's homegoing in 2021, scholars and critics have moved to bring attention to her work, which has become increasingly essential—and imperiled—intellectual labor, particularly in light of the recent removal of her work from the AP College Board curriculum amidst the ongoing national sweep of legislation and policy revisions that have banned "woke" education, and punished educators whose work can be construed under the widely misunderstood banner of critical race theory (CRT). Most recently, as we have seen with the encampment protests at universities across the country formed in response to the destruction of the Palestinian homeland of Gaza, the crackdown on student and faculty political resistance has become militarized, the punishments progressively violent and carceral. Many of us are now witnessing our institutions' administrators cave in to the pressures of Boards of Trustees and state legislatures, who demand that programming be halted and curricula be revised without the input of the faculty who teach the courses or consideration of the national and international accreditation standards of our disciplinary flagship organizations. Furthermore, faculty and staff affinity groups that once offered us space to support each other and organize together are being dismantled as another failure of our administrators to protect us from the overreach of these governing bodies, made up of members who often do not understand the full scope of what our responsibility to serve students and communities must entail. As we prepare ourselves, our students, and our communities to contend with the return of incipient right-wing fascism and oligarchical self-interests to our government, we are gradually more at risk—and yet more motivated than ever before to continue the work of leaning into and learning from hooks's vital wisdom and theorization of the potential of pedagogical spaces to empower, transform, and make space for resistance, love, and justice. This work has never been more pressing.

***

Born in 1952 as Gloria Jean Watkins, bell hooks credited her native place of Hopkinsville, Kentucky—or her "anarchic life of the hills"—with teaching her to be "self-reliant," and her elders with showing her the necessity of community, and the importance of maintaining a connection to one's "cultural legacy."[3] It was in Kentucky where hooks first became aware of what she described as "two competing cultures": "the world of mainstream White supremacist capitalist power and the world of defiant anarchy that championed freedom for everyone. And the way in which that culture of anarchy had distinct anti-racist dimensions accounts for the unique culture of Appalachian Black folks that is rarely acknowledged."[4] hooks learned early on how to navigate these competing cultures, to actively resist the strictures of white power by implementing the anarchic and antiracist knowledge she gleaned from her Black friends and family. hooks was influenced by her experiences in the classroom, particularly at Booker T. Washington Elementary School, the "all-black grade school [that] became the location where I experienced learning as revolution."[5] In those early classroom experiences, hooks witnessed radical educators "enacting a revolutionary pedagogy of resistance that was profoundly anticolonial," life-affirming and life-sustaining.[6] The classroom became, for hooks, a space where Black joy was central to the learning experience, where the process of learning was one of "ecstasy—pleasure and danger."[7] These early spaces "of counter-hegemonic cultural practice" would inspire hooks's radical pedagogy. And yet hooks's model of education was also fundamentally shaped by her ongoing navigation of and resistance to white supremacist, capitalist, patriarchal, and heteronormative structures, as she worked to forge a path through school segregation, desegregation, and university banking models that made it difficult for her to learn.

For hooks, school desegregation functioned as a permanent disruption of her formative all-Black education, opening her up to white educators who not only reinforced white supremacist norms, but enacted colonial domination and systematic violence, and enforced a system that demanded learning take place as a disembodiment from the self. hooks later discovered that, in duplicating the learning systems she had previously encountered in the Jim Crow South, the university also proved to be a site of quotidian violence, as she found herself actively dissuaded from pursuing radical Black intellectualism for the sake of "obedience to authority."[8] In graduate school at Stanford University, hooks argued that, in spite of her childhood love of learning, over time "the classroom became a place where I struggled to claim and maintain the right to be an independent thinker [...] a place of punishment and confinement rather than a place of promise and possibility."[9]

The disjunctions in her education led hooks to theorize "ways that teaching and the learning experience could be different," and could serve a liberatory, political, and transformative function for both students and teachers.[10] In her own classrooms as an educator, hooks insisted upon a praxis of freedom that was animated by "the interplay of anticolonial, critical, and feminist pedagogies."[11] hooks envisioned the classroom as a space where "students [can be] seen in their particularity as individuals," and a place where educators and learners alike "model and practice a genuine interest in one another, in hearing one another's voices, in recognizing one another's presence."[12] hooks described her praxis as "radical pedagogy," in which everyone's presence is acknowledged, as demonstrated through pedagogical practices. To begin, the professor must genuinely *value* everyone's presence. There must be an ongoing recognition that everyone influences the classroom dynamic, that everyone contributes to an open learning community. Often before this process can begin there has to be some deconstruction of the traditional notion that only the professor is responsible for classroom dynamics.[13] Emerging from her own experiences and in conversation with the Brazilian pedagogue Paulo Freire, radical pedagogy emphasizes relationality and transformation, the creation of an open and liberatory classroom community, and the collective creation—and holding—of spaces where teachers and learners can be actively engaged, as a coalition, in practices of justice, love, and resistance to oppression. Radical pedagogy most importantly, takes seriously working the "margin" as a site of possibility and "place of resistance," a location from which students and teachers can do necessary and radical work in spite of (and in opposition to) the violence of the superstructure.[14]

Radical pedagogy depends upon an understanding between teachers and students that learning spaces require a deeply political commitment to interrogating and interrupting systems of power and domination. Classrooms "as site[s] of creativity and power" demand transformation—"individually, collectively, as we make radical creative space which affirms and sustains our subjectivity."[15] These pedagogical imaginings seeded what we know as bell hooks's teaching trilogy: *Teaching to Transgress: Education as the Practice of Freedom* (1994), *Teaching Community: A Pedagogy of Hope* (2003), and *Teaching Critical Thinking: Practical Wisdom* (2009). Almost thirty years after the publication of *Teaching to Transgress*, hooks's theory of radical pedagogy continues to offer strategies, guidance, and hope for students and pedagogues who find themselves navigating insurgent antiblackness, the Covid-19 pandemic, and incipient state violence. For the teachers and learners who have treasured this work over the years, the notion of "education as the practice of freedom" continues to inform and animate their critical pedagogical praxis, and their efforts to create freer spaces of learning. We understand this work to be ongoing and adaptive, continuously shifting in practice, location, and exigent content—because the freer we get, the more we witness how systems of domination evolve to perpetuate themselves and challenge that freedom. hooks's collected works on strategies of pedagogical liberation and her critical reflections on the practice of freedom counter the ongoing and increasingly virulent devaluation of pedagogy by the far right, particularly in relation to the teaching of writing and culture, feminist and gender studies, and Black and ethnic studies. *Teaching Community* and *Teaching Critical Thinking* shift our thinking about pedagogy to the entanglement of the personal, political, and communal by centering her reflections on teaching outside of academia, constructed around brief "teachings" that stress political action and collectivism. By urging us to (re) commit to making revolutionary ideas accessible and, in doing so, expand our communities of resistance, hooks reminds us of our imperative to engage with and in public narratives about the development (and repression) of critical ethnic and cultural studies programs that promote justice in education. hooks underscores the urgent need for practical wisdom, or what she has described as "that union of theory and praxis" that "shows us that all genuine learning requires of us is a constant open approach, a willingness to engage invention and reinvention, so that we might discover those places of radical transparency where knowledge can empower."[16] hooks's moving recollections of her college experiences remind us that education is often mired in violent hierarchies of race, class, and gender, and that resistance to those forms of oppression can take many forms. hooks's recognition that teaching is a fundamentally political act, and her call for the creation of transformative learning spaces—inside and outside of traditional educational spaces—organized around counter-hegemonic and anticolonial praxes provides educators with the actionable roadmaps to co-create participatory spaces of self-recovery and collective liberation.

***

What does it mean to lead others toward freedom, encourage freedom as an intellectual practice, and practice freedom ourselves as teachers and learners? What specific modes of unfreedom are we experiencing today in the culture, classroom, and world? How can our education praxis meaningfully counter the rise of fascism, genocide, legislative violence, state surveillance, book banning, risk-averse and punitive administrators, and resistance to political and radical instructional material? *bell hooks's Radical Pedagogy: New Visions of Feminism, Justice, Love, and Resistance in the Classroom* is our attempt to gather answers to these and other vital questions, and an effort to continue to learn from the central tenets of hooks's teaching trilogy. The chapters in this collection include critical essays on educational praxes, personal reflections on pedagogy from learners and practitioners, and "teachings" that outline pedagogical activities designed to facilitate dialogue and promote a productive learning environment. Our inclusion of these narrative modes reflects our collective effort to mirror and honor hooks's intellectual structures in *Teaching Critical Thinking* and *Teaching Community*, and to strive for accessibility across audiences in various learning communities. Our contributors explore the complex ways teachers and learners from all educational levels, various disciplines, and locations both inside and outside of the university employ hooks's engaged pedagogical praxes. To that end, each chapter in *bell hooks's Radical Pedagogy* examines how her pedagogical theory and practical wisdom can serve as roadmaps for resisting antiblack, imperialist, white supremacist, capitalist, abled, and cisheteronormative patriarchal pedagogical practices, while simultaneously calling for a deep and sustained commitment to the work of "ending domination in all of its forms."[17]

This book embraces and takes seriously what hooks argued is our collective potential to establish caring, informed, and critical classroom praxis, spaces where we center and make possible pleasure, joy, and love in communal learning, and where we remain committed to the engagement that facilitates our cooperative resistance. As the first sustained collection of teachings, reflections, and critical essays, *bell hooks's Radical Pedagogy* addresses the full scope of hooks's teaching trilogy, and is intentionally and accessibly designed for pedagogues, community educators, students, and scholars in all learning environments—from prisons to book clubs to formal classrooms. The collection features twenty concise and highly readable critical essays, personal reflections, and instructive teachings, each crafted in response to and in conversation with hooks's teaching trilogy, as well as featuring a diversity of international perspectives from teachers in formal and informal teaching communities. We operate in light of bell's reminder in *Teaching Community* that "we can do work that can be shared with everyone. And this work can serve to expand all our communities of resistance so that they are not just composed of college teachers, students, or well-educated politicos."[18] For that reason, this collection explores hooks's pedagogical praxis beyond *Teaching to Transgress*, and offers an examination of her work that reflects her decades of continued practice and theoretical development in community spaces.

bell hooks's Radical Pedagogy is importantly designed to be a ready-to-use teaching resource. Educators and students across communities can take up, adapt, and personalize the many models of critical self-reflection and intellectual exercises in order to further develop their own transgressive praxes and strategies. We hope that students and teachers alike will marshal the insights in this collection toward the practical application of planning projects and rethinking assignments, and opening up dialog in classrooms, community centers, and at kitchen tables. Given that our contributors examine creative pedagogies and nontraditional educational spaces, in addition to emergent work in de/anticolonial pedagogies, *bell hooks's Radical Pedagogy* offers frank and vulnerable truth-telling by highlighting and strategizing around the ethical, practical, and self-preservational struggles teachers and students must face inside and outside the classroom. The contributors to *bell hooks's Radical Pedagogy* are making powerful and visionary interventions in their fields of study and in their local, regional, national, and international communities. They represent scholars and teachers affiliated with universities, K-12 schools, and community education cooperatives—they are also radically diverse in their identities, social and geographic locations, and scholarly interests. This collection is therefore designed to appeal to a broad expanse of educators, including administrators and educational leaders; elementary and secondary school teachers; teachers-in-training who are preparing to navigate hostile school boards, parent groups, and state governments; individuals in higher education working across disciplines; community organizers and public educators; and anyone committed to equity, decolonization, social justice, and increased access to education for all peoples. The goal of this collection is to provide teachers, students, and lifelong learners with critical tools, strategies, ideas, and connections for the creation of their own radical pedagogical communities—to that end, the diverse array of student, scholar-activist, artist, and teacher-scholar contributors embody hooks's "yearning to take my intellectual work and find forums where the practical wisdom it contained could be shared across class, race, etc."[19]

***

This collection is organized into four parts: "Engaged Pedagogies," "Pedagogies of Hope and Joy," "Pedagogies of the Bodymindspirit" and "Strategies of Resistance and Anticolonial Frameworks." In "Part One: Engaged Pedagogies," contributors offer insights and strategies for engaged instruction, or "progressive, holistic education" that, as hooks notes, focuses on the "whole person, and therefore emphasizes for students and teachers pedagogical processes that will aid them in their own struggle for self-actualization."[20] Engaged pedagogical praxis respects the unicity of each classroom, "necessarily values student expression," and "does not seek simply to empower students," but to employ a "holistic model of learning [...] where teachers grow and are empowered by the process. That empowerment cannot happen if we refuse to be vulnerable while encouraging students to take risks." To that end, engaged pedagogy (re)visions the classroom as an inherently collaborative space, a community where professors and students share with one another, are mutually vulnerable, and are equally committed to "being wholly present in mind, body, and spirit."[21] In Chapter 1, "Pedagogies of Care: Care Teams," Meika Loe argues that the establishment of care teams in student centers, classrooms, university structures, and public communities allows us to attend to the needs of the present moment alongside the demands of historical and generational trauma. hooks identified that care teams served a vital function for her "beloved community" in rural Kentucky, given that they required participants to practice radical openness, equanimity, integrity, and work to call one another in rather than out. Loe describes how care teams can be safely organized, and offers a guide for a compassionate praxis that can be immediately put to work. Chapter 2, "Death to PowerPoint, Life to Engaged Relational Pedagogy," features a dialogue between Lauren Reid, Judelysse Gomez, Erin Hipple, Michelle Mendez, Oluwanifemi Olugbemiga, and Jack Wolcott, multiply marginalized learners and educators who are actively practicing engaged pedagogy. Informed by hooks's call to cross boundaries and *break bread*,[22] the conversation explores the tensions inherent in practicing radical pedagogy in the classist, racist, ableist, and cisheteronormative university, and urges pedagogues to move away from traditional pedagogical techniques—represented by the PowerPoint presentation—toward subversive liberation-focused praxis that encourages working in creative ways, such as peer-mentoring, movement through campus, class discussions, holding space for students to make personal connections with one another, and establishing a community of care.

In Chapter 3, "Student Choice Projects as Engaged Pedagogy within the Neoliberal University," Jade Da Costa examines engaged pedagogy from the perspective of a teaching assistant (TA) who is required to work within certain pedagogical strictures. Da Costa describes turning to engaged pedagogy in order to develop a student choice project that values personal expressions, and therefore functions as a way to encourage students to interrogate the mechanisms of Western socialization, and to transgress senses of self that are rooted in hierarchical structures. In Chapter 4, "The Cultural Critique Paper: Teaching bell hooks in Philosophy," Hazel T. Biana outlines a cultural critique assignment that encourages students to read bell hooks as a feminist philosopher alongside— and in critical dialog with—Mary Wollstonecraft, Simone de Beauvoir Hélène Cixous, Judith Butler, Luce Irigaray, and other more mainstream women philosophers. Biana offers a critical justification for reading hooks as philosopher and a way to help students better engage in relevant sociopolitical and cultural critiques. In Chapter 5, "Engaged Pedagogies while Asynchronously Online: Students as Experimental Storytellers," Desi Self argues that hooks's teaching trilogy is a theoretical lighthouse and practical guide for Black queer learners and instructors. Self takes up hooks's pedagogical "call to action," and outlines a classroom praxis that allows for consistent reinterpretation, enables critique and reflexive responses that challenge dominant ideologies, prioritizes student feedback and classroom dynamics, and facilitates meaningful intellectual growth, interpersonal connection, and intellectual engagement across a range of assignment types, including creative modes of writing and narrating. Finally, in Chapter 6, "All about bell: Foregrounding bell hooks in the Classroom as Engaged Pedagogy," Megan Feifer makes the case that we must bring a wider sampling of hooks's work to the classroom, and that we should offer students a critical engagement with her work beyond isolated quotes. Feifer offers strategies for expanding materials in the classroom—for example, reading *Where We Stand: Class Matters* (2000) alongside *Bone Black: Memories of Girlhood* (1996)—in addition to thinking through hooks's close engagement with rural Kentucky, while advocating for students and learners to make critical use of hooks's papers and forthcoming digital archive.

***

"Part Two: Pedagogies of Hope and Joy" explores what hooks has described as the work of the "democratic educator [to] attemp[t] to create a spirit of joyful practice in the classroom,"[23] where teaching, learning, thinking, and working are serious, but can also lead to happiness. hooks acknowledges that radical pedagogy can be wearying, as the struggle against oppressive forces always is, no matter where we teach and learn. And yet, hooks argues that she maintains hope in the power of education to create necessary change, given that, to her, "the classroom continues to be a place where paradise can be realized, a palace of passion and possibility, a place where spirit matters, where all that we learn and know leads us into greater connection, into greater understanding of the life lived in community."[24] Central to this holistic labor for hooks is our need to renew the academy and society as we "renew our minds [...] so that the way we live, teach, and work can reflect our joy in cultural diversity, our passion for justice, and our love of freedom."[25] In Chapter 7, "Leaning into Discomfort: Grounding Our Identities as Teachers-learners to Confront Difficult Emotions and Build a 'Pedagogy of Hope,'" Jasjit Sangha and Kosha D. Bramesfeld argue that classrooms can become liberatory when instructors lean into discomfort and create space for students to grapple with the complexities of their emotions, connect more deeply with themselves, one another, and the course material. Sangha and Bramesfeld offer tactics for developing a praxis of hope that encourages students to build self-awareness, engage in mindfulness, curiosity, and compassion for self and others, and that privileges deep-listening, community-building, and opportunities to reflect on mistakes and grow. Patti Duncan engages the necessary risks when teaching for liberation in Chapter 8, "Transgressive, Transformative Feminist Pedagogies: Education for Hope and Healing," by turning to a critical reflection on hooks's feminist world-making of the 1990s, and exploring the urgency, potential and peril of making feminist worlds in hostile spaces. Through an exploration of Sara Ahmed's conception of feminist world-building and hooks's practice of world-making, Duncan offers concrete methods for putting into practice transgressive feminist teaching practices grounded in love, care, and community, in the service of healing and justice.

In Chapter 9, "Hope Survival, and Futurism as Creation," Bunny McFadden contributes a critical autoethnography of her struggle in a San Francisco school that, in spite of her efforts, continued to underserve BIPOC students. McFadden argues that even in the face of powerful opposition, pedagogies of love and hope inspired by Afrofuturism and Chicanxfuturism make possible decolonized visions of the future, open up space for new methodologies, and help students reimagine what can be. Chapter 10, "Connecting through Emotional Solidarity: Learning from Youths' Stories of Hope and Sorrow," features a discussion from organizers of the Literacy and Community Initiative (LCI), a nine-month community workshop for young people ages twelve to twenty-two that works to develop self-awareness, advocacy, and leadership skills. Katie B. Peachey, Caitlin M. Donovan, Jennifer C. Mann, María Heysha Carrillo Carrasquillo, and Crystal Chen Lee offer an explication of LCI's work, and describe in detail how we can learn to strengthen classroom relations by being vulnerable, creating space without judgment, developing student-led community, and centering student cultural and linguistic backgrounds. Chapter 11, "Rethinking the Classroom as a Hub for Intellectual Joy and Scholastic Passion: A Dialogue," features a conversation between Laiba Rizwan, Melanie Taddeo, and Kosha D. Bramesfeld. Modeled on hooks's long-standing dialogues with Ron Scapp, Rizwan, Taddeo, and Bramesfeld examine what it takes to make the learning environment stimulating and joyful—from creating an open classroom culture to leading with humor and levity to encouraging teachers and students to become partners in the learning process.

***

"Part Three: Pedagogies of the Bodymindspirit" engages hooks's emphasis on the importance holistic pedagogy, her advocacy for praxis that emphasized "spiritual well-being, […] [and] care of the soul," and her rejection of "bourgeois educational structures [that] seemed to denigrate notions of wholeness and uphold the idea of a mind/body split, […] that promotes and supports compartmentalization."[26] hooks imagines the instructor as healer, and the classroom as a space where all participants can attend to the needs of their mind, body, and soul in equal measure—central to the practice of freedom, hooks argues, is a praxis that attends to the whole person. In Chapter 12, Marlaina Martin examines the complexities of being inside and outside the academy, and offers tactics for instructors eager to bring their entire selves into learning spaces, including clear suggestions for providing students with compassionate flexibility, centering student affectual well-being, and encouraging holistic participation in all aspects of the learning experience. In Chapter 13, "Soul of the Syllabus," Dr. Rev. Natalie Coe examines the syllabus as a sacred pact that can make the invisible visible in order to create an engaged community of active learners. Coe explores the importance of nurturing self-development and self-actualization, and offers critical ideas for instructors and students interested in fomenting a spiritually focused classroom experience that makes it possible for students (and instructors) to move between the mind space to the heart space. In Chapter 14, "Freedom Teaching: Black Feminist Ethic and the Death of the Ego," Nicole A. Spigner explores hooks's indebtedness to Buddhist teachings, and demonstrates how the ethics of bringing oneself into the room, modeling vulnerability, and committing oneself to a deep exploration of the self outside of the classroom can foster a trusting, cooperative space for instructors and students. Spigner examines the effects of hooks's freedom pedagogy that emphasizes the role of instructor as healer, a positionality that requires eliminating the ego in favor of multidirectional learning. In Chapter 15, "Practical Wisdom: Praxis and the Urgency of the Moment," Joanna Davis-McElligatt explores bell hooks's practical wisdom in the form of a companion guide for instructors who are struggling to connect emotionally with their students, and want to sustain community in the classroom. Davis-McElligatt offers meditations on five excerpts from *Teaching Community*, and emphasizes the importance of physical, emotional, intellectual, and interpersonal connection, the function of radical love, and ways to move beyond the dysfunctional institution while also working within its constraints. Finally, in Chapter 16, "Spiritually Engaged Writing and Community Pedagogy: Honoring bell hooks' Legacy," Rachel Panton turns to hooks's eco-feminist writings, offering a "hydrofeminist" reading of water and water spirit veneration and explication of a three-day community learning event in Florida: *Ancestors, Orishas, and Ocean Conservation: The Rhetoric of (Mami) Water in Afro-Diasporic Environmentalist Education in Florida*. Panton argues that hooks's work demonstrates a deep ethic of care and the work of preservation that has for too long gone ignored, and suggests that the bodymindspirit connection must also reflect a "blue consciousness" committed to affirming subjugated knowledges, asserting a fluid symbiotic relationship between diasporic spiritual beliefs and practices and global environmental conservation.

***

"Part Four: Strategies of Resistance and Anticolonial Frameworks" takes seriously hooks's contention that her pedagogical praxis emerges "from the mutually illuminating interplay of anti-colonial, critical, and feminist pedagogies."[27] hooks's pedagogy of freedom was founded on a commitment to resist—and to teach resistance to—imperialism, class oppression, penal colonialism, racial capitalism, patriarchy, heteronormative social systems, and ableism. Ultimately, hooks believed that the classroom was a space where "we have the opportunity to labor for freedom, to demand of ourselves and our comrades an openness of mind and heart that allows us to face reality even as we collectively imagine ways to move beyond boundaries, to transgress."[28] In Chapter 17, "Indigenous (Zapotec) Queer Feminist Pedagogy: Accessible, Healing, and Transformative Theory," Nancy Morales argues that, as an Indigenous Zapotec feminist scholar-activist, hooks's engaged pedagogy has enabled her to develop collaborative learning spaces at a PWI that centers Women of Color scholarship, and centralizes radical compassion that also stems from the cariño, or critical care in Chicanx/Latinx feminist pedagogy. Morales argues that reading hooks alongside Chicanx, Latinx, and Indigenous scholars, including Michi Saagiig Nishnaabeg writer and artist Leanne Betamosake Simposon, offers up new ways to interrogate colonialism, rethink class difference, and generate a reciprocal relation between theory and praxis. In Chapter 18, *"Reading Circle as a Model of Cultivating Engaged Pedagogical Praxes*: The bell hooks Teaching Trilogy Reading Circle as a Model of Cultivating Engaged Pedagogical Praxes," Savannah Geidel and Maia Butler examine the possibilities, pitfalls, and impacts of doing diversity work in the neoliberal university, and make the case that teaching is fundamentally political work that demands transformative spaces of learning that are both counter-hegemonic and anticolonial. Geidel and Butler explore how the development of pedagogical reading circles—in this instance focused on hooks's teaching trilogy—can facilitate community building in the classroom, work against banking models of education, encourage a holistic ethics of care, and generate connections between class work on the family, community, region, and globe.

Chapter 19, "Intersectional Latinidad as a Critical Praxis Connecting College to Classroom: Lessons, Lineages, and Legacies of Liberatory Pedagogy from *Teaching to Transgress*," features a complete guide to the creation of a radical engaged pedagogical praxis that centers communal learning as an act of resistance, the creation of alternatives to traditional learning models that enforce hierarchy and domination, and the development of collective conscientization. Alyssa Garcia, Margarita Mojica, and Glenview Middle School students offer an extensive look at the "Tertulia and Hermandxd Workshop" that examines the importance of self- and community-care through explorations of culture and experience, body and media, resistance to violence, and community engagement and action. Finally, in Chapter 20, "Community Writing Programs as Communities of Resistance," Charles McMartin, Nicole Crevar, Maxwell Irving, and Charisse Iglesias examine how hooks's conception of communities of resistance has helped them navigate their existence on the margins of two corporatized educational contexts: standardized test scores for high school students and national rankings systems for colleges and universities. In a critical dialogue, McMartin, Crevar, Irving, and Iglesias explain how their creation of a community writing program—Wildcat Writers—enables students and instructors to consider how marginality can function as a site of oppression and also as a location of radical openness and possibility.

Notes

1   bell hooks, *Teaching to Transgress* (New York: Routledge, 1994), 10.
2   Ibid.,8.
3   hooks, *Teaching to Transgress*, 7–8, 13.

4 bell hooks, *Belonging: A Culture of Place* (New York: Routledge, 2009), 11.

5 Ibid.,2.

6 Ibid.

7 Ibid.,3.

8 hooks, *Teaching to Transgress,* 4.

9 Ibid., 4.

10 Ibid., 4–5.

11 Ibid., 10.

12 Ibid., 3.

13 Ibid., 8.

14 bell hooks, "Choosing the Margin as a Space of Radical Openness," *Framework: The Journal of Cinema and Media*, no. 36 (1989): 22.

15 hooks, *Teaching to Transgress,* 23–4.

16 bell hooks, *Teaching Critical Thinking* (New York: Routledge, 2009), 4.

17 hooks, *Teaching to Transgress,* xiii.

18 bell hooks, *Teaching Community: A Pedagogy of Hope* (New York: Routledge, 2003), xii.

19 Ibid.

20 hooks, *Teaching to Transgress,* 15, 17.

21 Ibid., 20–1.

22 bell hooks and Cornel West, *Breaking Bread: Insurgent Black Intellectual Life* (New York: Routledge, 2016), xii.

23 hooks, *Teaching Community,* 44.

24 Ibid., 183.

25 hooks, *Teaching to Transgress,* 34.

26 Ibid., 16.

27 Ibid., 10.

28 Ibid., 207.

Part One

Engaged Pedagogies

Transformational engaged pedagogy emerges from a collective of individual contributors who pursue and share critical knowledge that transgresses institutional standards, and creates possibility otherwise, elsewhere, in spite of the limitations of the system. Contextualized in our current political moment, characterized of the global rise of fascism and its attendant necropolitical logics, transformational pedagogy intentionally challenges systems and policies that inhibit our ability to speak out, dissent, and bring liberatory thinking and action into our classrooms and communities—or, in short, our dedication to creating more just futures. This section offers teachings and reflections that define and operationalize bell hooks's conception of engaged pedagogy in present contexts of "anti-woke" educational suppression and devaluation of humanity. In the thirty years since the publication of *Teaching to Transgress* (1994), the first book in hooks's trilogy, teacher-scholars have imaginatively woven hooks's concepts into their own "best practices" in order to cultivate engaged spaces of possibility. In *Teaching Community* (2003), hooks offers "practical wisdom about what we do and can continue to do to make the classroom a place that is life-sustaining and mind-expanding, a place of liberating mutuality where teacher and student together work in partnership"(xv). The chapters in this part answer the question: "Yes, but how?" The authors here confirm that an openness to improvisation, challenging narrow structures created by institutions, and incorporating student knowledge, concerns, and reflective insights leads to many "hows." As always, engaged pedagogy depends on the people in the room, the location of the room institutionally, regionally, and trans/nationally, and the outcomes each particular learning community hopes to realize in the midst of myriad barriers, and tenuous or shifting resources. The educators and learners included here facilitate engaged pedagogical environments that promote transformational learning. Their examples are touchstones that can be adapted to a multitude of diverse pedagogical situations.

The first two pieces in this part—written by Meika Loe and Lauren Reid, Judelysse Gomez, Erin Hipple, Michelle Mendez, Oluwanifemi Olugbemiga, and Jack Wolcott—challenge what hooks refers to as "dominator values," which prioritize conservative ideologies and white supremacist constructions, such as individualism and professionalism (*Teaching Community* 1–2). These authors undermine the primacy of the individual by teaching students to create bonds of care and learning with each other, and by avoiding differential treatment for those able to approximate or perform arbitrary standards of professionalism. Loe's "Pedagogies of Care: Care Teams" details how to intentionally build community in the classroom by creating trios of students, which helps students work through the isolation and collective trauma of the global pandemic, the climate crisis, and increased racial and political polarization. "Death to Powerpoint, Life to Engaged Relational Pedagogy" is a discussion between learner/teachers Reid, Gomez, Hipple, Mendez, Olugbemiga, and Wolcott, about the tensions inherent between engaged learning environments and academic settings that privilege professionalism, evaluation, and intellectualization, rather than an embodiment of emotions. hooks observes that "healing is an act of communion" (*All about Love*, 1999)—Loe's early semester community-building and the cultivation of solidarity forged in emotionally engaged pedagogy described in "Death to Powerpoint" create paths toward self-actualization—for students and teachers alike.

The next two chapters, written by Jade Da Costa and Hazel T. Biana, demonstrate how students' home communities can become places where students learn to confront the impacts of structural injustice on their lives through practices that prepare them to use their education toward transformative ends. These approaches recognize that students are members of diverse communities which they bring with them into the classroom, and urge them to consider how their education can strengthen and sustain those communities. Da Costa and Biana resist the "conventional dominator classroom [...] where students were simply given material to learn by rote and regurgitate," and instead offer students opportunities to find room outside of the classroom to examine and practice "how to think critically" (*Teaching Community* 8). Students learn how self-directed learning is necessarily critical of traditional canons and methodologies, and are empowered to confront the neocolonial forces acting upon their communities. Da Costa's "Student Choice Projects as Engaged Pedagogy within the Neoliberal

University," offers models that center student choice in assignment design, and demonstrates how students who are encouraged to draw on experiential knowledges are more able to move toward self-actualization by expanding the classroom's field of knowledge. Hazel Biana's "The Cultural Critique Paper: Teaching bell hooks in Philosophy" troubles the traditional canon of philosophy by challenging prevailing ideas about who can be philosophers, and the methods they must employ. Biana and her students' hooksian critique of popular culture reveals the centrality of systems-thinking to feminist philosophy, and pushes us toward a deeper critique of interlocking modes of oppression. Teaching hooks in the particular neocolonial context of the Philippines, Biana illustrates how cultural critique assignments can help students to explore how their personal experiences with marginalization can also inform their ability to challenge harmful representations.

We acknowledge that it is no easy feat to set the stage for holistic learning experiences in the classroom, and to make space for transformative self-actualization that makes possible rich and nuanced critique, reckoning, and action. We are tired. In "This Is Our Life," hooks discusses factors contributing to "stale, unproductive, deadening energy" into the classroom, which we recognize in our own late-pandemic teaching environments (*TC* 172). The trauma and exhaustion our students have been carrying for years often leave them with only enough energy for passive learning. Furthermore, collective anxiety about uncertain futures makes it challenging to embrace mindful presence in our carefully crafted learning moments, to say the least. hooks explained that she offered her students a "This Is Our Life" lecture in order to awaken them to the necessity of taking part in the co-creation of the "quality of life in the classroom [...] nurturing, life-sustaining [that] brings us into greater community" (*TC* 173). The next chapter in this part, by Desi Self, explores the challenges of establishing and sustaining an engaged learning environment in the post-Covid asynchronous learning environment. Self's efforts to keep her asynchronous introduction to feminist theory course engaged and responsive evidences the attention she pays to hooks's imperative that we make room for improvisation, which necessarily demands that we pay close attention to student feedback. In "Engaged Pedagogies while Asynchronously Online," Self describes an experimental storytelling assignment that asks students to research their assigned feminist thinker, and deploy flexibility forms as a mode of critical engagement with their theorist's imagined response to major cultural events. Self's student responses and peer reflections underscore how hooksian principles can impact developing praxes for both teacher-scholars and students.

Finally, this part bookends with Megan Feifer's invitation in "All about bell" to heed hooks's call for practical engaged pedagogy and justice-oriented student work. As the inaugural bell hooks Teacher-Scholar-in-Residence at Berea College, Feifer offers strategies for examining how hooks's works offer a clear-eyed study of systems of domination, particularly through the lens of class as a regionally specific collective entry point for her Appalachian student body. Feifer models course design grounded in a close cross-reading of hooks's texts, rather than a sprinkling of oft-cited quotes, which enables students to come to an understanding of their own positionality while simultaneously articulating their values by synthesizing hooks's coalition-building and resistance tenets with those of their home communities. Feifer, like other teacher-scholars in this part, models how to bring humanity, care, and collectivity into the classroom so that students may "embrace and explore the practice of knowing together" (*Teaching Critical Thinking* 22). The authors in "Part I: Engaged Pedagogy" provide several strategies for practicing transformational pedagogy under duress, so that we may be better equipped to examine, challenge, and resist interlocking systems of oppression and pursue more liberated futures for ourselves and communities.

Pedagogies of Care: Care Teams

Meika Loe

Pedagogies of Care in Theory and Practice

Now is the time to center care in our teaching; care for ourselves as scholar-activists, and care for our students, who attend to wellness like no other generation. We must center love and care in this time of brokenness. After all, what better skill set is there to pass along to students in such a time?

Pedagogy informed by an ethic of care is always an attempt to grapple with these questions: How do we attend to the now, to be fully present with each other? How do we name and center historical and generational trauma? How do we collectively sit in discomfort to grieve, but never become numb? How do we see each other as fully human, imperfect beings who need one another? How do we simultaneously embrace student-scholar-activist identities, or lean toward radical hope and realistic collective solutions to social problems?

These are questions many of us have, especially in the context of debilitating collective trauma, during a global pandemic, climate crisis, and extreme race and class polarization. To teach in this moment is to acknowledge these stark realities, to prioritize a commitment to being fully human together, and to ultimately generate social change efforts that reflect our complex human lives.

For bell hooks, what she describes as "beloved community" takes work—it requires being present with each other, through conflict and joy. In a conversation with John Brosi, hooks describes how building beloved community in rural Kentucky surrounding Berea College required "radical openness," a sense of equanimity and integrity, a "willing[ness] to know one another," by giving people the benefit of the doubt, even in a context of conflict.[1] Calling one another in is crucial to communities of care, as I have learned from Loretta Ross, as it is a practice built on trust and radical openness.[2] Ross challenges us to avoid the humiliation of calling people out or canceling one another, but instead suggests "calling one another in" with a level of respect and trust, to engage and work together on transformative change. Both of these Black feminist theorists suggest that community is a practice and a process, one that is well worth working toward.

What Are Care Teams? I work hard to build beloved community in all of my classes (usually no larger than twenty students). This requires assigning students to care teams starting at the beginning of our second week together. I began to formalize this method in the semester following the Covid-19 lockdown, when we all craved a new approach in the classroom. While many of us professors were focused on learning new technologies such as Zoom and Slack, I also turned my attention to weaving an ethic of care into everything I do. I knew we were returning to the classroom in a period of profound grief, and I wanted to be attentive to this shift. Especially in the context of social distancing and masking, we needed to re-learn how to actively care for one another and our larger community. Thus, I added a section to all of my syllabi called "Care Teams" that looked something like this:

> *CARE TEAMS: Each student will be assigned to a care team with 2-3 other students enrolled in this course.*
> This team will work together to dialogue and care for one another throughout the semester. When you have to miss class, you can turn to your care team for notes. You will also work together on the midterm exam.

Most weeks my students meet in care teams—small groupings of students who center and model the practice of care in the classroom, the university, and society. I explain to students that these are intentional communities—people you can count on, folks you can ask for help. These are smaller intimate spaces of trust and support—people who will call you in. Usually they are randomly assigned peer groups of three. That said, in my historically white-centering institution, I hesitate to put one student of color in a care team with two white students. In these cases, I try to put students representing majority groups in the numerical minority, so that our most precarious students are not made to feel further minoritized.

Preparing students to do the work of care involves assigning specific readings, listening exercises, dialogue assignments, and grounding practices. The first readings assigned in my classes focus on care, whether it be the "The Beloved Community" by hooks and Brosi, a speech called "Accompaniment as Policy" by Paul Farmer, or a poem called "Washing my Mother's Body" by Joy Harjo.

We discuss what care looks like and how these authors can guide us in building beloved community. Listening exercises early on in the term also helps to build strong relationships of care. For example, we may do a partnered LARA (Listen, Affirm, Respond, and Add information) exercise from Inter-Group Dialogue that asks one student to speak in response to a prompt for two minutes while the others in the team actively listen, affirm, and then switch roles. These listening exercises foreground vulnerability in order to build trust. Later in the semester we do regular ten-minute care team check-ins that are also structured around engaged listening and trust-building. In the first check-in, I might ask each care team to talk specifically about how they can support each other throughout the semester. Later on, small in-class dialogue assignments (see example below) set the stage for in-class group quizzes or midterms, when the team can work together to reflect on what they are learning in class. Finally, I model what it looks like to begin each class session with a grounding practice such as a breathing exercise, a short meditation, or gratitude exercise, many focused on the theme of community, and then ask students if they would like to make this a regular class ritual. Five years in, every class has requested that we continue these rituals; they say it enables them to re-set in their busy lives and reconnect with community.

Care teams are accountability groups that center care, in part, by honoring peer learning. Accountability requires being present for one another. And interestingly enough, this age group may be more attuned to learning from and not letting down their peers than their professors. They are always curious about what their peers are thinking, and they are eager for a different model of teaching in college that is less top-down than what they received in high school. Because peer learning is highly valued but rarely facilitated, students are intrigued and uniquely invested. The students in each care team learn each other's strengths and vulnerabilities, and how best to depend on each other and ask for assistance. Without realizing it, they are also learning and modeling practices of care for themselves and one another, practices they may well emulate in their post-college lives. After all, bell hooks was all about learning and practicing lifelong skill sets for community and dialogue.

What do care team dialogues look like? It depends on the content and pedagogical vision of the class. In my health class, these small groups meet to interrupt institutional, historical, and community silences so that students can work through and imagine their own ideal care practices and sex education. In courses on death and dying, these small groups normalize conversations about loss and grief on campus, and work collectively on a midterm exam on racialized mortality. In a class on aging and the life, care teams work through internalized ageism and reflect on intergenerational community as they partner with local elders. Below, I describe how the ethic of care is woven into my class on health.

Once trust is established in small groups, the larger work of bridge-building can begin. Bridge-building requires work on the micro or small-group level as well as with the class as a whole. Thus, small and intimate care teams help students to build trust, understand one another, and begin to seed big questions about justice and change. Then, the next step is for these teams to share some of their questions with the students as a whole to build bridges in the larger course. All care teams host dialogues with the class; specifically, they facilitate an hour-long learning session or teach-in for the class as a whole, asking big questions and taking time to imagine and dream within the lens of transformative justice. In this way, small efforts reverberate, and all students start to see each other and themselves as compassionate caregivers *and* change agents.

In Practice

In the first week of class in "Women, Health, and Medicine," we are reading about practices of care, focusing on hooks's concept of "beloved community" and Ross's "calling others in," as well as studying Paul Farmer's practice of "accompaniment" and Joy Harjo's poem and care practice in "Washing My Mother's Body." The syllabus for this course discusses care as both theory and practice, and outlines that students will be working in care teams to practice an ethic of care. Thus, students are prepared for embarking on their own individual and collective care journeys from day one. First in partners and then as a large group, we discuss community guidelines that will enable us to build beloved community together.

After I assign care teams at the beginning of week two, I set up a guided listening exercise for each care team, where one student speaks for two minutes in response to a prompt, such as, "Tell us about a moment when you felt another's care," while the other students in the group actively listen, then acknowledge and respond. They each take turns speaking and listening, and I keep time. This exercise normalizes sharing vulnerability to find common ground and build trust. After everyone has had a turn, the small team spends a few minutes dialoguing together about how to define and measure "care," and then sharing their ideas with the larger class. In the third week of class, I ask students to sit with their care teams and to share something they are currently struggling with in their lives, and then brainstorm how the team can help to support them through this challenge. Usually at this point in the semester, they have met with each other once or twice, and now are willing to be vulnerable enough to share one thing they are dealing with in their lives. I let them know that they are building relationships of care, a practice that will serve them throughout their lives, à la bell hooks; this vulnerability work is incremental, the building blocks of beloved community.

Importantly, community-building is taking place throughout the semester, in and out of care teams. If a class meets twice a week, one of the days will be focused on partnered or large-group activities, and the other day will be focused on care teams. So, while trust-building starts with care teams, listening and dialogue become commonplace across the board. In the health class, each student facilitates a class session with someone *outside of* their care team so that they continue to build connections and learn from others. By the end of the term, the goal is to ensure that every student has partnered with or gotten to know and understand the vast majority of their classmates. This sets us up for having large-group reflections about whether we have achieved beloved community at the end of the semester, and if/how we might replicate this process in other social groups.

One of the final health class sessions is devoted to a sex-ed teach-in. This is their dialogue project. I have asked for sex-ed questions/confusions in advance, and now the classroom is transformed into a dialogue space devoted to 6–9 questions (posted on the walls). Students are told to sit next to a theme they are curious about in small groups (no more than five), and dialogue about their responses, focusing on curiosity, listening, and support, rather than right answers. For example, a small group may coalesce to discuss "queer-friendly sex ed" and another to focus on "normalizing asexuality." As they dialogue, they actively interrupt institutional and collective silences. In the final ten minutes of the teach-in, care teams come together intentionally to discuss their takeaways, and policy recommendations.

By the time they reach the end of the term, each care team has met together, in class at least five times, and they have come to know and depend on each other. Some groups have even made efforts to meet outside of class, or rely on regular GroupMe information-sharing. At the end of the semester, the bulk of the culminating work takes place within care teams. Team members work collectively to prepare for their team to complete a thirty-minute oral exam together, talking through the key concepts of the course and imagining social change. By and large, these teams have put in the work to be able to create a safe and supportive (noncompetitive or perfectionist) setting, building on each other's points and ideas, and, afterward, assigning themselves both individual and team grades. Thus, even the final exam is a culmination of beloved community, as students walk away feeling a deep sense of personal accomplishment, group solidarity, and visions for social change.

In class evaluations, many students reflect that they have made new friendships and crucial connections across difference. They have learned about how to study and practice care personally and politically. And they have also spent several months together enacting small acts of change and seeing these efforts reverberate in their own social groups outside of the classroom. From the sex-ed teach-in to their discussions of reproductive justice, birth justice, and intersectional feminist health care, they have been interrupting institutional silences, confronting shame and stigma, listening, collaborating, and facilitating dialogue, and imagining a better world and a beloved community. Perhaps most importantly, instead of feeling weighed down by the content of a critical sociology course, they carry a sense of hope knowing they have a radical skill set for social transformation, and a peer network that is similarly devoted to care, dialogue, and change.

Notes

1   George Brosi and bell hooks, "The Beloved Community, a Conversation between bell hooks and George Brosi," *Appalachian Heritage* 40, no. 4 (2012): 76–86.
2   Loretta J. Ross, "Don't Call People Out, Call Them In," TED Talk, August 4, 2021, https://www.youtube.com/watch?v=xw_720iQDss.

2

Death to PowerPoint: Life to Engaged Relational Pedagogy

Lauren Reid, Judelysse Gomez, Erin Hipple, Michelle Mendez,
Oluwanifemi Olugbemiga, and Jack Wolcott

I celebrate teaching that enables transgressions—a movement against and beyond boundaries. It is that movement which makes education the practice of freedom.

—bell hooks

We are learners and educators with multiple marginalized identities who practice engaged pedagogy in social work, psychology, and counseling programs. What follows is a conversation where we navigate the tension of inherently classist, racist, ableist, and cisheteronormative higher education settings. This dialog is informed by hooks's call to cross boundaries and *break bread*.[1] In doing so, we create generative tension to transgress and transform how we engage with and relate to one another—crossing the prescribed boundaries of "teacher" and "learner." This pedagogy is not valued or reinforced by traditional structures in academia—a system that prizes and incentivizes assimilation and overtly and covertly punishes teaching in a way that pushes against and transgresses the status quo (the "banking system").[2] One such tension is the pull to buy into the system while resisting its impacts in radical and subversive ways—engaging in this way is costly *and* necessary. This praxis looks like subversive liberation-focused educators working and being in creative ways, including mentoring in and outside institutional walls, on walks across campus, during office hours, in some class discussions (sometimes nonverbally), over text messages and Zoom calls. It can also look like setting aside the agenda to hold space for students to connect with one another and the professor around recent collective stressors, eliciting lived experiences, and centering our spirits in order to prioritize the embodiment of our collective learning (hooks's concept of "engaged pedagogy"). It is inviting and sharing our humanness in the classroom space. This, in an academic setting where "intellect" and "objectivity" are primary currency, is transgressive. We honor that there is a cost to sitting in this tension as educators, and yet, the greater harm of giving in to traditional academia performance would be spiritual death. We manage the cost in dynamic ways, through radical self and community care,[3] and by disrupting systems where we can.

A Dialog Reflecting on How Engaged Pedagogy Shows up in the Classroom

Erin: What does it look like to create transgressive spaces in classrooms for students?

Judy: It looks like culture changing work, such as, "*Hey,*" at the top of a meeting, "*How are you all doing?*" rather than jumping into the agenda, "*How did you get rest this weekend? How did you self-care this weekend?*" Some people are taken aback when you shift the space from the start to recognize their humanity. As the professor, I have the agency and power to do that. I am the person responsible for creating culture.

Lauren: I hear that, Judy, in certain spaces, it feels like you must adhere to the traditional culture. Traditional pedagogies (e.g., teacher in complete control of the learning) check all of the boxes: how do we evaluate the objectives? What are the "smart" goals? Yet, traditional approaches are rooted in these oppressive systems. All the different ways that we might see the whole human experience don't get the same credence. It goes back to who created and continues to benefit from these systems. Who evaluates what is good and what is "rigorous," or "robust," or whatever coded language? Part of that is our sense of our power, our role, the way we feel beholden to a syllabus or PowerPoint. That's what I hear you saying: you can feel the energy of expectation. When you have the power to shift that energy, you can sit with the tension a little differently than when you feel like you have less power in the room, and you're being judged. People have the power to judge you and impact you based on their assessment of your adherence to traditional teaching practices.

Jack: Students see how you all sit in that tension, and take note of the times you're authentic versus the times you uphold the schedule on the syllabus.

Michelle: Coming to my graduate program from my undergraduate was a shift, because of how open and genuine it is—it is a different environment that I have come to appreciate. Also, many feelings emerge when sitting in the tension. Being in inherently oppressive educational settings contributed to this idea that there is an expectation for me to fail due to my identities. I still get that icky, uncomfortable feeling that there are expectations I fear not meeting, and thus need to work harder. Feeling I must produce until I am burnt out, and feeling guilty whenever I try to refill my cup.[4] On one hand, I know I am successful as I have come this far. On the other hand, I still hold the fear of being unsuccessful if I don't assimilate to this idea of the "ideal" student. Even writing my biography, I felt the need to assimilate and strictly talk about my academic experience—but there is more to me than academia. I am a human first: imperfect, flawed, and doing my best. I am not expected to know it all, but I am expected to try my best with what I know, and continue to learn as I experience life. Which makes me wonder, when did these inadequate feelings arise?

Erin: We are in different professional contexts and identity plays a role—I use an agenda for my classes, but I tend to say to students: "This is to let you know what's coming." I use it as a way to talk about care. I want the parameters of the space to be known just as a means for us to understand what may come up today, and I try to be really intentional about that, while also trying to balance the relational aspect of it. If a conversation needs to happen, then we're going to let it. Each space is unique to the individuals inhabiting it, and I would rather stay with the conversation that needs to be had than move it along for the purpose of productivity.

Lauren: Similarly to Michelle, I fear not meeting expectations as the professor and fall into the productivity trap that Erin mentioned. I felt like I had to do the PowerPoint to meet expectations. I was responding to times where people felt we didn't get to the "whole agenda" because of conversations or fear they wouldn't be prepared for licensing exams. It's this internal and external pressure—or an external pressure that we've internalized. PowerPoint does not align with engaged pedagogy. And yet, there was some internalized piece that I felt … Shame? Guilt? Some discomfort around whether I had done my job. Again, I am in the position of power, as the professor, and I get to decide. No one was saying I had to go back to the PowerPoint, but I had internalized pressure.

Erin: How do we teach students to practice complicating relations of power? There is an exercise I use from a transformative justice training I took. Students are asked to identify a minimum of six types of power happening between us. Lauren, as I'm hearing your story, I am thinking about how the pressure you feel to do that is not just internal, as you mentioned. There is the pressure of licensing boards and students, who might perceive themselves to be consumers. Some of us live in identities that make the prospect of engendering/courting dissatisfaction scarier because there can be direct consequences for our refusal to conform.

Judy: PowerPoint follows a traditional model. As an educator I am expected to present learning content and perform my expertise, pouring knowledge into students.

In this model, students are expected to act as passive containers—receptacles of knowledge. It creates an "expert" and "learner" binary that de-emphasizes relational, engaged, and critical work.[5] As an educator, I believe the skills students really need are empathy and relationship building, however, the academic system we currently exist in considers these "soft" skills. Engaged pedagogy, that is dropping down into your body and focusing on what's going on internally, to sit with each other's stories and the discomfort, to think about why you're here and what you're interested in, that is the world where (to me) learning exists.

Erin: And it's much easier to do more traditional classroom work if we don't have relationships or don't see the complexity of someone's humanity. PowerPoint can be a useful tool, but when we elevate our relationship to the PowerPoint over our relationship with each other, we miss opportunities for learning that are more deeply contextualized, felt, and remembered. Recently, in one of my classes, students got into small groups, taking turns as interviewer, interviewee, and witness in ten-minute increments. When in the role of interviewee, each student was prompted to think of a person who contributed to their decision to pursue their degree. They were asked to tell a detailed story about this person that demonstrated the nature of this relationship. Then they were asked, "If this person was going to introduce you to our class, what would they say?"[6] When I looked at the written feedback students gave about that assignment, I cried. More than one student said, "*I learned more about my classmate and who/what is important to them in ten minutes than I have known about them my entire time in a cohort with them.*" Engaged pedagogy can cause a lot of anxiety for people socialized in a system that favors productivity and banking knowledge. But it's such an impactful thing when you're calling in relatives, ancestors, communities—in this activity, people who matter, people with knowledges outside the academy, were being called into relationship, too.

Michelle: From the student perspective, I hear how we are impacted by the hierarchy, the power, the pressure to do things one way. I went to a large state school for my undergraduate studies and felt like I was on autopilot. Similar to Judy's point of being passive containers or receptacles. I feel that I was only taking in information to produce, not to retain. But I had an epiphany during the pandemic—that I am a human being. It's okay to take time for myself, to actually listen to my body and breathe.

Nifemi: I'm trying to understand or fight through putting language and vocabulary to my time in higher ed, which, for me, often turns into intellectualizing emotions. I think that's where we miss the heart. When we tap into the heart, it almost feels like it's oppositional. I'm in this space where I'm trying to understand how we got from defining emotions, to completely missing feeling them. Understanding what that looks like from a teacher aspect, it's like, am I just creating a bunch of people who can intellectualize their emotions, but not feel them? And where do I leave them? It's about pushing back and trying to feel the emotions of what I'm going through.

Lauren: Nifemi, I'm sitting with how disembodied it is—getting disconnected from the feeling, because you must figure out how you talk about it in an "academically acceptable" way. Performing in order to rise up this ladder of white supremacy and be valuable—also, the role of internalized capitalism. That we have to show up a certain way to be seen, or be valuable, or be heard. Then we get so disconnected, even from ourselves. While we don't want to engage this way, if we are true to ourselves, if we honor people, if we are messy and embodied ... we may get fully rejected. I keep tapping my heart, because each of us has a story—many stories—where we've experienced this and what it feels like in our bodies: this anxiety and dread. To avoid it, I think, "*Let me go look at the rules again and show up in the performative way that they expect.*" If I show up as my true self, and it gets bypassed, I'm left sitting with rejection and disconnection. And the thought that I wasn't what they wanted in this space.

Erin: I want students to notice their bodies in the space—are they connected? How are they responding beyond being a passive recipient? How do we increase our capacity to do the work that needs to be done if we don't notice what we are embodying and perpetuating? The work becomes just another set of PowerPoints to memorize and move on from. We ask students to be disembodied brains. And I think too often we are primed to assume that classroom space is for intellectual things but what might be a point of intellectual interest for one student is a lived and felt reality for another. Relational spaces offer a way to sit with the messier stuff.

Lauren: The other tool that we all use is the community we have with each other. I can go to y'all and say, "*Oh, this tension, can we speak about how it's sitting in my body?*" Or, "*This is what somebody said to me, and it made me feel this way.*" So that we don't have to carry this alone. Part of engaged pedagogy is knowing who you debrief with, who you talk to when you're sitting in a class, and something doesn't sit right with you.

Erin: I'm constantly just balancing the co-creation of a space of community care and grading because they are antithetical. Like, "*It's all cool here except you also get a participation grade.*" This is why I have students grade their attendance and participation at the end of the semester by writing a brief in-class reflection, to reflect on how they feel they showed up, and why they did. What would they give themself as a grade? And then I give them all A's.

Nifemi: To your point, Erin, a grade is also involved. I, as the student, have to intellectualize, code-switch, and even compartmentalize my entire experience into theory and discipline, processed through outdated material to prove that I am a scholar. Academic excellence becomes performance; imposter syndrome becomes survivor's guilt. Because I got the grades, I participated, I performed, but I am still unsatisfied, unfulfilled. I am trying to unlearn all of that now that I have graduated because that work was for my GPA or for an accolade. Yet, they don't pay the bills. They don't measure my worth.

Michelle: Right! I'm learning to not perform and just show up. I find that I'm sitting with the "shoulds." I "should" know how to do a case conceptualization, "should" know how to apply these theories. But I'm realizing that it's my first time learning this, and I'm new to this. I'm not going to know it right off the bat; it comes with practice and experience. Letting go of that guilt, that shame, that feeling of being incompetent, that sense that "*I don't know what I'm doing, I don't know if I'm in the right space.*"

Jack: Speaking to Lauren's point about internalized capitalism and disembodied emotions, I have realized that going for my MSW degree was a survival decision made in response to the government's failures during the beginning of the Covid-19 pandemic. In that period of my life, I was traumatized and in survival mode, which was reinforced by academia's disengagement in engaged pedagogy. There isn't much feeling in my body when it comes to capital and producing. We are alienated[7] from our bodies, from each other, from the work we do. In the classroom, we are alienated from our peers, and our work, and are pushed to fall into boxes, to condense our experiences into PowerPoints. There are connections we will truly never make because of our positionality in capitalism. I cannot even begin to fathom what human connection and love would feel like in my body, or sadness, or joy—if I had all my basic needs met by the state. I know love and pain in my body as it relates to the deprivation of capitalism—as it relates to being a working-class person. I find ways to be overtly who I am within the constructs that are given to me.

Nifemi: Community practices are often difficult in times dominated by buzzwords— "soft life," "self-preservation"—as a means to streamline and co-opt the conversation of individual wellness. Capitalist commodification has no time for process or the building blocks we need for self and community—you either follow suit or get left behind. As our worlds blend under one house and one virus (i.e., Covid-19), all the spaces where we practice community have also collapsed or morphed into a hybrid-communal independent model. Our domiciles have become our place of work, and our place of recovery (from viruses, from our day), their maintenance, our means of survival, no longer serving as spaces of communing and healing. Under these conditions community becomes a luxury, an unaffordable budget line item. Community has to share space on the internet cloud or a group trip that never makes it out of the group chat because the general world we live in continues to be built less for community engagement and more for corporate gain. Every social interaction is billed and taxed (the ride/flight to the hangout, the parking fee, the meal, the Zoom pro account), which in turn has resulted in community engagement as an optional luxury rather than a necessity. Communing requires more planning, coordination, resources, and capacity. When community is optional, we inherently teach that showing up, making room, extending invitations, and calling one another in are also optional, and that leaves the individual with one tool: self-preservation. Community is no longer readily available; it has to be penciled in. The academic response reflects the general world because even though college campuses are physically built for social engagement, entry is determined by cleared tuition checks mostly financed through student loans, and the experience filtered through masks, social distancing, and PowerPoints.

Michelle: I'm unlearning a lot of things and trying to figure myself out, to figure out who I am and how I want to present myself. I have to let go of the common norms and expectations—white supremacy, capitalism, educational hierarchy, etc. I'm trying to give myself grace, and know that I've learned through socialization. I'm figuring out how to let that go and move away. I find that I'm doing that not just in academic and professional settings, but, as Nifemi was saying, even in my family and social groups.

Erin: Capitalism has twisted educational spaces in so many ways, but one primary way is through language purity. If issues aren't being meaningfully and messily addressed—because it will be messy—and in relationship to each other, if we aren't fucking up and repairing, learning stagnates because the work is relational. How do we teach students to repair? Or do we just correct one another, memorize the language, and go about our day? Because that is not learning, especially in professions like counseling and social work. How can we be with one another in generosity? How can we recognize that marginalized people experience disproportionate exhaustion in classroom spaces and encourage students to actively notice the space they take?[8] And how do we acknowledge that we're going to mess up—how are we going to foster repair when we do? And are we able to hold that interpersonal repair may not always be possible but still there is potential to be in solidarity?

Judy: That makes absolute sense—how lifelong this process and journey is. I really like ending with "repair." Meaning, when we mess up, say the wrong thing, when we don't see each other's humanity, how do we come back to each other and reconnect? How do we move away from disposing of one another (as capitalism would have us do) when we misstep? Because, to me, that is the essence of doing, living and breathing engaged pedagogy. Messing up, reconnecting, relying on each other, repairing—as part of the lifelong journey and work of community and collective building. How do we do that? The answer is in the doing, I think that that is a key part of this offering.

We're sitting in this tension; we don't have answers because we're still going through it and we're still figuring it out. That is the action of praxis and working in service of liberation.[9]

Erin: And if we know that we change over time, we know that we are developed in relationship, then repair is also developed in relationships—it's not another bullet on a PowerPoint. Bulleted lists are satisfying in their concreteness, and some things need to be concrete—but it's not the whole picture. Trying to distill repair processes in that way feels like one of the fundamental errors that we make.

Nifemi: I probably needed this space more than I realized. Thank you all.

Notes

1   Refers to a discussion between people with different perspectives who come together over a meal; see bell hooks and Cornell West, *Breaking Bread: Insurgent Black Intellectual Life* (Boston, MA: South End Press, 1991).
2   The banking system as defined by a transactional cycle where educators deposit knowledge into learners, and learners merely memorize and reproduce rather than understand and deeply analyze; see Paulo Freire, *Pedagogy of the Oppressed* (New York: Herder and Herder, 1970). See bell hooks, *Teaching to Transgress: Education as the Practice of Freedom* (New York: Routledge, 1994).
3   We derive our conception of self- and community care from Black and Latiné/x feminist work; see bell hooks, *Sisters of the Yam: Black Women and Self-Recovery* (New York: Routledge/ Taylor & Francis Group, 2015). Audre Lorde, *A Burst of Light: Essays* (Ithaca, NY: Firebrand Books, 1988). Cherríe Moraga and Gloria Anzaldúa, eds, *This Bridge Called My Back: Writings by Radical Women of Color* (New York: State University of New York Press, 2015).
4   This is the mind/body split referred to by hooks (1994, 18), hooks, *Teaching to Transgress*, 18.
5   See hooks's dialog with Gloria Watkins on Paulo Freire's Pedagogy in Process: The Letters to Guinea-Bissau, in hooks 1994, 53–4; hooks, *Teaching to Transgress*, 53–4.
6   This was an activity adapted from a training with the Narrative Therapy Initiative in Boston, Massachusetts. Narrative Therapy Institute, "Narrative Therapy Certificate Program," Narrative Therapy Initiative, Boston, Massachusetts, September 2021 to May 2022, https://www.narrativetherapyinitiative.org.

7   See Karl Marx's concept of alienation; Karl Marx, *Economic and Philosophic Manuscripts of 1844*. Translated and edited by Martin Milligan (Mineola, NY: Dover, 2007).

8   Some of these questions are promoted by the work of Frantz Fanon and Michael Foucault; see Frantz Fanon, *Black Skin, White Masks* (New York: Grove Press, 1952). Frantz Fanon, *The Wretched of the Earth* (New York: Grove Press, 1968). Michel Foucault, *Discipline and Punish: The Birth of the Prison* (New York: Vintage Books, 1995).

9   See Ignacio Martín-Baró, *Writings for a Liberation Psychology* (Cambridge, MA: Harvard University Press, 1994).

3

Student Choice Projects as Engaged Pedagogy within the Neoliberal University

Jade Da Costa

Between September 2016 and April 2023, I was a teacher's assistant (TA) for the Department of Sociology at York University. I held this position throughout my Ph.D. program and, with the exception of my first contract, I worked for my doctoral supervisor, Dr. Amber Gazso. Each year, I taught with Amber, she would assign a Tutorial Activity Project in which students were asked to complete two ten-percent assignments designed by their TA. At first, I opted to assign more traditional projects, such as in-class participation and group presentations. Although I made an effort to make these assignments a bit more creative, they never strayed too far away from the familiar pressures and constraints of academic rigor and professionalism. This all changed, however, in the Fall of 2020, when I began assigning a Student Choice Project.

The design of the project is as named: students are asked to choose a platform through which they can explore and apply course material. The only requirement is that students must select a platform that is either creative and/or personalized. The images peppered throughout my reflection are examples of some of the assignments I have received over the years. Additional assignments are also featured on the Student Project page of my professional website.[1] I got the idea for the project from my friend and mentor, Dr. Carla Rice, who assigned a similar project in her co-designed graduate course, Re-Thinking the Human at the University of Guelph, which I took in Fall 2019 as a visiting student. The actual impetus for the project came months later, however, with the onset of Covid-19 and the subsequent turn to online learning. As university educators pivoted to this new way of teaching, many of us reckoned with the need to be more accessible, and it was through this experience that I decided to adapt Carla's project into my tutorial activity assignment.

In many ways, the Student Choice Project has been a wild success, culminating in countless submissions of wonder, beauty, and intellect. Given that academia is a colonial institution haunted by a post-positivist mindset that has long disavowed creative and personal thought,[2,3] it is unsurprising that university students would jump at the chance to be creative and personal with their studies. This is especially true in the context of York University, where the majority of undergraduate students are nonwhite and/or immigrants. Not only are students from these backgrounds more likely to have attended underfunded public schools with limited resources and cultural capital, but they are also more likely to be of a social world in which creativity, art, and personal expression are considered viable, if not vital, modes of knowledge transmission and articulation.[4]

At the heart of the Student Choice Project is hooks's praxis of engaged pedagogy, which is rooted in her larger teaching philosophy of "teaching to transgress."[5] This philosophy positions education as a site of freedom, whereby the liberatory power of social thought can be harnessed against the hierarchical infrastructure of modern Western society, or what hooks describes as "white supremacist capitalist [cis-hetero]patriarchy."[6] Critical thought empowers and encourages human beings to interrogate the mechanisms of Western socialization that have systematically taught us to think of ourselves as either better or worse than one other—as either dominant or subordinate—and instead situate ourselves within a diametrical "matrix of domination."[7] Through the praxis of engaged pedagogy, students and teachers alike are able to tap into this liberatory power and transgress a sense of self rooted in hierarchy and qualified difference.[8]

Engaged pedagogy achieves this goal by activating the mutual self-actualization of both the student and the teacher. For the student, this activation occurs through the recognition of the complex ways in which folx learn.[9] Through engaged pedagogy, the practice of education (as it is hegemonically defined) is shifted from an "assembly-line," where "all students need to do is consume information fed to them by a professor and be able to memorize and store it,"[10] to a place where students are known as "unique beings" and their "intellectual and spiritual growth" is taken seriously.[11] With its combined focus on student agency, personal expression, and accessibility, the Student Choice Project takes the self-actualization of the student as its point of departure, offering a practical incantation of the ethos behind engaged pedagogy: student expression is not only valued but made both the authority of the assignment's infrastructure and the aim of its learning objective.

But, as hooks notes, "Engaged pedagogy does not seek simply to empower students," but teachers as well.[12] With the Student Choice Project, this occurs through the transgression of expertise. When students are invited to transgress validated knowledge forms and articulate their learning based on personalized and creative energies, they render both their experiences and their unique talents into sites of sociological mastery. In this way, the knowledge of the educator is not only challenged in content—through our exposure to the lived sociologies and intimate political knowledges of our students' everyday lives—but in actual form, too. The student who can paint the "bifurcated consciousness"[13] of their worlding into existence (Figure 3.1), or who uses memes to convey the sociocultural complexities of Bangladeshi families (Figures 3.2 and 3.3), or sketches the anonymous artist's[14] *Looking Glass Self* into perfect symbolism (Figure 3.4), knows a technique and form that I do not (i.e., representational painting, sketching, and meme creation/knowledge). These students also know

Figure 3.1 *Bifurcated Consciousness, c.* Winter 2020. Painting of the back of a woman's head looking into a split view of her home and workplace, with a counter, lunch bag, television set, and laundry machine featured on the right, and a gray office with a single man coworker on the left. Reproduced by permission of the artist, Leandrea Sanchez.

Figure 3.2 Cover Page for Meme Essay on Bangladesh Families, *c*. Fall 2020. Image features an iconic meme of Canadian rapper and singer Drake split into two images on the left. The top image shows Drake gesturing to someone off camera to stop what they are doing. The bottom image shows Drake smiling. Right of top image, text in large, black center text reads "Assignments requiring readings, research, essay, citations." Right of the bottom image, text in large, black center text "Assignments requiring meme knowledge." Reproduced by permission of curator, Adri Ananya.

experiences and realities that are beyond me, from the particulars of their own standpoint or sense of self to the generalized norms of transnational Bangladeshi families.

Take the magazine article below by Rianna Brown (Figure 3.5), as a further example. Not only am I unable or unlikely to explore mainstream feminism's exclusion of Black women through a fictitious magazine, but I also lack the situated and experiential knowledge that Rianna, as a Black woman, has on the topic. By bringing both their practical and lived knowledges into the classroom through the Student Choice Project, students like Leandrea, Adri, Rianna, and their anonymous classmate, bring forth knowledges that exhort me, the educator, to expand my sociological imagination, and with it, my teaching practice. Leandrea showed me how to visualize a bifurcated consciousness; Adri taught me about meme knowledge and its sociological power; the creator

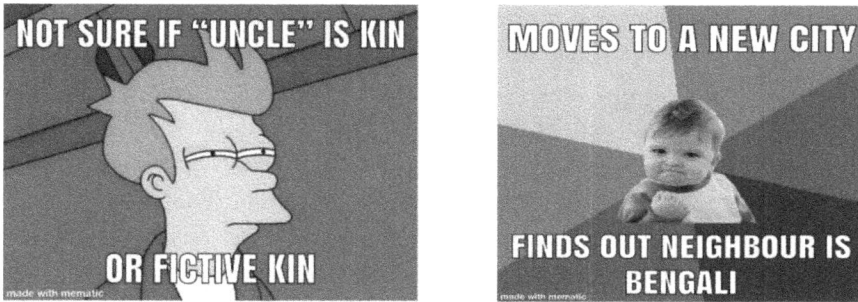

Figure 3.3 Bangladesh Family Memes, *c.* Fall 2021. Two memes are placed side-by-side. Meme on the left is of an iconic meme image of the character Fry from the cartoon sitcom, *Futurama*. He is squinting his eyes at someone off screen. White center text at the top of the image states "NOT SURE IF 'UNCLE IS KIN.'" White center text at the bottom of the image reads "OR FICTIVE KIN." Meme on the right is of an iconic image of a white baby making a fist in a sign of victory. White center text at the top of the image features "MOVES TO A NEW CITY." White center text at the bottom of the image contains "FINDS OUT NEIGHBOUR IS BENGALI." Reproduced by permission of curator, Adri Ananya.[15]

of Figure 3.4 made salient the effect of the Looking Glass Self, and Rianna contextualized the exclusions of mainstream feminism within the context of her own life. Thus, at the same time the student choice assignment acts as a mode of self-actualization for the student, it also produces a knowledge form that aids in the self-actualization of the teacher.

That said, I would be remiss if I said students didn't also struggle with the assignment. When I first implemented the Student Choice Project, I found myself having to repeatedly assure students that it was *meant* to be creative, fun, and accessible. But even with my constant reassurances, I received countless emails and in-tutorial questions from students pondering the merit of their ideas and whether to include more concepts and citations. Their assignments similarly reflected their anxieties—I received many submissions that went so far beyond what was expected that they rivaled the most challenging of academic projects. These projects were exhaustive (and exhausting) in their efforts as opposed to engaging, fun, and personalized. It seemed the freedom that I'd given the students had not only failed to challenge the colonial boundaries of academic rigor and professionalism but had conversely made these boundaries limitless. Socialized and trained in the *assembly line* of dominant colonial schooling, these students had come to mistrust the wisdom of their own embodied knowledges and therefore turned to excellence out of a sheer fear of failure.

Students have similarly responded to the Student Choice Project (and its adaptations) every year since its inception. To clarify, the excellence to which I write is not the excellence of genuine creativity or passion. Such excellence *is* exemplified by the projects I've included above: the thoughtfulness of Leandrea's painting and the *Looking Glass Self* drawing; the personality and innovation of Adri's meme essay and Rianna's magazine. The projects included below feature these same elements, with a propulsive child abuse activity workbook by Kinjal Patel and an experiential sociology poem by Feben Yitbarek. I remember grading Kinjal's assignment and being moved by both the novelty and the overwhelming

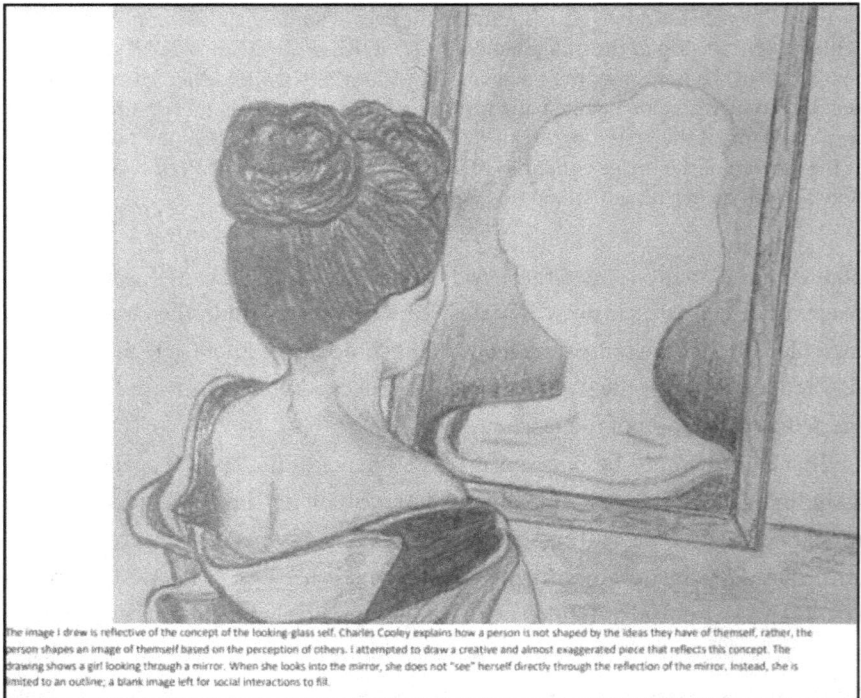

The image I drew is reflective of the concept of the looking-glass self. Charles Cooley explains how a person is not shaped by the ideas they have of themself, rather, the person shapes an image of themself based on the perception of others. I attempted to draw a creative and almost exaggerated piece that reflects this concept. The drawing shows a girl looking through a mirror. When she looks into the mirror, she does not "see" herself directly through the reflection of the mirror. Instead, she is limited to an outline; a blank image left for social interactions to fill.

Figure 3.4 *Looking-Glass Self, c.* Winter 2020. Heavily shaded drawing of a woman looking into a mirror without a reflection. Small black, left text at bottom states "The image I drew is reflective of the concept of the looking glass self. Charles Cooley explains how a person is not shaped by the ideas they have of themselves, rather, the person shapes an image of themself based on the perceptions of others. I attempted to draw a creative and almost exaggerated piece that reflects this concept. The drawing shows a girl looking through a mirror. When she looks into the mirror, she does not 'see' herself directly through the reflection of the mirror. Instead, she is limited to an outline; a blank image left for social intersections to fill." Reproduced by permission of the artist, who wishes to remain anonymous within this publication.

sincerity of the project. The booklet *felt* like something she had wanted to do and had enjoyed doing. With Feben's poem, I was struck by the personality and art of her words, as well as a sense of gratitude for the project's elegant simplicity. Combined, these assignments capture what femme education scholars might call the "soft" side of the Student Choice Project,[16] in that they represent the wondrous felt knowledges of students in embodied and accessible ways, thereby exemplifying the potentials and promises of engaged pedagogy as a teaching praxis. What they negate, however, is the constant work I did throughout each term to reassure students that a meme essay was a valid option or that a poem is knowledge.

Throughout the years, I've made intentional, consistent efforts to reassure students that their Student Choice Projects would not be penalized, either for being creative and/or simple and thus accessible. (Indeed, of the assignments featured here, all but the painting and the drawing, arguably the most extensive pieces, are from later TA contracts). But even with these efforts, students' anxiety remained palatable, and I continued to receive projects that were exceptional, not for their beauty and personality, per se, but for their extreme rigor. In contrast to the soft exceptionalism of Figures 3.1–3.7, these assignments were hard: intense, overzealous, and often lacking the very personality and ease that I'd designed the project for.

For me, such responses to the Student Choice Project gesture to the current climate of postsecondary education: the neoliberal university. Neoliberalism is a socioeconomic ideology that represents the state's attempt to reassert a free-market capitalist economy characterized by private property, freedom of exchange, and the growth of business interests.[17] Mintz notes that "neoliberal thought considers higher education a financial investment for students, and it assumes that colleges and universities should compete for customers, just like any other sector."[18] When students are treated like customers, they are taught to invest in higher education as a necessary form of human capital, while also being made to feel solely responsible for the extent to which said "investment" yields a measurable return. The value of education is reduced to a student's quantitative success within a course (the grade that they receive) and whether this success can be leveraged into a job, internship, law degree, graduate degree, etc. As a result, students are funneled into the exact assembly-line hooks spoke against when conceiving of engaged pedagogy—courses are designed like products that students buy, and information is dispensed to them in a standardized fashion that they are then asked to regurgitate to complete the transaction.

It makes sense why students have struggled with the Student Choice Project: the neoliberal university, with its concerted standardization, quantification,

---

Friday, December 8, 2022   **BROWNS BUZZ**   Issue #10

Do Black Women Feel Represented in Feminism?

Inspired by Tohe's One Indigenous Perspective from One Standpoint

Tohe has emphasized that feminism is historically situated and contextualized by scholars of the Global North. She notes that when she crosses the Western world, she notices that women are different and that feminism is a concept, action, theory, and movement primarily for white women (Gazso, 2022).

By: Rianna Brown

White women's voices are the main ones highlighted in the movement and sociologists creating feminist theories around Eurocentrism neglect the voices and ideas of women that do not fit into the Eurocentric identity. All in all, feminism has historically excluded women of colour in the past like women's suffrage and this exclusion has been shut out of the media and conversation.

With the rise of conversation on Tohe's idea of feminism, Browns Buzz decided to do a round-table talk conversation with various Black women and see their takes on if they feel represented in feminism. This experiment was created to see if there has been any change in this movement since historical events.

"When I think of *feminism* my first thought is white women," said an interviewee when asked how they would describe their feeling of representation in feminism. During the interview, this thought received various head nods in agreement. Feminism has highlighted white women's experiences in the past while ignoring the experiences of other women and nonbinary. Because of this primary focus on white women, when people think of feminism, they have a character associated with a movement. This Black woman's answer answers the question that there has not been a significant change in this movement.

Another interviewee brought up that as Black women they feel silenced in feminism. She states there are issues that Black woman face that have yet to be addressed and changed such as issues in healthcare, employment pay and more. Black women are at high risk of being ignored during childbirth and not catered to properly during labour. This puts them at a higher mortality rate when giving birth. To avoid this some Black women avoid having children as a whole and some primarily go to Black doctors and Black midwives.

> "If we aren't intersectional some of us, the most vulnerable, are going to fall through the cracks"
> - Kimberlé Crenshaw (coined the term Intersectionality)

However, the ratio of Black to white workers is unfortunately lower. Therefore, even if Black women wanted to go to workers that look like them to avoid these problems, they must deal with the barriers of not having many Black healthcare workers.

To allow all identifying women or non-gender-conforming individuals to feel a part of this movement, the movement needs to highlight the experiences of all to make the world equitable for all. That includes looking at experiences from different racial groups, different abilities, sexuality, classes, ages and more. However, will the movement be able to satisfy all groups while working towards their main goal – creating equal rights and opportunities among all genders?

Page 1

Figure 3.5 Black Feminist Standpoint Magazine Article, *c*. Fall 2022. Image of a fictitious magazine entitled *BROWNS BUZZ*. An image of the cartoon outlines of mostly racialized women/people is top center. Brown, bold, left text underneath reads "Do Black Women Feel Represented in Feminism?" Underneath is the text of a fictitious magazine article. Reproduced by permission of the creator, Rianna Brown.

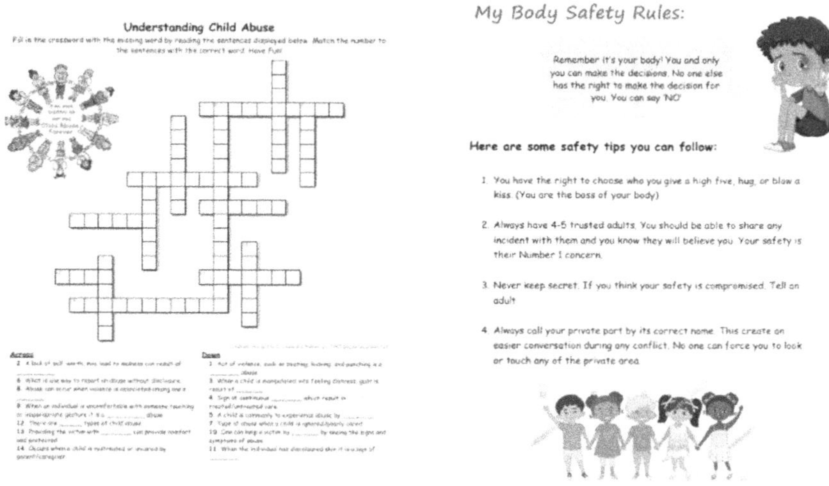

Figure 3.6 "I Say No," a Child Abuse Activity Book, *c.* winter 2021. Two images from a children's activity book on child abuse. One image is of a crossword and the other is of rules for children's body safety. Reproduced by permission of the curator, Kinjal Patel.[19]

and consumerization of knowledge, constitutes the diametrical opposite of the project's anchor—engaged pedagogy. Under neoliberalism, universities have become capitalist businesses, and business is not a place for self-actualization, for creativity, or for learning through the political contours of the personal. On the contrary, businesses are places where you listen to your boss (or your teacher) and do exactly what they tell you to do. Agency is not only ignored but discouraged, and students within this educational hellscape have fallen into a linear rhythm where they are far more comfortable taking multiple-choice tests than they are genuinely contemplating the matrix of domination in which we all live. As a result, the creativity, agency, and personality of engaged pedagogical approaches, quite literally, scares them.

What I've learned from this experience is that engaged pedagogy within the neoliberal university is as necessary as it is challenging. When hooks advocated for a philosophy of teaching to transgress, she was advocating for the pedagogical refusal of an educational system that reproduces a world dependent on exploitation, violence, and abjection, and instead fosters transformative change from the ground up, starting with the embodied knowledges of the oppressed, from those living in and amid the world of violence that academics are tasked

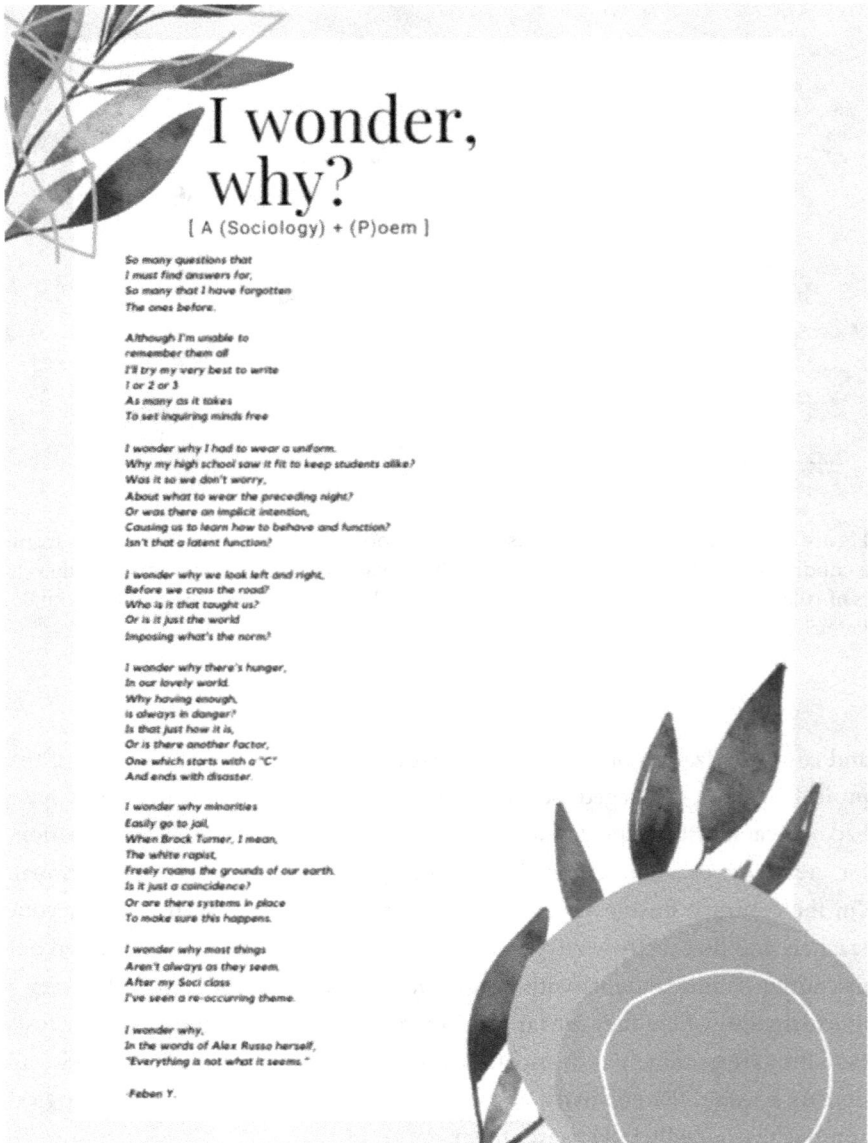

I wonder, why?

[A (Sociology) + (P)oem]

So many questions that
I must find answers for,
So many that I have forgotten
The ones before.

Although I'm unable to
remember them all
I'll try my very best to write
1 or 2 or 3
As many as it takes
To set inquiring minds free

I wonder why I had to wear a uniform.
Why my high school saw it fit to keep students alike?
Was it so we don't worry,
About what to wear the preceding night?
Or was there an implicit intention,
Causing us to learn how to behave and function?
Isn't that a latent function?

I wonder why we look left and right,
Before we cross the road?
Who is it that taught us?
Or is it just the world
Imposing what's the norm?

I wonder why there's hunger,
In our lovely world.
Why having enough,
Is always in danger?
Is that just how it is,
Or is there another factor,
One which starts with a "C"
And ends with disaster.

I wonder why minorities
Easily go to jail,
When Brock Turner, I mean,
The white rapist,
Freely roams the grounds of our earth.
Is it just a coincidence?
Or are there systems in place
To make sure this happens.

I wonder why most things
Aren't always as they seem.
After my Soci class
I've seen a re-occurring theme.

I wonder why,
In the words of Alex Russo herself,
"Everything is not what it seems."

-Feben Y.

Figure 3.7 "I Wonder Why?" A Sociology Poem, *c.* 2023. A poem depicted in a visual format. Top left-aligned black text, "I Wonder Why?" Below in smaller font, "[A (Sociology) + (P)oem]". Beneath this is a nine-paragraph poem in small black font. Top right, graphic of green leaves and yellow lines. Bottom left corner, graphic of blue circle in front of a yellow circle with green leaves sticking out from behind. Blue tinted page with darker blue border. Reproduced by permission of the artist, Feben Yitbarek.

with theorizing. With the rise of the neoliberal university, which functions not only to reproduce this world but to do so with startling precision and through intellectual bureaucracy, engaged pedagogy feels like a radical dream. It can keep us moving toward freedom through a social justice-based education, but it's constantly weighed down by the neoliberal anxieties and productive colonial thinking of our waking reality.

It's not that elitism and inequity are new to the university. Universities are, after all, colonial by design.[20,21] It's that the neoliberal university repositions this colonial impetus into a universal credential. Within this apparatus, engaged pedagogy becomes a constant struggle not just with the institution but with the students themselves, which, in turn, limits our ability as educators to activate engaged pedagogy as a relational praxis. Through enabling students to self-actualize in and through their education, engaged pedagogy pushes teachers into our own self-actualization through the expansion of critical thought. However, when teachers have to fight the neoliberal energies within students while also fighting the neoliberal systems of the university, it becomes increasingly difficult to appreciate their educational outputs beyond their evaluative quality—beyond measurable grades.

There are, of course, many educators who continue to dream up a liberatory curriculum, but we are always acting against neoliberalism (where our efforts are undervalued and underfunded) and are thus systematically burnt out of these transgressive practices. Educators must face this reality with truth and vulnerability. Those of us who teach to transgress will continue to do so—it is who we are. But the neoliberal university makes it harder for us to be who we are *at all levels* of teaching, and if we don't reckon with this fact on a regular basis, pushing against the chronic burnout in an effort to embrace and harness critical thought, we might forget the core lesson upon which engaged pedagogy depends and which hooks herself so firmly believed: teaching is a practice of *freedom*.

Notes

1   Jade Da Costa, "Student Projects," *Jade Crimson Rose Da Costa* (November 2023): www.jadecrimson.com/studentprojects.

2   Fitsum Areguy, "Exploring the Boundaries of Critical Pedagogy," *New Sociology: Journal of Critical Praxis* 1 (2019): 10.

3   Katherine McKittrick, *Dear Science [...] and Other Stories* (Durham, NC, and London: Duke University Press, 2021), 7.

4   Ibid., 5.

5   bell hooks, *Teaching to Transgress: Education as the Practice of Freedom* (London: Routledge, 1994), 7–10.

6   bell hooks, *Talking Back: Thinking Feminist, Thinking Black* (London: Routledge, 2014), 124.

7   Patricia Hill Collins, *Black Feminist Thought: Knowledge, Consciousness, and the Politics of Empowerment* (London: Routledge, 2000), 22.

8   hooks, *Teaching to Transgress,* 20.

9   Ibid., 21.

10   Ibid., 13–14.

11   Ibid., 13.

12   Ibid., 21.

13   Dorothy E. Smith, "Sociology from Women's Experience: A Reaffirmation," *Sociological Theory* 10, no. 1 (1992): 89.

14   Charles H. Cooley, *Human Nature and the Social Order* (New York: Charles Scribner's Sons, 1922).

15   View the full meme essay at: https://www.jadecrimson.com/_files/ugd/12dff3_79bf 37b14e364e66b54393636ccafff3.pdf.

16   Lindsay Cavanaugh, "Embracing Queer, Fem(me)ine & Crip Failure: Arriving at Dream-mapping as a Speculative Tool for Queer and Trans Educational Research," *Theory, Research, Action in Urban Education* 8, no. 1 (Spring 2023): para 14.

17   Beth Mintz, "Neoliberalism and the Crisis of Higher Education," *Marxist Sociology Blog: Theory, Research, Politics* (October 27, 2021): para 1–3.

18   Ibid., para 3.

19   View the full activity book at: https://www.jadecrimson.com/_files/ugd/12dff3_130 0f43c74e14df1aa974900b41bc67e.pdf.

20   Areguy, *New Sociology: Journal of Critical Praxis,* 10.

21   McKittrick, *Dear Science [...] and Other Stories,* 1–7.

4

The Cultural Critique Paper: Teaching bell hooks in Philosophy

Hazel T. Biana

Although I never told anyone, it gave me great pleasure to be called a philosopher, when I learned that the root meaning of the word was "lover of wisdom."

—bell hooks

Recently, there has been a call for feminizing the philosophy curriculum in the Philippines. This call, however, limits its suggestions to adding Filipino women philosophers' works or reading materials to the syllabus or offering some courses on foreign women philosophers. While claiming to address the "gender gap" and lack of inclusiveness in philosophy,[1] such proposals seem superficial, as they do not use gender, place, race, or ethnicity in a subversive way.[2] bell hooks, in *Teaching to Transgress: Education as the Practice of Freedom,* where she has a conversation with Ron Scapp, talks about how there are "many professors who have been willing to change their curriculum" or add radical texts to traditional lists in philosophy classes, but "have refused to change the nature of their pedagogical practice."[3] In the Philippines, "mainstreaming" by adding women thinkers' writings to reading lists is seen as a win,[4] but does such inclusion shift paradigms? Without acknowledging diverse political stances, such practices delegitimize progressive pedagogy and render students passive consumers of conventional education.[5] Merely replacing Filipino male philosophers' works with Filipino female philosophers' could be risky without fully understanding that the shift in representation must be accompanied by a shift in ways of thinking about ideas.[6]

In this context, I write this personal reflection on my integration of bell hooks's works into *Feminist Philosophy* and *Women in Philosophy* classes at both the undergraduate and graduate school levels at my university in the Philippines. Unlike other local colleges and institutions fighting for women's inclusion in the syllabi or curricula,[7] *Feminist Philosophy* has always been a major course in our graduate program. Additionally, *Women in Philosophy* is mandated in our university's philosophy curriculum. Such mandates are a result of a "gender-balanced" faculty roster and the department's commitment to inclusive education. However, the challenge of teaching such courses is ensuring that pedagogical practices do not fall into the pitfall of superficial change. At the same time, my academic social contract with my students should celebrate creativity, fearless speech, and honest self-disclosure.[8] The innovation I thought of was integrating bell hooks's works, frameworks, and concepts into the philosophy courses, not just as an added feature, replacement, or token but as a means for students' active engagement in serious sociopolitical and cultural critiques.

In this chapter, I discuss the most common feminist and women's works discussed in philosophy classes. I also delve into how bell hooks's theory and cultural criticism are inspired by critical theory and feminist philosophy. I enrich and contextualize discourses on feminist philosophy and tackle the need to integrate hooks into the philosophy curriculum. I also share a class requirement, a particular cultural critique paper that uses hooks's framework on interrogating cultural representations and social systems that students have fulfilled in their courses.

Teaching Feminist Philosophy

In 2009, I was hired as a part-time lecturer in the Department of Philosophy of De La Salle University in Manila to teach primarily *Introduction to Philosophy* and *Gender Studies*. In addition to this appointment, I was working toward a Ph.D. in Philosophy. I knew I wanted to work on gender, race, and representation as a dissertation topic, but I was unaware of how to proceed. Most of my academic work revolved around traditional and mainstream philosophical concepts—none of which tackled the central themes of gender and race. To help me, my Postmodernism Professor Feorillo Demeterio introduced hooks's work by giving me a second-hand copy of *Salvation: Black People and Love,* which he bought for 50 Philippine pesos (approximately US$1) in a thrift shop. Inspired by *Salvation,* I acquired hooks's other books and wrote my dissertation on her feminist theory and cultural criticism. I successfully defended my dissertation in 2012, after which I was tasked to teach *Feminist Philosophy* to graduate students.

In this scenario, I decided to recalibrate the syllabus to integrate hooks into my philosophy courses.

My early *Feminist Philosophy* course's syllabus was mainly composed of white feminist philosophers' works, their critique of the philosophical canon, and their ideas of patriarchy and womanhood. For example, one of the first readings of the course is Charlotte Witt's "How Feminism Is Re-writing the Philosophical Canon."[9] Witt's work is an essential introductory reading to the course as she discusses the role of feminist philosophers in reformulating the philosophical canon and pinpointing the "problem of historical exclusion" and denigration. Witt states that the debates on the canon composition are very similar to the disagreements regarding feminism in feminist philosophy. While Witt affirms the multiplicity of feminisms, she is branded an essentialist since she asserts that other variables, such as race, presuppose gender.[10]

From a historical perspective, my course also requires readings from the first wave of feminist philosophers, such as Mary Wollstonecraft's *A Vindication of the Rights of Woman* and John Stuart Mill's *The Subjection of Women*. Simone de Beauvoir's *The Second Sex* is, of course, one of the primary references of the course. Beauvoir is considered a "feminist thinker for our times," as she puts feminism into perspective through her discourse on philosophy and identity.[11] Bringing to the fore the discussion of woman as the *Other*, Beauvoir's most significant contribution to feminist philosophy is her conception that "one is not born, but rather, becomes, a woman." In true existentialist fashion, Beauvoir challenged existing notions of sex by distinguishing it from gender, thereby establishing that women can cut across social constructions (such as gender). Witt acknowledges that Beauvoir (along with Wollstonecraft and Hannah Arendt) is elevated to the canon of philosophers, debunking the myth that "all philosophers are male." Feminist philosophy would not be feminist philosophy, after all, if it were not for Beauvoir.

Interestingly, however, despite the ideas of intersectionality and multilayered oppression discussed in the nineteenth century by Anna Julia Cooper, the feminist philosophy tradition was still limited to the works of Wollstonecraft, Beauvoir, Hélène Cixous, Judith Butler, Luce Irigaray, and other more mainstream women philosophers. While the course in *Feminist Philosophy* attempts to include women and feminists in a philosophic tradition, I noticed no works from philosophers of color or women philosophers of color included in the syllabus!

With my background on hooks, I noted her feminist theory was excluded from the discourse, despite enhancing and clarifying feminist philosophy. The differences raised by hooks between reformist and revolutionary feminism, for instance, shed light on the motivations of white, privileged feminist philosophers. Furthermore, her expansion of patriarchy into "White Supremacist Capitalist Patriarchy" highlights the complicated system of subjugation that not only targets women by their sex but other intersecting factors as well. I concluded that marginalizing hooks's feminist theories in the course rendered the course incomplete. Furthermore, aside from merely "adding" hooks to the course design, I used her critical framework to ensure students acknowledged their diversity and actively engaged in their learning.

Is bell hooks a Philosopher?

Aside from addressing the obvious "historical exclusion" of philosophers of color and marginalization of what George Yancy refers to as "inappropriate subjects"[12] in the course content, a challenge I posed to myself was how to integrate bell hooks's theories in a philosophy course while disrupting the passive method of transmitting philosophy and affirming the progressive nature of feminism. However, I had to justify hooks's inclusion before I could do this, given that hardcore philosophers and academicians have a strict definition of who and what a philosopher is. For instance, David Bournet and David Chalmers characterize professional philosophers as faculty members of philosophy departments or members of national philosophical associations.[13] Using Bournet and Chalmer's classification, hooks does not fall into the professional philosopher category. On the contrary, looking at Julian Baggini and Jeremy Stangroom's differentiation of philosophers and "non-philosophers," they discuss how physicist Alan Sokal, zoologist Richard Dawkins, and those from other professions are non-philosophers but have "strayed into philosophy, by accident or design."[14] These thinkers have become philosophers "temporarily" because they dealt with "trademark philosophical questions" and approached subject matters that are "primarily philosophical in nature."[15]

Similarly, the distinction between philosophers and non-philosophers who dabble in philosophy is an ongoing debate in Filipino philosophy. Jeremiah Joven Joaquin and I question the traditional concept of a Filipino philosopher, especially when scholars are labeled as mere non-philosophers, even if they engage with philosophy or apply philosophical methods in their work.[16] When I defended my dissertation on hooks, reviewers commented that she was not a philosopher, but my study was philosophical and, thus, acceptable.

Thus, including hooks in a philosophy course would assume that (1) she is a philosopher, first and foremost, or (2) she uses a philosophical method.

Pamela Sue Anderson asserts that the role of feminist philosophy is to critique the incumbent philosophical canon.[17] A feminist philosopher, therefore, questions "default interpretations of philosophical texts" and examines works developed by male, heterosexual, white, middle-class philosophers. hooks, however, takes Anderson's assertion further and critiques sexist biases such as those of Karl Marx and Antonio Gramsci and multilayered biases presented by other feminist philosophers as well.[18] This practice alone not only uses a feminist philosophical lens but also employs critical theory. This is also why Filipino academic Delia Aguilar is considered a feminist philosopher in her own right when she took part in analyzing Marxist and radical feminist theories.[19]

In my article "The Philosophical Heritage of bell hooks's Radical Feminism and Cultural Criticism," I argue that, as a cultural critic, hooks is not far from the canonical critical theorists such as Max Horkheimer, Friedrich Pollock, Herbert Marcuse, and Theodor Adorno.[20] hooks, after all, not only critiques feminist theory and improves the discourse of cultural criticism but enriches it by emphasizing the significance of eradicating multilayered oppression and transforming culture through a feminist perspective (Biana, 2020a).[21] If critical theory, as a philosophical approach to culture, aims to change the world by addressing injustices and inequalities by combining theory and praxis, hooks's cultural criticism makes the cut. In *Outlaw Culture: Resisting Representations*, hooks talks about her theory, praxis, and pedagogy and how she challenges the existing systems of domination, particularly racism, sexism, and class elitism.[22] This is also evident in her earlier, more philosophical and systematic works, such as *Feminist Theory: From Margin to Center.*[23]

Although American philosopher Sally Haslanger does not explicitly refer to hooks as a philosopher, she commends hooks as a "cultural theorist and a cultural critic doing really important work."[24] Furthermore, Haslanger also observes that hooks's work "shows us how symbols and norms and ideology play a role in understanding social categories" and explains "the role of culture in oppression."[25] With hooks at the helm of the postfeminist turn to culture, why are her works not included in the list of the postmodern greats who highlight securing meaning in cultural productions and texts when she has contributed not only to the critique of feminist theory but critical and social theory, as well? hooks has also enabled the oppressed to reimagine counterhegemonic actions.[26] This practice is epistemological in discipline, particularly with the trend of studies on epistemic injustice. Even before British philosopher Miranda Fricker's

(2007) *Epistemic Injustice: Power and the Ethics of Knowing* was published, hooks
had already discussed the oppressed groups' lack of capacity to know, their lack
of voice, which renders them susceptible to the power of dominant groups in
Talking Back: Thinking Feminist, Thinking Black. hooks analyzed the unique
injustices experienced by Black women as a product of white supremacist
capitalist patriarchy, while Fricker attributed them to epistemic injustices of
Blackness and womanhood.[27] These two concepts, however, are just the same,
with Fricker being (more) analytic. Perhaps the exclusion of hooks from the
philosopher title can be traced to accusations that her writing is ahistorical,
disorderly, lacking in methodology, and unscholarly.[28] Furthermore, she has been
criticized as forgetful of theories, lacking in critical awareness, and dismissive of
academic research formats.[29] Perhaps, as well, this exclusion could be attributed
to a type of "philosophical territorial arrogance" mentioned by Yancy.[30]

bell hooks as a Framework for Critique

I firmly believe that hooks is a philosopher and that her methods are
philosophical. Albeit controversial, I assert that she is what philosophers
consider a critical theorist, epistemologist, ethicist, or even a metaphysician!
Mako Fitts claims that hooks's work provides a "discursive understanding of
intersectional modes of oppression" and "a conceptual roadmap for creating
the conditions for social transformation," which stabilizes the work of women
philosophers and feminist philosophers of color.[31] This is perhaps why, besides
Scapp, other philosophers, such as Iris Marion Young and Kathryn Sophia
Belle, have likewise philosophically and politically engaged with her work. With
this in mind, I situate hooks's work in philosophy, and I use her conceptual
roadmap to evaluate the work of white and Filipino women philosophers. Most
significantly, however, I highlight her "praxis-oriented transgressive politics"[32]
and ensure that her framework is applied to the learning outcomes of my course.
Aside from integrating hooks's *Feminist Theory: From Margin to Center* as one
of the main references in my *Feminist Philosophy* course, I require students to
submit a cultural critique paper as one of their final requirements. This paper
will be preceded by analyzing the students' unique diversity dimensions to
situate their perspectives and privileges. This practice is my way of encouraging
students to understand existing hierarchies of power and their diverse political
stances. I then ask students to select a local film, advertisement, song, news
program, or any other cultural production and critique the text using hooks's

Table 4.1 Interrogating sex, race, and class representations[33]

Sex	Race	Class
In what period and social context is the representation conferred?		
How are individuals of a certain sex/class/ race portrayed in pop culture?		
• Are they given equal status? • Are they ignored? • Are they patronized? • Are they demeaned? • Are they idealized?		
• How important are the female characters? • How individual are they in their own right? • Are they credited with their existence and character? • How are they treated, in their relationship with others? • How much interest do the male characters exhibit in women's concerns?	• How important are the Black characters? • How individual are they in their own right? • Are they credited with their existence and character? • How are they treated in their relationship with white characters? • How much interest do the white characters exhibit in the Black characters' concerns?	• How important are the poor characters? • How individual are they in their own right? • Are they credited with their existence and character? • How are they treated in their relationships with affluent characters? • How much interest do the rich characters exhibit in the poor characters' concerns?

framework for interrogation. I instruct them to think critically and look at motivated representations in these productions. As an exercise to stay faithful to hooks's call for critical consciousness and her assertion that pop culture is where the pedagogy is,[34] I use this the Table 4.1 above as a guide for their cultural critique paper.

I also invite students to critique cultural productions by looking at representations through the lens of the oppressed, which presupposes an examination of the authenticity or truthfulness of portrayals and the possible impact of representations. This is evident in the following questions: "Granted that these portrayals are what they are, how do they influence certain ideals and ways of thinking? Do they enforce systems of domination? Are they helpful in constructing pathways towards liberation from oppressive White Capitalist Supremacist Patriarchal systems?"[35] Since hooks uses the lens of Blackness and whiteness for the column on race, students tend to replace this lens with a decolonizing mindset. For instance, there have been a lot of papers that tackle the prevalence of mestiza or mestizo-looking models that promote skin products. Such representations result from the Spanish and American colonization of the country. Similarly, some replace the race column with the concept of place. Since the Philippines is not as multicultural as the United States, the United Kingdom, or Singapore, where differences in race and skin color are more obvious, students become evaluative of representations in terms of regionalist and placist notions. They are also critical of the portrayals of aspects of place, such as language and linguistics, food, and other indicators.

The exercise aims to develop students' capacities for critical consciousness and strengthen their radical voices. While one critique cannot ultimately transform culture, awareness contributes to a culture resistant to problematic representations. Any recognition of the impact of pop culture images is a skill necessary for feminist philosophy students. As I have observed, this activity has promoted a student paradigm shift. It allows them to put theory into action and engage in critique and praxis. However, I stress in my classes that hooks's method can be improved to recognize *other* groups. For instance, hooks focuses specifically on binary oppositions (male/female, white/Black, rich/poor) when other marginalized groups may not be authentically represented. For instance, the LGBTQIA+ community, younger or older people, members of the middle class, persons with disabilities, women from developing nations, Indigenous peoples, etc. These groups are also important, particularly in the Philippine context, where intersectional factors of oppression are quite different from those of comparatively developed nations. The Western feminist lens (which includes hooks's lens) has likewise ignored the uniqueness of Asian women.[36] For instance, hooks collectively refers to Asian women as "third world diva girls." Many feminist scholars from Asia assert that women's experiences in their various nations are diverse and cannot be reduced to simply being *Asian*. Students must also be aware of the multiple voices of women and people excluded from hooks's discourse. With this in mind, we can think of hooks's roadmap not just as a cause of African Americans, but as a framework that can also be applied to the plight of Filipino women and other marginalized groups. This type of understanding enacts critical self-reflection true to the spirit of hooks's vision of mutuality.

Final Thoughts

The reformulated *Feminist Philosophy* course brings to the fore the concept of intersectionality or multilayered oppression. With my invitation to teach the revived course *Women in Philosophy* in 2020, I also included Sojourner Truth, bell hooks, and Filipino women philosophers such as Mary John Mananzan and Delia Aguilar in the course content. By including hooks's feminist theory and applying her cultural criticism framework to interrogate representations of pop culture, students gain a feminist consciousness that is both critical and intersectional. With inspiration from the course, some of my students have even culminated their philosophy graduate degrees by working on hooks's ideas on engaged pedagogy, cultural criticism, and the feminist philosophy of education—something quite unthinkable in the rigid discipline of philosophy. Such student work further expands hooks's development of feminist philosophy as they genuinely make new knowledge themselves, further destabilizing the idea of who "does" philosophy.

Some students have also published cultural critique papers using hooks's framework. My doctoral student Ruel Nalam, co-authored a piece entitled "Terms of Endearment: The Displacement of Inday" based on his critique paper of the representations of *Inday* in movies and shows. Joseph Martin Jose has a forthcoming journal article, "bell hooks' Postfeminism and Indigenous Women in the Philippines." He wrote this paper for my class seven years ago and claims that hooks changed his view of feminism. Jonathan Florendo, whom I supervised for his dissertation "A hooksian Critique of Spady's Outcomes-based Framework as Applied in the Philippines," inspired his published work, "Re-examining the Philosophy of Outcome-Based Education." These works prove that hooks fits the philosophical bill and motivates an active critique of representations and sociocultural structures and institutions.

In a mini-autobiography where hooks narrates the philosophical career of Beauvoir in contrast to Jean Paul Sartre, she mentions that she considers herself a feminist philosopher despite the common view of academic circles that she is not one.[37] Scapp affirms this by debunking the myth that one has to have a philosophical system similar to Hegel to be a philosopher:

> hooks asks the question what is good, what is real, and what is it that we know. She does so in relation to race, class, and gender and so she is best understood as philosophizing about the dynamics and relationships that exist within a social and cultural context. What someone who is genuinely philosophical does is ask certain kinds of questions. expressing a profound commitment to freedom, justice and love, hooks' work should remind us that this is a philosophical position and a philosophical worldview.
>
> (Scapp in hooks 2012, 234)

Although hooks was not initially thought of as a philosopher or *philosophical* per se, Rebecca Buxton and Lisa Whiting name bell hooks in their list of *Philosopher Queens*, which puts her on the same level as the Hypatia and Diotima of ancient

Greek philosophy.[38] While still questionable in some philosophy circles, hooks's
work is essential to teaching feminist philosophy and promoting critical thinking
and subversive consciousness. She is not only a feminist theorist and cultural
critic but "a philosopher in the truest sense of the word," and we must not simply
"add" her to the syllabus but make the most out of her transgressive politics in
philosophy.[39]

Notes

1   Gina A. Opiniano, "Introduction: Envisaging a More Gender-responsive
    Philosophy," *Suri* 9, no. 1 (2021): 1–13; Marella Ada V. Mancenido-Bolaños, "From
    Exclusion to Inclusion: The Case of Filipino Women Philosophers," *KRITIKE* 17,
    no. 2 (2023): 1.
2   bell hooks, *Teaching to Transgress: Education as the Practice of Freedom* (New York:
    Routledge; Edition Unstated, December 1, 1994), 140–1.
3   Ibid., 143–4.
4   Mancenido-Bolaños, "From Exclusion to Inclusion," 3–7.
5   hooks, *Teaching to Transgress*, 143–4.
6   Ibid., 144.
7   Mancenido-Bolaños, "From Exclusion to Inclusion."
8   Maria del Guadalupe Davidson and George Yancy, *Critical Perspectives on Bell
    Hooks* (New York: Routledge, 2009), 6.
9   Charlotte Witt, "How Feminism Is Re-writing the Philosophical Canon," *The Alfred
    P. Stiernotte Memorial Lecture in Philosophy at Quinnipiac College*, October 2, 1996.
10 Natalie Stoljar, "The Metaphysics of Gender," in *A Companion to Applied
    Philosophy* (Malden, MA: John Wiley & Sons, 2016), 211–23, https://doi.
    org/10.1002/9781118869109.ch15.
11 Karen Vintges, "Simone de Beauvoir: A Feminist Thinker for Our Times," *Hypatia*
    14, no. 4 (October 1999): 133–44, https://doi.org/10.1111/j.1527-2001.1999.
    tb01257.x.
12 George Yancy, *Reframing the Practice of Philosophy: Bodies of Color, Bodies of
    Knowledge* (New York: State University of New York Press, 2012), 1.
13 David Bourget and David J. Chalmers, "What Do Philosophers Believe?"
    *Philosophical Studies: An International Journal for Philosophy in the Analytic
    Tradition* 170, no. 3 (2014): 465–500.
14 Julian Baggini and Jeremy Stangroom, *What Philosophers Think* (New York: A&C
    Black, 2005).
15 Ibid., 6.

16 Hazel T. Biana and Jeremiah Joven B. Joaquin, "Questioning Demeterio's Approach to Filipino Philosophy," *Philosophia: International Journal of Philosophy* 24, no. 1 (2023): 131–55.

17 Sarah Gamble, *The Routledge Companion to Feminism and Postfeminism* (New York: Routledge, 2004), 117–18.

18 Hazel T. Biana, "The Philosophical Heritage of Bell Hooks' Radical Feminism and Cultural Criticism," *Scientia* 9, no. 2 (2020): 40.

19 Biana and Joaquin, "Questioning Demeterio's Approach to Filipino Philosophy," 139.

20 Biana, "The Philosophical Heritage of Bell Hooks' Radical Feminism and Cultural Criticism," 42–4.

21 Ibid., 40.

22 bell hooks, *Outlaw Culture: Resisting Representations* (Routledge, 2006), 3.

23 bell hooks, *Feminist Theory: From Margin to Center* (Pluto Press, 2000), 3–5.

24 Jeremiah Joven B. Joaquin and Hazel T. Biana, "From Social Construction to Social Critique: An Interview with Sally Haslanger," *Hypatia* 37, no. 1 (February 2022): 9, https://doi.org/10.1017/hyp.2021.82.

25 Ibid., 9.

26 del Guadalupe Davidson and Yancy, *Critical Perspectives on Bell Hooks*, ix.

27 Maggie Clarke, "Epistemic Injustice and White Supremacy in Information Literacy Instruction," *LOEX Conference Proceedings 2021*, January 1, 2022, https://commons.emich.edu/loexconf2021/20.

28 Patricia Bell-Scott, "The Centrality of Marginality," ed. Bell Hooks, *The Women's Review of Books* 2, no. 5 (1985): 3–4, https://doi.org/10.2307/4019632; Cynthia G. Franklin, *Academic Lives: Memoir, Cultural Theory, and the University Today* (University of Georgia Press, 2009), 227, https://www.jstor.org/stable/j.ctt46n9kp; Barbara Christian, "Black Feminism and the Academy," in *Theories of Race and Racism: A Reader*, eds. Les Black and John Solomos (London: Routledge, 2001), 462–77.

29 Hazel T. Biana, "Organizing bell hooks' Frameworks for Interrogating Representations," *Plaridel* 19, no. 1 (June 2022): 3–4.

30 Yancy, *Reframing the Practice of Philosophy*, 2.

31 Mako Fitts, "Theorizing Transformative Revolutionary Action: The Contribution of bell hooks to Emancipatory Knowledge Production," *The CLR James Journal* 17, no. 1 (2011): 112.

32 Ibid., 112.

33 Biana, "Organizing bell hooks' Frameworks for Interrogating Representations," 17.

34 bell hooks, bell hooks—Cultural Criticism & Transformation, 1997, 2, https://www.mediaed.org/transcripts/Bell-Hooks-Transcript.pdf.

35 Ibid., 18–19.

36	Hazel T. Biana, "Extending Bell Hooks' Feminist Theory," *Journal of International Women's Studies* 21, no. 1 (February 24, 2020): 13–29.

37	bell hooks, "True Philosophers," in *Beauvoir and Western Thought from Plato to Butler*, eds. Shannon M. Mussett and William S. Wilkerson (New York: State University of New York Press, 2012), 233–4.

38	Rebecca Buxton and Lisa Whiting, *The Philosopher Queens: The Lives and Legacies of Philosophy's Unsung Women* (London: Unbound Publishing, 2020), 199.

39	hooks, "True Philosophers," 236.

5

Engaged Pedagogies while Asynchronously Online: Students as Experimental Storytellers

Desi Self

The radical pedagogical legacy of bell hooks is invaluable to me as a queer Black scholar and academic. I regularly refer to hooks's teaching trilogy (*Teaching to Transgress,*[1] *Teaching Critical Thinking,*[2] and *Teaching Community*[3]) as both a theoretical lighthouse and a practical guide leading me through my course development as well as day-to-day student engagements. For the purpose of this particular reflection, I focus primarily on *Teaching to Transgress* because of the significant impact that particular text had on my development of the course I explore here. Similarly to what hooks shared in *Teaching to Transgress,* as I began to teach, I, too, was inspired to think more critically about class dynamics within and outside of learning spaces as a result of my academic experiential history, which in most cases enforced a hierarchical tenor. The hierarchical tenor structuring these learning spaces either made me feel wrong about my scholarly perspective, or had me constantly on-call to intellectually represent aspects of the many intersections of identity the space inscribed upon me. hooks's wisdom helped me to know that there are ways to engage the learning space and everyone within it to challenge more traditional hierarchical pedagogical legacies propagated throughout institutions of higher education.

I function precariously as a graduate student teacher, where I'm not exactly autonomous, but am at a level where I bear responsibility for teaching undergraduates. I enter the academic scene as a queer Black femme-presenting women's, gender, and sexuality studies (WGSS) scholar, which brings epistemic tensions in itself, one being a preconception of any course I teach lacking intellectual rigor. There are also preconceptions of my value as an instructor when the WGSS courses I am allowed to teach are often systematically flagged as courses that qualify as institutional diversity credits. The shift to online learning that the Covid-19 pandemic brought in spring of 2020 led to my online asynchronous courses being full each semester, which initially was quite exciting having students who were presumably there out of their interest to learn and think critically. However, with each online asynchronous course I taught, I began to see trends in class dynamics where the diffuse state of the virtual classroom brought additional pedagogical obstacles. These included less student engagement without the demand for regular facetime, less critical engagement with the course content, and more demand for graded results without critical feedback from me. Notwithstanding that, hooks helps me to feel excited about entering any learning space—whether in-person and/or virtually—as a student-teacher where I hopefully receive whatever outcomes the course content might bring and use it to inform the direction(s) in which my courses progress.

By the time I was entering my introduction to feminist theory online asynchronous course, I had a few semesters of teaching asynchronously online under my belt. I was entering with an idea that to create an open space for learning and engagement, I had to begin by acknowledging the fact that each person entering this digital learning space comes from a unique lived experience, including myself. There is a precipitating tension inherent in realizing the diversity happening within the course I am teaching for an institutional diversity credit, just as hooks asked in *Teaching to Transgress*, "How many feminist scholars can respond effectively when faced with a racially and ethnically diverse audience who may not share similar class backgrounds, language, levels of understanding, communication skills, and concerns?"[4] While hooks raised a significant consideration that many WGSS teachers regularly face, I come to this signification also thinking about how to account for this with little to no facetime. I started addressing the issue by providing mixed-media content because perhaps one method of learning doesn't work for everyone entering the course. The mixed-media I had us cover throughout the course included short informative videos from various conferences and interviews, documentaries, films, readings, poetry, speeches, and more. I also anchored the course in Black feminist theory and legacies of Black feminist activism because Black feminism centers the perspectives and experiences of the multiple oppressed in order to make and sustain systemic change. A component of Black feminist thought is an openness to try new and different things in an effort to grow toward liberation. As such, in following this philosophy, I also was experimental with the types of assignments I would have the students take on and corresponding spaces for student feedback.

Creative Storytelling Assignment

In essence, the Creative Storytelling assignment is a unique combination of a biography and creative narrative. The assignment remixes the quintessential biography assignment by having students build a creative narrative that combines a biographical element, a corresponding social issue, and all of it has to be fact-driven. Each student is individually assigned a feminist thinker from underrepresented communities. The experimental aspect of the assignment is the autonomy given to students to choose the type of narrative they develop about their given feminist thinker. I describe the assignment in present tense because I still use and refine this particular assignment and am recognizing its ongoing vitality. Throughout, I closely reflect on key passages throughout hooks's *Teaching to Transgress* in order to expound upon my process of seeking and exploring experimental storytelling as engaged pedagogy in my online asynchronous introduction to feminist theory course. I also include examples from the many types of stories my students have produced as well as portions of student contributions to online asynchronous class discussions in an effort to give more of an idea of the creative and critically engaged work their experimental storytelling yielded.

The course flow was the first thing that came to mind when developing my syllabus. Since we didn't have any particular time or physical place to meet and engage, I immediately began brainstorming potential assignments that might spark and maintain engagement regardless of when and where they happen. I initially presumed I'd provide the quintessential discussion boards that online courses usually employ. However, upon reflection, I realized that was my compulsion to maintain the status quo for online class dynamics that typically result in minimal engagement and generate little-to-no meaningful connections among students, either intellectually or otherwise. The passage from *Teaching to Transgress* that spoke to me focuses on our purpose when entering and engaging the learning space. hooks notes:

> To enter classroom settings in colleges and universities with the will to share the desire to encourage excitement, was to transgress. Not only did it require movement beyond accepted boundaries, but excitement could not be generated without a full recognition of the fact that there could never be an absolute set agenda governing teaching practices.[5]

From this excerpt, I gleaned critical insight about a generative way to strategize various intellectual possibilities that might catalyze the space in effort to get students' eyes on the course page and keep them regularly checking in and engaging one another about class content as the course progresses. I realized I wouldn't have a chance to see any critical changes in engagement if I didn't open my mind to different ways of exploring the course materials in the asynchronous online learning space.

The Creative Storytelling assignment was the most engaging, even if the storytelling development process wasn't entirely ideal, considering that most students in the course had never been given such a creativity-based assignment to submit. Initially, upon posting the assignment sheet and explaining it via recorded assignment overview, I was inundated with questions for clarity and general trepidation via email. On the whole, students seemed uncomfortable with the creative freedom they were given to present on an assigned feminist thinker. Some thought it was a trap. I fell back on another passage from *Teaching to Transgress* to remain open to debriefing students both individually and collectively throughout the time they had been given to complete their storytelling assignments with the intention to communicate the autonomy therein:

> Progressive, holistic education, "engaged pedagogy" is more demanding than conventional critical or feminist pedagogy [...] it emphasizes well-being. That means that teachers must be actively committed to a process of self-actualization that promotes their own well-being if they are to teach in a manner that empowers students.[6]

I realized that I must do my part to instill some sense of comfort in my students regarding their creative process, their willingness to be vulnerable when any questions or concerns arise, and let them know the variety of ways that I am supporting them through the process. I had to show them my own thought process through sharing my own creative narrative. By doing this, I not only gave my students a brief example of my expectations, but I also gave them a glimpse into my own thought process including particular creative interests and stylistic flair. I also think that by sharing my own creative narrative as a model, students were able to have a tangible example that indicated my eagerness to show that I want the space to flow against traditional student-teacher hierarchical dynamics, uplifting their voices and unique perspectives.

Although giving the students creative control did bring a bit of anxiety, it also seemed that the autonomy inspired creative curiosity and openness when submitting their stories to the class discussion board. As a result, student responses were filled with creative ideas, meaningful insights, and open critical discourse. It seemed to help foster a sense of well-being and community within our digital classroom, as after the storytelling assignment, students were more open to raising their questions and feedback to one another as the class proceeded. I was blown away by this, especially considering that I doubt I would have even thought about such an experimental assignment without hooks's pedagogical reflections.

Self-reflection and Feedback

It is worth restating that all of the method/ologies I employed were deeply rooted in histories of Black feminisms and activisms, including critical reflexivity. Throughout the semester, I deliberately set up times to sit and reflect on my process in relation to any student feedback received and a more general sense of class pace. I had to regularly be present with myself and consciously open to addressing any pedagogical barriers the course might have been in danger of hitting. At the end of each content segment, I generated self check-ins with a set of questions I responded to, which shifted the way the course proceeded. This is particularly important when reflecting on the Creative Storytelling assignment—academically unconventional—and offering students more agency about the trajectory of the content they produced, which was also new to them. Using self-reflexive check-ins, I was able to modify the questions and frequency in order to be more attentive and responsive to student questions and/or concerns regarding any impending pedagogical barriers. This required that I be present with myself throughout the assignment process to ensure that the assignment did not derail our critical engagement with the feminist thinkers we discussed.

Another method I heavily relied upon during the course relates to the improvisational aspect of teaching. hooks's words about teaching as a performative act[7] helped me to hone the ability to identify and implement strategies that meaningfully impacted my students' attentiveness. I understand this as the pedagogical pivot. I, for one, love the idea of being able to pivot based on class response, and the Creative Storytelling assignment allowed for a lot of opportunities for me to do so. Pivoting manifested in various ways throughout the storytelling assignment process, most clearly through assignment sheet modifications. I could fine-tune and grow the Creative Storytelling assignment as a result of receiving student questions and concerns about the assignment structure, including how I worded the assignment instructions, and then modified based on students' trepidation. I also received gratitude from my students for being attentive and making changes based on collective responses. Through end-of-semester reflection, students let me know that they felt like they had a voice in the class, and I listened and was there with them throughout the process. On the whole, I was able to see the content become more effectively consumed as the content was constantly being reinterpreted and reshaped through the variety of student stories flowing through it throughout of the semester.

Although it requires a lot of vulnerability, flexibility, critical thought, and reflexive moments, being open to trying different ways of learning from students provided invaluable opportunities to grow my pedagogy with my online asynchronous feminist theory introductory course. hooks is there to remind me to be open to change, student feedback, and to novelty within learning spaces because the potential there is to grow engagement with the important content outside of the bounds of the learning space, a particularly prescient move considering an asynchronous online course. What kept me encouraged at the start of the course and helped me stay present is the following passage, which I turned to right before the first day of classes. hooks notes:

> Engaged pedagogy not only compels me to be constantly creative in the classroom, it also sanctions involvement with students beyond that setting [...] The important lesson that we learn together, the lesson that allows us to move together within and beyond the classroom, is one of mutual engagement [...] I could never say that I have no idea of the way students respond to my pedagogy; they give me constant feedback [...] When students see themselves as mutually responsible for the development of a learning community, they offer constructive input.[8]

The passage was and is a pedagogical call to action and analysis for me. hooks's words propelled me to facilitate the class in ways that sought to challenge the quintessential classroom set-up where there was consistently an atmosphere of possibility not only for my students to engage course content in ways that best suit their unique learning styles but a possibility to connect, critically engage, and learn from one another through their own words and research. There was also a class atmosphere of possibility for me as the queer Black scholar/teacher I am, to learn new and different ways to engage foundational feminist theory, which is priceless to me personally, pedagogically, and most crucially, to my dissertation writing.

Student Narratives and Thoughtful Peer Engagement

In concluding, I will move to share a few examples from the inaugural Creative Storytelling assignment. While there were a range of narratives presented in the Creative Storytelling discussion board, most of them were structured as either an editorial piece on the feminist thinker, in relation to their engagement with a fictional event, or an entirely fictive scenario in which students infused biographical information and factual events about their given feminist thinker. The first example is an excerpt from a student story about how their assigned feminist thinker initially responds to a current event:

> It started like a normal day for adrienne maree brown. She woke up early, wrote in her blog while sipping her morning coffee, and then all of a sudden, she got a notification: "Roe v. Wade Has Been Overturned." Her heart sank, her throat felt tight. She felt everything and then nothing. How can a country that allows weapons to sneak into elementary schools now force people to give birth and send those children to schools and hope they make it home every night? A country currently facing a formula shortage that even if people are able to carry their children and birth them, may now face issues feeding them and making sure such a basic need is met?[9]

The student used their research and creative process to engage in an experimental embodiment of their feminist thinker addressing an actual current event. From the point of view of adrienne maree brown, the student imagines the ways their given thinker contributes to the betterment of US culture by critically responding to the current event that the story initially raises.

The next example from a student's story was framed in the voice of the feminist thinker: "If you happen to search up my name, Michelle Alexander, and find 'New Jim Crow Law,' don't be alarmed; I didn't actually create new Jim Crow laws. That would simply feel like a crime against myself [...] But I'll explain myself instead of letting google click bait you into thinking I may be controversial."[10] I chose to share this example because it seemed like this student wanted to enter their story with humor, in which they attempted to explain their assigned thinker's famous works and tried to imagine how they would want their contributions to help work toward their larger goal. I chose to share these two examples because they both began a bit sensationally, yet gave my students space to discuss their assigned feminist thinker's factual information and sociocultural contributions.

Since critical student engagement and feedback were major factors for the progress and success of the course, I will share some meaningful moments of student engagement with each other during the Creative Storytelling assignment on the discussion board in our digital classroom. The following passages are indicative of the sense of openness and community fostered throughout the semester. The first example I share is from one student responding to what resonated with them from their peer's story:

> I think this was such an inventive way to bring Leah's accomplishments and works of notability to light by depicting it as a fantasy superhero story. Your piece reminded me of a children's book, but in a clever way where you're describing a role model for their contributions to social change. This would be a cool way to teach children about updated modern practices with acceptance of one's sexual orientation, gender identification, and disabilities. We look up to Superman, Wonder Woman, Spiderman, but painting social figures provides the youth a sense of belonging that they can relate to.[11]

This student seemed to respond meaningfully to their peer's story by identifying the parts that stood out to them and why. This to me indicated that this student took time to read and think about their peer's story in ways that helped them develop informed and supportive feedback. The next example comes from a student who attempted to discuss critical insight from their peer's story:

> Hi there! I really loved your creative narrative and the way it demonstrated empathy in response to situations that are difficult to find solutions to sometimes. In allowing Aimee to not hold judgment towards, the girl and her experience, and sharing her the options that she needed, she helped the girl help someone she cared about. Aimee gave the girl and her family or those she shared it with the power to change their lives for the better. In addition, I noticed how you made subtle mention of the discrimination and stigma that illegal immigrants face and how it is often something that is kept hidden to avoid its consequences. In my opinion there was an underlying sense of shame and a hint of sadness in the tone of the girl's voice when telling Aimee her circumstances.[12]

I consider this student feedback to be very compelling because it indicates how their peer's story provoked them to continue looking into their peer's assigned feminist thinker. I also shared this because of the insight the student points to within the limited word count they were given. Students were encouraged to develop their stories and feedback in a casual, open fashion, which is evidenced throughout the examples I've included here. I found that allowing them to engage with the Creative Storytelling assignment more casually made them less anxious about sharing their respective contributions, more open to the research they were required to do, and also to the vulnerability required in the storytelling class discussion. According to student feedback about the course more generally, students appreciated having a range of assignments where some allowed for more casual engagement, and others had more formal structural requirements, because it helped them to practice time management skills while growing their critical thinking.

Ultimately, it is hooks's pedagogical process that rethinks the quintessential classroom in ways that allow for constant reinterpretation, critique, and reflexive moments that challenge dominant ideology throughout academic systems and structures that really helped me to critically pivot. Using hooks's teaching trilogy, in this case more specifically *Teaching to Transgress,* gave me the tools to think and act in ways that changed the entire trajectory of the course. My hooksian openness to pedagogical change and attentiveness to student feedback and reaction allowed me able to remain vigilant in assessing classroom dynamics. I was also able to achieve my goal of facilitating meaningful intellectual growth and interpersonal connection and engagement in an asynchronous virtual learning space, which comes with barriers of distance and spatiotemporal disconnect. We were able to shape our digital classroom by engaging experimental ways of learning that included a range of assignments where student experience was centered throughout. *The Creative Storytelling assignment allowed me to see how we all were able to contribute to the online asynchronous class while learning different analytical techniques and teaching in our own respective ways.*

Notes

1   bell hooks, *Teaching to Transgress: Education as the Practice of Freedom* (New York: Routledge, 1994).

2   bell hooks, *Teaching Critical Thinking: Practical Wisdom* (New York: Routledge, 2010).

3   bell hooks, *Teaching Community: A Pedagogy of Hope* (New York: Routledge, 2003).

4   hooks, *Teaching to Transgress,* 112.

5   Ibid., 7.

6   Ibid., 15.

7   Ibid., 11.

8   Ibid., 205–6.
9   Anonymized example from student work A.
10   Anonymized example from student work B.
11   Anonymized example from class discussion.
12   bell hooks, *Teaching Community: A Pedagogy of Hope* (New York: Routledge, 2003).

6

All about bell: Foregrounding bell hooks in the Classroom as Engaged Pedagogy

Megan Feifer

Appointed as one of the inaugural Teacher-Scholars in Residence at the bell hooks center of Berea College, I thought, *this is it*; the years spent reading, thinking about, and teaching bell hooks's work had led me to a college with a bell hooks center, a bell hooks Institute, and the special collections and archives housing her papers. Finally, a place *all about bell*! Alas, upon settling into my position at Berea, I was alarmed by the percentage of students who had no idea who she was. Here, I encountered the stark reality that bell hooks, the visionary feminist and dissident intellectual of the late twentieth and early twenty-first century, was unheard of in the *one place* where her legacy appears most visible. In this reflection, I consider what it means when students who "should" know who bell hooks is, do not, while reflecting on my own strategy for addressing this lack of awareness in the classroom. Namely, I think through how we move from merely citing a quote or two from bell hooks's work to foregrounding her multi-genre texts in our classrooms as acts of engaged pedagogy and praxis, a labor all the more exigent in the face of hooks's untimely transitioning in 2021, the penchant toward historicizing her work, and the call to erase her from High School Advanced Placement courses in the United States.

I came to know bell hooks's work during my first year of college. I was a working-poor, first-generation student with no language to describe my place in the world. I felt the rage of and had internalized the sense of never being good enough or having enough, but I lacked the words to describe the systemic structures that defined my life. Freighted with experiential awareness, I arrived at her collected writings longing for clarity and profoundly hurting. In her words, I found language and guidance, a means to imagine otherwise while feeling a sense of deep belonging. I quickly became a forth-teller, a herald, or what my students would call a "serious fan-girl," proclaiming hooks's work to anyone who would listen. I have since spent the last fifteen years as an educator, grounding my scholarship and pedagogical practices in her life's work.

Arriving at Berea College in 2021, I was tasked with teaching general studies courses, co-organizing two summer symposiums, designing and participating in weekly programmatic center events, and engaging in scholarship. My two primary research projects included this edited collection and the *bell hooks digital archive project.* I imagined *bell hooks's Radical Pedagogy* as a co-created body of work addressing the wealth of knowledge found in hooks's pedagogical trilogy. Like many, I had used her collection in the various classrooms in which I had taught, but had yet to see a sustained body of work engaging with all three books. I yearned for dialogue, a conversation with educators across learning spaces who were applying and expanding upon her suggested practices. The second project, the *bell hooks digital archive,* is a forthcoming public humanities website dedicated to preserving hooks's life and works through a curated selection of digitized artifacts found within her papers alongside a community archive, biographical, and critical biographical features, interviews, and pedagogical materials. Freely accessible online, the digital archive will preserve hooks's artistic, intellectual, political, and personal works while ensuring space for ongoing engagement. Throughout my three-year fellowship at the bell hooks center, I was committed to thinking about ways to continuously elevate and engage with hooks's work—before and after her passing.

Now looking back, it was naïve of me to think any institution would hold, let alone honor the late bell hooks in her fullness. She, herself, had long decided to walk away from higher education for its embodiment of the very "imperialist, white supremacist, cis-hetero patriarch[al]" systems and practices she fervently critiqued, in addition to its trenchant politics of extraction and exploitation. Nor should I have been surprised when I stepped into a classroom of twenty or so first-year college students, entirely unaware of her work. Berea College, despite its abolitionist beginnings, is a predominantly white institution (PWI) serving a large majority of students from Appalachia, a population of students coming out of minimally resourced K-12 school systems that are often contested battlegrounds for the dictates of conservative politicians.

It became clear to me that to bring hooks's work into the classroom, I needed to think about the liberatory possibilities of such within local and temporal contexts. Teaching bell hooks in Kentucky would require a deeper understanding of how dis/ability, race, class, gender, and sexuality were not only historically codified in rural Appalachian spaces but actively interpreted and shaped by contemporary conservative and neoliberal rhetoric. Also necessary to building adequate context for our work together was building a critical understanding of the college's mission. Since its founding in 1892, Berea College has prided itself on its integrated, co-educational origins and free tuition policy. As one of ten federal work colleges in the United States, Berea waives the cost of attendance in exchange for ten hours of student labor each week, a project aimed at shifting students' material and economic conditions that is politically and rhetorically rooted in boot-strap ideologies around becoming degreed.

Here, the mutually shared experiences a college degree could not erase, for my students and me, were the grief and death that accompany the grinding poverty of our respective origins. Moreover, the cumulative traumas ascribed to generational poverty and lack, or those affective experiences of growing up poor in extractive and negligent economies. The college's promise of "coming out of poverty" will not heal intergenerational wounding, let alone bring back the dead. Simultaneously, we shared knowledge and skills taught to us by resistant members of our home communities actively working to do more than just survive. In the context of Berea, I found it necessary to begin with the one critical entry point with which we shared intimate knowledge: class.

Poverty, and the myriad ways it manifested, was a unifying force that determined our life experiences. In the classroom, using our intimate knowledge of class and classism became a starting place for critical thinking and engagement with the dictates of economics in our lives and the various forms of homegrown resistance we had come to practice. The general studies classroom quickly became a space where bell hooks's writings took center stage. Together, we read *Bone Black: Memories of Girlhood* (1997) and *Where We Stand: Class Matters* (2000) alongside examining artifacts from the bell hooks papers as guides to develop a clearer understanding of the influence of class positionality on not only bell hooks's life and theory, but also on our own processes of self-creation and survivance.

It was not long before we realized the impossibility of talking about class without considering how the intersections of dis/ability, race, gender, and sexuality also inform our lives. But, starting with one critical point of entry allowed for what hooks describes as

> a context for building solidarity [...] [one] that cannot be expressed solely through shared critique of the privileged, [but that is rooted] in a politics of resistance that is fundamentally anti-racist [and] that recognizes that [...] students from poor and working-class backgrounds had common experiences history had not taught us how to sufficiently name or theoretically articulate.[1]

Each text in hooks's teaching trilogy contains a close analysis of class and the importance of building solidarity across lines of shared experiences and differences. This is because radical engaged pedagogy for hooks required not only inspiring transgressive political thought and action but also community-building, wherein individuals actively engage in collective struggle through a commitment to transformative justice via critical thinking, self-analysis, difficult dialog, critique, and ultimately, transformation. This type of solidarity does not happen in spaces where only flat critiques of power and the cancellation of individuals exist; instead, community building requires modeling and practicing relationality.

Using class as a critical entry point to examine systems of domination provided space for us to consider the oscillating relationship between privilege and oppression in each of our lives. In doing so, we applied the very feminist thinking and practices hooks laid out in her teaching trilogy. Through a set of framing questions for the course and the close reading of hooks's multi-genre works, we witnessed how class, in addition to race and gender, deeply impacted her own life. Here, rather than relying on a quote or two of hooks, or as Mikki Kendall argues, the practice that favors "a handful of favorite and easy to absorb quotes" we took the time to engage holistically with hooks's oeuvre.[2] The outcome was a witnessing of the ways in which hooks grappled with the very questions we were beginning to think through ourselves:

- How does one's socioeconomic status impact health and well-being, educational attainment, and access?
- What are the emotional impacts of class?
  - What are the affects/effects of narratives associated with class status?
- How have the communities we come from shaped us, encouraged survivance, joy, and resistance?
- What skills, practices, and ways of being have we learned and embodied from our home communities? How have these skills played a role in how we identify as individuals and community?

As we paged through the chapters of *Where We Stand: Class Matters*, we developed a common language to interrogate and critique our own political passivity toward economic conditions in the United States. For students, this meant learning to hold a critical stance toward the narratives that compelled them to seek a college degree in the first place. Through a short writing exercise, we listed and analyzed the narratives we were told about obtaining a college degree. One by one, we noted which sentiment was standard/different amongst us and how so before unpacking its influence on our perceptions of where we came from. We intimately discussed the demand of academia on working-class, working-poor, folks of color, and first-generation students "to surrender memory, to forget the past and claim the assimilated present as the only worthwhile and meaningful reality."[3] From there, we could reflect on the psychic and emotional wounding, the sacrifices made, and the wealth of contradictions we were navigating while recognizing the need for critical vigilance and the continuous reexamination of our political understandings and practices.

In tandem with *Where We Stand*, we listened to podcasts like *Strapped: A Look at Poverty in America* and the *Poverty Research & Policy: Institute for Research on Poverty* to debunk the myth of the United States as a classless society wherein individuals from any background can rise to economic ranks. We examined the history of, and present actions by, those in power to splinter solidarity movements across lines of difference as a means of stymying grassroots political power. Moreover, we took a close look at consumer culture. Namely, we examined our role as consumers in exploiting environments and workers worldwide for fast and cheap goods through a rhetorical analysis exercise. Here, we looked at the language found in popular advertisements to persuade consumers into the cycle of purchasing "updated" versions of the same items, specifically technology. In doing so, we uncovered the long history of planned obsolescence in US marketing and manufacturing. Collectively, we engaged in sharpening our class consciousness while thinking long and hard about how intersectional oppressions further impacted our experiences and understandings of class.

Simultaneously, *Where We Stand* created space for students to do the one thing hooks modeled so well: to critique. Here, students took issue with hooks's call for minimalist practices, including living simply, interdependency, and the commitment to sharing goods to resist what she perceived as "hedonistic consumer culture." For students, hooks's critique countered everything they'd been told about capitalism, going to college, and earning a degree to make money. Raised on narratives that emphasized the value of one's worth based on the amount of money they would make caused students to struggle with the very idea that their desire for and acquiring of material goods was avaricious because that was the behavior expected of them by everyone around them. As the generation having grown up in the period of late capitalism and neoliberalism, students did not take issue with the notion that "the good life has come to be seen as the life where one can have whatever one wants, where no desire is seen as excessive."[4] hooks's critique not only engendered students to think critically about her commentary, but also the very narratives they had come to accept and believe. Through this critical entry point, we were able to think about the propagation of boot-strap and good life narratives, who benefits from them, what the costs are, and who bears the weight of those costs. As such, the classroom became a space for critical and transgressive thinking and reflection.

While *Where We Stand* guided us to think through some of the framing questions of the class, *Bone Black: Memories of Girlhood* fostered the beginning of a process of healing and recovery for students. In broad strokes, *Bone Black* reveals the beauty and complexity of coming of age, coming to self, and finding one's voice while grappling with systems of domination in the world at large and at home. The memoir encourages readers to think about the importance of homeplace, ancestors, and the values learned early on. hooks's memoir modeled the reconfiguration of dominant narratives of homeplace while holding space for students to do the same. While challenged to think critically about existing narratives, students identified and honed homeplace values while coming to voice and collectivity around the pressing issues of their time.

Teaching general education courses over the last three years has again affirmed the importance of radical engaged pedagogy. Namely, one centered on feminist practices of accessibility, accountability, self-reflection, and meaning-making— as modeled in hooks's work. Here, pedagogy matters as much as ensuring our praxis aligns with the specific localities wherein we teach. Working as an educator at a PWI like Berea requires feminist practices rooted in self-critiques of whiteness and my own shifting class positionality. Here, I must engage in the work *with* my students, actively modeling transformative thinking and praxis. Creating accessible entry points for critique and community building is also just as essential if we hope to create liberatory learning spaces and engage with "education as a practice of freedom," especially in the contemporary political context of anti-woke circumscription of academic freedom.

It bears repeating: opting for a citation of hooks's work here and there simply cannot and will not do the work that a holistic engagement with her texts does. Instead, the construction of classes centered on her multi-genre oeuvre and course activities rooted in her pedagogy and praxis is the only way we co-build liberatory educational spaces. Here, hooks's canon provides a roadmap to engage critically, reflexively, and learn/teach transgressively. In community, as educators, we must keep her work at the forefront of our pedagogy, praxis, and course design to ensure she is never again rendered invisible by the same institutions and systems she spent a lifetime fighting.

Notes

1   bell hooks, *Where We Stand: Class Matter* (New York: Routledge, 2000), 118–19.
2   Mikki Kendall, *bell hooks: The Last Interview and Other Conversations* (New York: Melville House, 2023), xiv.
3   hooks, *Where We Stand*, 37.
4   Ibid., 63.

Part Two

Pedagogies of Hope and Joy

The authors in Part Two prioritize working with and through emotions as central to a pedagogical praxis that embraces students' full humanity and nurtures "the self-development and self-actualization of students in the classroom" (*Teaching Critical Thinking* 3). The first chapter from Jasjit Sangha and Kosha D. Bramesfeld, entitled "Leaning into Discomfort," discusses how mindful grounding can prepare teachers for the work of holding space for an often unpredictable display of emotions arising in a classroom. Sangha and Bramesfeld are teacher-learners who offer key questions and exercises that help develop a practice of vigilant mindfulness, one that is ideally open to revision, in light of the hooksian practice of "talking back" that students can embrace when they are valued co-constructors of classroom space. When educators undertake work on their own persons and embrace a foundation of groundedness and commitment to one's own nonlinear path of healing, their praxis can make possible new ways to meet and respond to the discomfort of growth and change.

In Patti Duncan's reflection, "Transgressive, Transformative Feminist Pedagogies," care and connection make possible the use of theory in the classroom space a potential site of healing, although not without caveats. For those of us working in academic institutions predicated on hierarchical power imbalances, and driven by programmatic outcomes and assessments, Duncan provides strategies for "making feminist worlds" in otherwise hostile spaces, and shows us that a commitment to growing caring collectives must extend to local organizations by supporting students' development as community leaders. Duncan affirms hooks's claim that students who come to educational spaces in order to develop practices of resistance, spaces where their community values and investments are honored will thrive and where they will become equipped to expand their communities' pathways to freedom (*Teaching Community* 48–9). This imperative also drives Bunny McFadden's piece, "Hope, Survival, and Futurism as Creation," in which she describes her implementation of a pedagogy of futurism in San Francisco, California, where schools often function as locations of "spirit murder" for Black, Indigenous, and other students of color. McFadden speaks to the "devaluation and degradation […] [at] play in maintaining racial subordination, especially in the arena of education" that hooks describes in "Moving Beyond Shame," a continuation of a "pedagogy of race and racism" endemic to dominator culture in education (*Teaching Community* 94–5). McFadden offers a grade-school classroom activity based on curriculum she developed at Tenderloin Community School. Her students' work decolonizes visions of the future as separate and distinct from the past by bringing Tenderloin sights and sounds into conversation with Afrofuturist and Chicanafuturist art pieces, a project that ultimately unfolded into student-created portals that linked their family roots to imaginative futures.

The last two pieces model sharing and openness to emotional experiences as avenues to transformational possibilities. In "Connecting through Emotional Solidarity," Katie B. Peachey, Caitlin M. Donovan, Jennifer Mann, *María Heysha Carrillo Carrasquillo*, and Crystal Chen Lee highlight the lessons youth participants taught them in co-writing activities. Whether working with previously incarcerated youth, refugee youth and their families, high-risk students, or students for whom English is an additional language, these North Carolina State University faculty hold writing sessions that encourage vulnerability without judgment. With community organizations co-crafting their curriculum, activities centering students' cultural and linguistic repertoires take their leadership potential seriously as they imagine hopeful futures and tell liberating stories. Finally, Laiba Rizwan, Melanie Taddeo, and Kosha D. Bramesfeld's dialogue, "Rethinking the Classroom as a Hub for Intellectual Joy and Scholastic Passion: A Dialogue," offers us an examination of joy, fun, and passion in the classroom. The piece begins with an explication of the challenges strict disciplinary and professional evaluation standards pose to students and instructors, and examines the tensions between liberatory teaching and circumscribed course design autonomy. Rizwan, Taddeo, and Bramesfeld provide strategies that center student interests and experiences with humor and levity, and offer exploratory activities that encourage wonder and inspire intellectual joy. Their insights remind us that "hopefulness empowers us to continue our work for justice even as the forces of injustice may gain greater power for a time" (*Teaching Community* xiv).

7

Leaning into Discomfort: Grounding Our Identities as Teacher-Learners to Confront Difficult Emotions and Build a "Pedagogy of Hope"

Jasjit Sangha and Kosha D. Bramesfeld

Leaning into Discomfort

As I closed the breakout room, the sound of two students in heated discussion pierced the silence of the virtual classroom. Their anger and frustration were palpable. In the past, I would panic and try to deflect my students' anger when conflict arose. This time, I took a deep breath, grounded myself, and leaned into their reactions as an important teaching tool. We worked through the anger, without anyone having to feel shame, embarrassment, or animosity. And in the process, students became deeply engaged in the discussion, eager to analyze the strong reactions and learn from them.

—Kosha

Early in my career, I gave students a chance to share their fears and frustrations as we discussed race, social injustice, and systemic barriers in society. Then I received a teaching evaluation in which a racialized student commented that my course reinforced for them that they would experience barriers no matter how hard they tried because of the racism they would encounter. I was crushed. This was not my intention. Now when I invite students into difficult conversations, I also invite them into moments of mindfulness, self-compassion, and embodiment, so they can feel a sense of inspiration, in a supportive community with others.

—Jasjit

bell hooks notes that classrooms can be spaces of liberation "when there are progressive educators who give [learners] space to feel their shame, express those feelings, and do the work of healing."[1] When we lean into discomfort and create space for our students to grapple with the complexities of their emotions, we help them connect more deeply with themselves and the content. But inviting people to bring complex emotions into a classroom is difficult and requires careful consideration. To avoid feelings of discouragement and vulnerability, we must ensure that these discussions are coupled with messages of hope, healing, and empowerment; opportunities for community building; and efforts to reduce the stigma of asking for help from student support services and mental health resources.

In this teaching, we discuss how we have worked to develop self-awareness and mindfulness so we can ground ourselves as teacher-learners, capable of leaning into the discomfort of emotions, while also cultivating a pedagogy of hope.

Developing Deep Self-awareness

In my own journey, I have had to both learn and unlearn how I have been impacted by internalized racism. It has been a difficult journey but incredibly rewarding, as I am able to see more clearly how my view of the world, my view of my "place" in society, and of my worth as a human being has been impacted by buried "thinking traps" or thought processes. By freeing myself from these limitations, I can see the possibilities ahead of me, despite what messages I may hear, see, or experience from society. This is a journey that I undertook with community support, guidance from meditation teachers, and a daily practice of self-exploration.

—Jasjit

When I first started teaching, I was terrified to talk about racism and oppression because, as a white woman, I felt completely unprepared to have, let alone, lead these conversations. Since then, I have spent years seeking out workshops, readings, and conversations with colleagues to gain a deeper understanding of myself. As I have become more grounded in who I am, I have been able to move past my white guilt to better hold space for others and to better engage students in difficult conversations about race and oppression.

—Kosha

In *Teaching to Transgress*, bell hooks reminds us, we must be "actively committed to a process of self-actualization that promotes our well-being if we are to teach in a way that empowers students."[2] Developing self-awareness begins by reckoning with our identities and positionalities and addressing our feelings of shame, guilt, sadness, rage, helplessness, and hurt that arise from living in a society in which racial hierarchies, injustice, and division are embedded into its ethos. As Renita Wong reminds us, it requires us to "confront our implication in the interlocking systems of power relations, without judging ourselves or others as inherently bad or unworthy, or denying our responsibility in the world."[3]

To develop this deep self-awareness, we can begin by asking ourselves:

- How has my identity, my access to power and privilege, or my experiences with oppression shaped how I teach?
- *Who* am I prepared to teach?
- Whose life experiences do I struggle to understand?
- What gaps do I have in *my learning*?
- What about *me* needs to be changed so I can create a more inclusive classroom?

Reflecting on these questions should occur through a process of deep self-reflection, with raw honesty and community support. Often, as we delve into deeper self-awareness, we may feel overwhelmed by our insights. In these moments, we need to feel supported through our journey. This support can come in many different forms, including meeting with trusted colleagues, attending university-hosted workshops or collaborative discussions, joining a racial affinity group, attending community-based events, or seeking out family, friends, advisors, or mental health professionals who can serve as sources of support and inspiration.

Doing this work can feel exhausting and draining emotionally. It can bring to the surface our own past traumas and experiences with injustice that we have not yet fully processed or understood. We may feel like our self-worth is wrapped up in the success of our labor or feel a deep sense of responsibility for student's empowerment and healing, to "right" the "wrongs" of society. This can make us feel isolated and alone, like we are the *only person* who can do this work. It forces us to ask ourselves, "What emotions and feelings have I had to bury so I could succeed in a racist and unjust institutional and societal environment?" "How can I learn to love and heal all parts of myself?"

It is awareness of these internalized feelings of shame that allow us to move forward on the path of self-actualization *through our work as educators*. If we can better understand the circumstances that result in our experiencing strong emotional reactions and triggers, we can be less afraid of encountering similarly strong emotional reactions in our classrooms and even begin to welcome them as teachable moments. However, this process of greater self-understanding must be grounded in a process of mindfulness, curiosity, and compassion. As bell hooks writes, "[W]hen we can give ourselves the unconditional love that is the ground for sustained acceptance and affirmation [...] we are able to reach out to others from a place of fulfillment and not from a place of lack".[4] Building our capacity to feel our strong emotions and fully accept who we are despite our perceived flaws and inadequacies is a powerful antidote to internalized oppression. It can help us feel more empowered so we can tap into a deeper well of compassion that we can bring forth in our teaching.

Grounding Ourselves in Mindfulness, Curiosity, and Compassion

I could feel the discomfort of the racialized students in the room as I opened up a conversation about internalized oppression, micro-aggressions, and feeling like an imposter in academia. The students' responses were raw as they grappled with the realization of the many ways they were hurt by racism. Their sorrow was palpable and felt very familiar. I put my hand on my heart, grounded myself, and listened to their stories.

—Jasjit

In *Teaching to Transgress*, bell hooks reminds us that one of the most radical things that we can do is to "genuinely *value* everyone's presence"[5] and voice in the classroom. But if we are genuine in inviting our students' voices into the classroom, we must accept that, at least occasionally, students' contributions will be raw, painful, shocking, triggering, or even offensive. We need tools in our pedagogical toolbox to help us ground ourselves as teacher-learners and become role models and collaborators with students so we can turn these raw reactions into teachable moments.

Building off the work of Ruth King[6] and Tara Brach[7] we have found that mindfulness-based practices such as RAIN (Recognitive, Allow, Investigate, and Nurture) can be helpful for grounding ourselves in the moment. RAIN teaches us that we must first ***recognize*** the thoughts, feelings, and reactions happening within our body. What are we experiencing? Is it anger? Sadness? Fear? As we recognize and name our thoughts, feelings, and reactions, we must ***allow*** ourselves to experience these reactions, without shame or judgment. Only then can we ***investigate*** those thoughts, feelings, and reactions with compassionate curiosity. What narratives and stories are we attaching to these reactions? For example, "my students hate me," or "I don't belong here," or "everyone is looking at me to say the right thing." Finally, in order to move past these harmful narratives, we must ***nurture*** ourselves with compassionate messages of strength and empowerment. For example, "you do belong here," or "anyone would be nervous in this situation," or "you're doing great."

Cultivating this mindful approach takes time. Ideally, it is practiced before you encounter a stressful or triggering situation because as Lee Warren reminds us, "sometimes things seem to explode in the classroom."[8] Warren refers to these explosions as "hot moments," which can be defined as points in time when "people's feelings—often conflictual—rise to a point that threatens teaching and learning".[9] Warren advises that educators can effectively manage these hot moments by (a) managing their own emotional reactions to the situation and (b) finding ways to turn students' reactions into teachable moments. To ensure that students are prepared to engage in these discussions respectfully, Warren recommends that educators seek to establish and model discussion norms earlier in the term.

In our own courses and workshops, we strive to lay a foundation of trust and relationship building through mindfulness and a deep listening activity (see the referenced book chapter for instructions for the activity).[10] We start by creating a welcoming space at the beginning of our sessions so participants can settle, integrate their mind and body, and bring their full presence into the room. This sets the tone for the deep listening activity, in which we invite students into dialog with a partner about equity and social justice. Before we begin, we role model our own vulnerability about having these conversations so students feel comfortable doing the same.

We stress that the activity's goal is to deeply listen to one another, without interruption or judgment, while the other person shares their experiences.[11] We start with a mindful moment, and then participants take turns sharing their reflections, while their partner listens intently. After each person has spoken, they are given time for free-flow conversation. We then discuss as a group what it felt like to (a) listen to another person with the goal of truly hearing what the other person is saying and (b) what it felt like to know that you were being listened to and heard. We find that this activity helps us model what it looks like, in practice, to ground ourselves for discussion, listen to others with curiosity and compassion, and engage in an open, honest, and respectful discussion of people's lived experiences.

Creating a Pedagogy of Hope

On several occasions, I have found myself becoming the biggest champion of those that others have written off. When students are struggling, I try to avoid labels like "lazy" or "unmotivated" and instead try to learn more about why they are struggling. When I do, I am often amazed at how much that student has going on in their lives, and how much strength and perseverance is required just for them to show up. Teaching becomes so much more rewarding when I take the time to learn about my students, their struggles, and their accomplishments.

—Kosha

Creating a "pedagogy of hope" may feel daunting, especially if we have not experienced a classroom like the one we wish to create for our students. For many of us, this requires avoiding the models of teaching of our own educational experiences, in which a teacher attempts to use authority and power to create a shield between themselves and their students. As bell hooks illuminates, "authoritarianism in the classroom dehumanizes and thus shuts down the 'magic' that is always present when individuals are active learners. It takes the 'fun out of study' and makes it repressive and oppressive".[12] In contrast, creating classroom communities in which the "magic" is present—and students can feel safe, secure, and hopeful—requires that we genuinely care about our students and desire to know them.

As Wong shares, teaching in this way offers students a chance to engage in more embodied learning in which they can connect with their hearts while learning, so they can feel and express their "wounds from colonization and social injustice" as well as their "yearning for healing and restoration of spirit."[13] Conventional teaching practices, in which engagement of the "discursive-analytical mind" is the key focus, does not lend itself to this depth of self-understanding and instead can see students "deflated into despair or paralysis"[14] when learning about how they are impacted by societal injustice. As Dei notes, creating hope in the classroom requires that we support students in healing from "the spiritual, cultural and mental alienation of the self."[15]

One of the best ways to support students in this process is to empower students to set their own learning agendas and to be their own agents of change. A great way to accomplish these goals is through the introduction of inquiry-based learning that challenges students to seek out information and examples that help them apply the course content to their own lives. One of Kosha's former students, Brianna, captures the "magic" of inquiry-based learning when she writes, "[B]y allowing students to contextualize [course] issues by using their own lived experience, they are able to find the power of their own voice and perspective. I did not realize how impactful my story could be and seeing it incorporated into the [course] alongside other people's stories and research findings was an incredibly empowering experience."[16]

Empowering students as co-educators in the classroom requires a great deal of trust, respect, and care for students. As bell hooks notes, "[T]eachers who extend the care and respect that is a component of love make it possible for students to address their fears openly and to receive affirmation and support."[17] Through doing our inner work and bringing our authentic selves into the classroom, we offer our students permission to do the same. In this way, education becomes a liberatory experience.

Matching Intent with Impact

We opened this teaching with two examples. In each of these examples, we reflected on how our teaching has changed over time. When Kosha was new to teaching, she desired to avoid conflict. And when Jasjit was new to teaching, she desired to give space for students to share their pain. Our intentions were good. We wanted to protect our students in the best way that we knew how. But intention is different from impact. By avoiding conflict, Kosha was denying her students the opportunity to explore and understand their complex emotions: good and bad. And by creating space for pain, but not for hope and empowerment, Jasjit inadvertently created feelings of helplessness in some of her students. To make an impact, educators must pair their intentions with knowledge, action, and insight. Below we discuss how we use readings, community engagement, and continuous feedback and reflection as methods of matching our intentions with our impact.

Readings

In the book *Teaching Critical Thinking*, bell hooks reflects on the role of reading in her own life and recounts her father's belief "that learning to read and think critically about the world we live in was more important than a college education or college degrees."[18] As avid readers ourselves, we strongly agree. Reading has played a key role in our formation as educators. Throughout this chapter, we cite several works that have been influential to us in developing our own teaching philosophies and practices. We also reference two of our own published works focused on the deep listening activity[19] and inquiry-based learning project[20] we discussed earlier. We encourage readers to view our endnotes as a list of resources for "doing" the work of creating a pedagogy of hope.

Engagement

In the preface of *Teaching Community: A Pedagogy of Hope*, bell hooks notes that "one of the dangers we face in our educational system is the loss of a feeling of community, not just the loss of closeness among those with whom we work and with our students, but also the loss of a feeling of connection and closeness with the world beyond the academy."[21] Teaching can be a very lonely and isolating endeavor; having trusted colleagues that we can turn to for advice, support, humor and encouragement has been core to helping us develop as educators, grow as people, and maintain a sense of motivation and enthusiasm for the work that we do. As such, we strongly recommend that educators cultivate a community of trusted and engaged educators, scholars, friends, family, and community members with whom they can regularly connect with to exchange ideas and get feedback and support.

Reflection

Finally, like bell hooks,[22] we recognize that when we are doing our work authentically, mistakes are inevitable. But if we listen to students, colleagues, and the inner voices that provide us with important feedback on what is working and also, what is not working, then our mistakes can offer valuable opportunities for self-awareness and growth. Instead of focusing on perfection, we urge educators to continuously seek out feedback from students, colleagues, and themselves to assess if intent is matching impact. Receiving constructive feedback on our teaching is not always easy. As bell hooks writes:

> There can be, and usually is, some degree of pain involved in giving up old ways of thinking and knowing and learning new approaches" [...] "The exciting aspect of creating a classroom community where there is respect for individual voices is that there is infinitely more feedback because students do feel free to talk – and talk back. And yes, often this feedback is critical.[23]

Change can be hard. As we expand our perception of what teaching as a liberatory process is we are going to be pushed outside our comfort zone by our students, and this may hit hard, especially when a well-thought-out lesson plan is rejected or criticized by our students. However, remembering our commitment to our self-actualization through our work as educators, can serve as our guidepost or compass to help us in these moments.

Despite these challenges, it is our hope that our reflections shared within this teaching have provided others with the motivation and tools to lean into this discomfort with a deeper sense of self-awareness and a desire to approach students' and one's own emotional reactions with mindfulness, curiosity, and compassion in order to develop a pedagogy of hope that has a lasting impact on teachers and learners alike.

Notes

1   bell hooks, *Teaching Community: A Pedagogy of Hope* (New York: Routledge, 2003), 102.

2   bell hooks, *Teaching to Transgress: Education as the Practice of Freedom* (New York: Routledge, 1994), 15.

3   Yuk-Lin Renita Wong, "Knowing through Discomfort: A Mindfulness-based Critical Social Work Pedagogy," *Critical Social Work* 5 (2004): 14.

4   bell hooks, *All about Love: New Visions* (New York: William Morrow Paperbacks, 2016), 99.

5   hooks, *Teaching to Transgress*, 7.

6   Ruth King, *Mindful of Race : Transforming Racism from the inside Out* (Boulder, CO: Sounds True, Inc, 2018).

7   Tara Brach, *Radical Compassion: Learning to Love Yourself and the World through the Practice of RAIN* (New York: Penguin Random House, 2020).

8   Lee Warren, "Managing Hot Moments in the Classroom" (Derek Bok Center for Teaching and Learning Harvard University, 2006), para. 1.

9   Ibid.

10   Jasjit Sangha and Kosha D. Bramesfeld, "Using a Mindfulness-based Deep Listening Exercise to Engage Students in Difficult Dialogues about Diversity, Equity, and Inclusion," in *Incorporating Diversity in Classroom Settings: Real and Engaging Examples for Various Psychology Courses* [Vol 2: Intersectionality], eds. Maria S. Wong, Lauri Weiner, Jessica Cerniak, and Lydia T. S. Yee (Washington, DC: Society for Teaching of Psychology, 2021), 7–11, http://teachpsych.org/ebooks/diverse2).

11   Ibid.

12   hooks, *Teaching Community*, 43.

13   Yuk-Lin Renita Wong, "'Please Call Me by My True Names': A Decolonizing Pedagogy of Mindfulness and Interbeing in Critical Social Work Education," in *Sharing Breath*, eds. Renita Yuk-Lin Wong and Sheila Batacharya (Athabasca, Alberta, Canada: Athabasca University Press, 2018), 259.

14   Ibid.

15   George J. Sefa Dei, "Chapter One: Rereading Fanon for His Pedagogy and Implications for Schooling and Education," *Counterpoints (New York, N.Y.)* 368 (2010): 3.

16   Kosha Bramesfeld, B. Leslie-Joachim, A. Hailemichael., and D. Veliz, "Using a Community-engaged Knowledge Mobilization Project to Build Students' Capacity for Personal and Community Empowerment," in *Empowering Students as Change Agents in Psychology Courses*, eds. Melissa Fortner and Iva Katzarska-Miller (Washington, DC: Society for the Teaching of Psychology, 2022), 222–3.

17   hooks, *Teaching Community*, 132.

18   bell hooks, *Teaching Critical Thinking: Practical Wisdom* (New York: Routledge, 2010, https://doi.org/10.4324/9780203869192), 129.

19   Jasjit and Bramesfeld, "Using a Mindfulness-based Deep Listening Exercise to Engage Students in Difficult Dialogues about Diversity, Equity, and Inclusion," 7–11.

20   Bramesfeld et al., "Using a Community-engaged Knowledge Mobilization Project to Build Students' Capacity for Personal and Community Empowerment," 218–29.

21   hooks, *Teaching Community*, preface.

22   hooks, *Teaching to Transgress*, 33.

23   Ibid, 42.

8

Transgressive, Transformative Feminist Pedagogies: Education for Hope and Healing

Patti Duncan

Introduction: An Offering of Care and Connection

It was mid-November 2014, and bell hooks was giving the keynote address at the National Women's Studies Association annual conference, held in San Juan, Puerto Rico. The theme of the conference that year was "Feminist Transgressions," resonating with the title of hooks's acclaimed 1994 book, *Teaching to Transgress: Education as the Practice of Freedom*. She took the stage in front of a huge audience in the ballroom of the conference hotel. Listening to her speak about feminist practice and pedagogy, and the necessary risks of teaching for liberation, I was reminded of the way her writings shaped my own early consciousness and understandings of feminist teaching and learning back in the 1990s. I remembered how hooks was the first feminist scholar I read who brought up class in relation to race and gender, and how class privilege—along with other forms of privilege—structures the practice of education. Her words helped me understand the sense of isolation I experienced during graduate school as a woman of color and first-generation scholar from a working-class background. I thought about my mother—my first teacher—who had grown up in poverty during the Korean War and had never been formally educated yet managed to teach me about survival and instill in me a love of learning. bell hooks's writings helped me to recognize and affirm the knowledge and generational wisdoms that my mother passed down to me.

Later that evening, after her keynote, hooks was the guest of honor at a party upstairs in the presidential suite of the conference hotel. When I entered the crowded room with my friend, Mehra, we immediately saw her surrounded by conference attendees of various ages and backgrounds. I can't tell you why, but in that moment bell hooks's eyes met mine and she stepped toward me with her arms open. Instinctively, I moved forward into a long, warm hug. We had never met in person before that night, but somehow, she offered me a deep sense of recognition and belonging. Without exchanging words with me, how did she know exactly what I needed at that moment? To be literally embraced by bell hooks that evening felt like a powerful encapsulation of the effect of her writings on my work and life over the years: an offering of care and connection, an inspiration to transgress social norms in favor of love and community, justice, and healing.

Making Feminist Worlds in Hostile Spaces

In a recent essay, "How I Learned to Love Teaching: bell hooks and the Possibilities of the Feminist Classroom,"[1] I detail the way that hooks's writings have shaped my teaching practices. Inspired by her discussions of transgressive feminist teaching practices grounded in love, care, and community, always in the service of healing and justice, I seek to center these values in my own teaching and interactions with students. But what does it mean to practice the values of love and community in the academy? And how do we create sites of resistance— what Sara Ahmed describes as building feminist worlds[2]—within institutions structured by hierarchy, that are so frequently sites of oppression and violence for minoritized students and faculty? For me, this means actively demonstrating my care for students, beginning from the first class meeting with learning their names and pronouns, listening to their reasons for taking my classes, and trying to understand what it is that they each need from our shared learning experience. It also means collaborating with them, sharing decision-making, shifting power dynamics, and actively building community. In this time of deep uncertainty, I prioritize students' well-being, remembering that many of them are dealing with multiple hardships each day, from food insecurity to trauma. I ask students to bring their full selves to our shared space, and I acknowledge that I must do the same, even—or especially—when doing so makes us feel vulnerable. I ground myself by remembering why I do the work I do, and even in the most difficult interactions, I try to be as compassionate as possible, to recognize students as "whole human beings with complex lives and experiences."[3]

Recognizing students as whole human beings feels particularly urgent in this moment, marked by trauma, as we consider what is happening in Gaza and elsewhere in the world. In the introduction to *Pedagogies of Crossing*, M. Jacqui Alexander writes:

> I did not awake this morning to the deafening noise of sirens or the rocketing sound of nonstop bombs. I did not awake to the missiles that fall like rain from the sky, exploding on contact with land. [...] Breathing grief for a lifetime can be toxic. [...] What do lives of privilege look like in the midst of war and the inevitable violence that accompanies the building of empire? We live in the privilege of believing the official story that the state owns and can therefore dispense security, that war is over, that silence is a legitimate trade for consent in the dangerous rhetoric of wartime economy; [...] to consume an education that sanctions the academy's complicity in the exercise and normativization of state terror.[4]

Alexander's words help me consider the ways we think about and understand feminist knowledge production, and our varied contexts. As feminist scholars, how do we write and teach and learn—how do we do our work—in the midst of this violence, and in the midst of so much pain and grief? And how do our students experience this space?

We continue to try to navigate the academy, and the processes and politics of feminist knowledge-making practices, even during an apocalypse, in the midst of war, a global pandemic, climate crisis, racialized state violence, attacks on reproductive justice, and increasing anti-trans legislation. Recently, more than 250,000 households were without power in the Portland area where I live, and several people died in a brutal ice storm. Like many others, there were a few days when I lost power, dealt with a burst pipe, no electricity, no water, no heat, but still the emails arrive, the grading continues, the deadlines loom. And I know this doesn't compare to what many others experience throughout the world. Over the last three years, over a million people in the United States and nearly seven million people worldwide have died from Covid-19. In Gaza, since early October, more than 26,000 people have been killed (or one in every 100 people), including more than 10,000 children. I'm reminded of something Priya Kandaswamy said in an *Ideas on Fire* podcast early in the Covid-19 pandemic: "I never imagined that when the apocalypse came, my biggest concern would be about how to do my job."[5] She was referring to our academic institutions pushing forward even during a global health crisis, with "business as usual" models, where we were all expected to keep teaching and learning, maintaining "productivity" even if remote, even if sick, or lacking childcare or eldercare, or grieving losses. How might returning to bell hooks's writings offer an intervention? What can hooks's framing of feminist theory and practice teach us about disrupting the normative structures of "business as usual" and state violence and terror?

Both hooks and Alexander articulate the importance of intervening in the spaces where knowledge is produced, to consider feminist pedagogies as political practices that engage the spirit. I follow their lead here, and especially the argument for a pedagogic imperative of teaching for justice, to imagine a framework for feminist scholarly work in precarious times that centers women of color feminist frameworks of care and connection. And I return to Alexander's question: "What do lives of privilege look like in the midst of war and the inevitable violence that accompanies the building of empire?" For us and our students, what does it mean to "consume an education that sanctions the academy's complicity in [...] state terror"?

To reflect on these questions, I revisit memories of my earliest teacher—my mother—whose formal education ended abruptly when she was a young child, after the small school she attended in the outskirts of Seoul was struck by a bomb. The teacher shouted that the students should run home and hide. My mother's retelling of this incident connected to her grief—when she shared the story, I understood this grief as complex and related not only to the Korean War, multiple losses within our family, trauma, and the loss of a childhood, but also her loss of the possibility of a formal education. For my mom, as I was growing up, there was absolutely nothing more valuable than education, and I want to recognize and affirm the knowledge and generational wisdoms she passed down to me.

But affirming the importance of education and knowledge production sits alongside the many harms enacted by and within institutions of higher education. In *Teaching to Transgress*, hooks poignantly describes the deep depression she experienced after earning tenure in the academy. Writing about how education ideally operates as the practice of freedom, she reflects on how so often this is not the case, as faculty frequently reinforce domination through unjust rituals of power and control in the classroom. Receiving tenure brought these tensions into sharp relief and highlighted a central conflict bell hooks grappled with in her life, explored in *Teaching to Transgress* and other writings.

Reflecting on her experiences in graduate school, hooks writes:

> The classroom became a place I hated, yet a place where I struggled to claim and maintain the right to be an independent thinker. The university and the classroom began to feel more like a prison, a place of punishment and confinement rather than a place of promise and possibility.[6]

This notion of the classroom as a place of punishment is of course a reality for many students of color, queer, trans, and gender-expansive students, students with disabilities, and students from working-class and poor backgrounds. And hooks's analysis highlights the ways that the carceral dynamics of education, including practices of social control and surveillance, connect in explicit ways to the violence of the carceral state. In *Black Girls Matter: Pushed Out, Overpoliced, and Underprotected*, Kimberlé Crenshaw details the racialized, gendered dimensions of the school to prison pipeline in the United States, and how discriminatory disciplinary policies negatively impact Black girls and other girls of color, primarily in K-12 education.[7] However, for many, there is an expectation that for those of us who manage to survive and thrive not only in K-12 but also college, graduate school will be different, that higher education offers the promise of liberation and hope, and that this is where real transformation is possible. However, hooks notes that the majority of professors in her program "often used the classroom to enact rituals of control that were about domination and the unjust exercise of power."[8] Later, she describes her intense isolation and loneliness:

> I and many other students, especially non-white students from non-privileged backgrounds, were unable to accept and play this "game." Often we were ambivalent about the rewards promised. Many of us were not seeking to be in a position of power over others. Though we wished to teach, we did not want to exert coercive authoritarian rule over others.[9]

In these writings, hooks explains how the rules of higher education felt like a "game" to be played, in which interactions with students were viewed as transactional, with rewards (degrees, tenure and promotion, fellowships, awards, and the like) promised to those who won. And in response to those who claim "academic freedom" to justify their actions, hooks asserts that education is not a neutral process: "Again and again, academic freedom is evoked to deflect attention away from the ways knowledge is used to reinforce and perpetuate domination, away from the ways in which education is not a neutral process. Whenever this happens, the very idea of academic freedom loses its meaning and integrity."[10] Her desire to become a critical thinker and question these normative practices resulted in her being seen as a threat to authority and furthered her sense of estrangement in the academy.

Similarly, Roderick Ferguson, in *The Reorder of Things,* argues that "the academy became the 'training ground' for state and capital's engagement with minority difference as a site of representation and meaning."[11] In linking the academy to the state and capital, Ferguson demonstrates the ways that previously "insurgent formations"[12] became part of normative structures, incorporated or "absorbed" into institutional power.[13] Academic concepts such as "excellence," tied to notions of productivity, competition, and administration contribute to the exclusion of minoritized subjects, bolstered by ideas of "merit," "standards," and "qualifications" that are racialized, gendered, and structured by social class.[14] Minoritized subjects seek affirmation and recognition in an institutional structure that works to regulate their (our) difference.

For those of us entering the academy as minoritized subjects, including first-generation and BIPOC scholars, institutionalization—or assimilation into the academy—appears to offer the promise of belonging, but in fact results in even greater pressure to fit within and uphold institutional norms. In these ways, similar to hooks's discussion of the classroom as a space of punishment and control, Ferguson describes the "limits of institutionalization,"[15] where institutionalization is a process of socializing subjects into the state. I continue to feel ambivalent about the ways institutions of higher education, in Shirley Hune's words, function as instruments of both social change and social control, "help[ing] preserve the status quo by perpetuating existing hierarchies and reproducing gender, race, class, and other inequities."[16]

The Classroom as a Site of Possibility

Almost thirty years later, the tensions described by hooks remain relevant in considering feminist pedagogy and the classroom, especially as we continue to live through the Covid-19 pandemic, multiple forms of racialized state violence targeting Black, Indigenous, and other people of color in the United States, and increasingly complex settler colonialist, imperialist, militarized forms of violence worldwide. I have felt these tensions most acutely when I have been expected to align with institutional norms and values that contradict my own values, and it is in these times where I have felt most embattled about the perils and promises of the academy. It has frequently been in these moments—especially when I express ambivalence about the systems of structures of academic institutions— that I, too, have been seen as the threat hooks describes, and the feminist killjoy theorized by Sara Ahmed.[17]

Considering the site of the US academy, bell hooks identified points of intervention in these dynamics via practices of "engaged pedagogy" and "theory as liberatory practice." She urged feminist teachers and minoritized subjects to bring our full selves into academic spaces in order to recognize students, too, as "whole human beings with complex lives and experiences."[18] Doing so includes recognition of our embodied experiences and lived realities, enabling us to understand the ways our experiences shape our ways of knowing and learning. hooks argued for transgressing normative practices in higher education in order to be open to different ways of knowing and new epistemologies,[19] informed by students'—and our own—experiences, identities, and communities. At times this may require innovative feminist pedagogies including bringing in aspects of service learning to address the needs of specific communities, or collaborative approaches in the service of social justice. Through such practices, hooks connected theory and practice, disrupting a false dichotomy between the two, and offering theory as a "location for healing."[20] But, she argued, "Theory is not inherently healing, liberatory, or revolutionary."[21] While often co-opted and/or commodified, feminist theory can also be liberatory when it names our pain, "emerg[ing] from the concrete, from [one's] efforts to make sense of everyday life experiences, from [one's] efforts to intervene critically in [one's] life and the lives of others."[22] Thus, lived experience forms the base for liberatory feminist theory.

In considering how to live and work within the academy, I have kept bell hooks's writings close, especially her reminder that "[t]he classroom, with all its limitations, remains a location of possibility."[23] By advocating for care and connection, hooks's writings outline the expansive possibilities of feminist pedagogy as transformative, liberating, and healing for many of our students, our communities, and ourselves. Recently in my work with students, I have focused more explicitly on her discussions about engaged pedagogy and feminist theory as a potential site of healing. I have imagined how she might have responded to students in this moment in time, when so many of us are struggling with grief and loss. What I continue to learn from hooks has to do with the importance of recognizing the complex realities of our students' lives, and the critical and urgent need to prioritize love and healing over hierarchy and administrative forms of discipline and violence.

Recently in my course, Women of Color Feminisms, several students became distraught over increasing anti-trans legislation in the United States. While trans and nonbinary students of color were the first to express their fears in our class discussions, before long all the members of the class shared a recognition of the urgency of resisting the oppression of trans, intersex, Two-Spirit, and gender nonconforming people and connecting this oppression to the policing of bodies and gender presentations of people of color due to settler colonialism, white supremacy, and heteropatriarchy. As a collective response, we drafted a public statement opposing the anti-trans and anti-gender nonconforming legislation, naming the potential harms of such bills, including increased precarity, medical and state violence, and criminalization. And, as a group of mostly BIPOC feminist scholars, many of whom were queer and trans, we expressed our love and solidarity for *all* members of our overlapping communities. In another class, a graduate seminar called Social Justice: Theory and Practice, I extended this approach, replacing a paper assignment with a writing collaboration, based on the idea of theorizing feminism and justice from our own lived experiences. Again, all members of the class actively participated in shaping the topic for the manuscript, deciding together what to address and how to do so. What started as a response to living through precarity during the pandemic eventually resulted in a co-authored article, "What Do We Long For? Reflections on Feminist Movements for Social Justice."[24] In it, we found space to grapple with the meanings of social justice in contemporary contexts and movements.

In moving away from grading toward a practice of "ungrading," I join scholars who suggest that conventional grading systems operate as disciplining technologies, grounded in capitalism, hierarchy, surveillance, and neoliberalism.[25] While initially difficult to put into practice, moving beyond conventional grading practices has dramatically changed the dynamics in my classroom. Students feel freer to experiment with various approaches; they are able to focus more on the learning process rather than how their work will be judged; and they often develop greater initiative in claiming an education. To move away from disciplinary practices rooted in individualism and competition—such as conventional models of grading—opens up space to consider new forms of collaboration, connection, and knowledge production. It creates possibilities of creating new ways of being together, even within the neoliberal university.

To return to Ahmed's notion of building feminist worlds in connection to hooks's practices of world making, I consider her argument that "[f]eminism is at stake in how we generate knowledge; in how we write, in who we cite."[26] Describing feminism as "a building project," Ahmed describes citations as "feminist bricks,"[27] suggesting that texts are worlds, and that "[f]eminist theory is world making."[28] Thus, hooks made feminist worlds, insisting on accessibility, embodiment, and connection. Moving forward, I take heart in Ferguson's words that we can continue to build feminist worlds, little by little:

> A syllabus, a job ad, a recruitment strategy, a memo, a book, an artwork, a report, an organizational plan, a protest—such are the little things that we can deploy in order to imagine critical forms of community, forms in which minoritized

subjects become the agents rather than the silent objects of knowledge formations and institutional practices.[29]

I remember bell hooks's warm embrace, and her argument that the classroom "remains the most radical space of possibility in the academy."[30] Even within contexts of political turmoil and state violence, through a commitment to engaged feminist pedagogy we can make meaning together in ways that often feel simultaneously mundane and momentous, opening possibilities for healing and hope. And then our work becomes an expression and an enactment of the care and connection hooks articulated so powerfully in her work.

Notes

1   Patti Duncan, "How I Learned to Love Teaching: bell hooks and the Possibilities of the Feminist Classroom," *Feminist Pedagogy* 3, no. 1 (2023): 1–2.

2   Sara Ahmed, *Living a Feminist Life* (Durham, NC: Duke University Press, 2017).

3   bell hooks, *Teaching to Transgress: Education as the Practice of Freedom* (New York: Routledge, 1994), 15.

4   M. Jacqui Alexander, *Pedagogies of Crossing: Meditations on Feminism, Sexual Politics, Memory, and the Sacred* (Durham, NC: Duke University Press, 2005), 1–2.

5   Cathy Hannabach and Ideas on Fire, *Priya Kandaswamy on Embracing Permanent Change*. Imagine Otherwise, Episode 138. August 4, 2021. Available online: accessed April 5, 2024, https://ideasonfire.net/138-priya-kandaswamy/.

6   hooks, *Teaching to Transgress*, 4.

7   Kimberlé W. Crenshaw, with Priscilla Ocen and Jyoti Nanda, *Black Girls Matter: Pushed Out, Overpoliced, and Underprotected* (New York: African American Policy Forum and Center for Intersectionality and Social Policy Studies, 2015), accessed June 23, 2023, https://scholarship.law.columbia.edu/cgi/viewcontent.cgi?article=42 36&context=faculty_scholarship.

8   hooks, *Teaching to Transgress*, 5.

9   bell hooks, *Talking Back: Thinking Feminist, Thinking Black* (Boston, MA: South End Press, 1989), 59.

10 Ibid. 64.

11 Roderick Ferguson, *The Reorder of Things: The University and Its Pedagogies of Minority Difference* (Minneapolis: The University of Minnesota Press, 2012), 11.

12 Ibid., 8.

13 Ibid., 214.

14 Ibid., 198.

15 Ibid., 35.

16 Shirley Hune, "Asian Pacific American Women and Men in Higher Education: The Contested Spaces of Their Participation, Persistence, and Challenges as Students, Faculty, and Administrators," in *"Strangers" of the Academy: Asian Women Scholars in Higher Education*, eds. Guofang Li and Gulbahar H. Beckett (Sterling, VA: Stylus, 2006), 15–36; 15.

17 Ahmed, *Living a Feminist Life*, 251–68.

18 hooks, *Teaching to Transgress*, 15.

19 Ibid., 41.

20 Ibid., 59.

21 Ibid., 61.

22 Ibid., 70.

23 Ibid., 207.

24 Aman agah, Emerson Barrett, Libia Marqueza Castro, Val Chang, Patti Duncan, and Adrianna Nicolay, "What Do We Long For? Reflections on Feminist Movements for Social Justice," *Journal of Feminist Scholarship* 21, no. 21 (2022): 46–59.

25 Carolina Alonso Bejarano and Stina Soderling, "Against Grading: Feminist Studies beyond the Neoliberal University," *Feminist Formations* 33, no. 2 (2021): 208–32.

26 Ahmed, *Living a Feminist Life*, 14.

27 Ibid., 16.

28 Ibid., 14.

29 Ferguson, *The Reorder of Things*, 232.

30 hooks, *Teaching to Transgress*, 12.

9

Hope, Survival, and Futurism as Creation

Bunny McFadden

I pass by the grimy windows and triple-locked doors of the Tenderloin Center. It is June of 2023, nearly a year since I resigned from 826 Valencia, but there on display in the hollow is a familiar Black paper princess with a golden crown and dozens of bees swarming around her proud smile. She's faded in the year since I came early to the street to help the artist install her in my writing lab, her edges curled with humidity. For 365 days, I was the programs director for 826 Valencia at this center. My curriculum project, Doors to the Future, is available for free on 826 Digital.[1] Although my site of action was my former employer, I want to focus this chapter on common threads like awareness, connection, and creation that will feel applicable to a variety of contexts while holding space for the unique circumstances that surrounded my ability to craft and deliver this curriculum.

Schools in San Francisco continue to be underserved sites of "spirit murdering through racialized exclusion and extraction" for Black, Indigenous, and POC students, as characterized by Asif Wilson[2] and set forth by Bettina L. Love.[3] Structures, policies, and practices reproduce oppression to the detriment of students through implicit and explicit rejection. bell hooks describes how love is a transformative mechanism that may be sought out in family, friendship, and community. In order to actualize the love of which bell hooks writes and resist the spirit murdering, we must first understand and acknowledge these conditions and then work toward imagining a future of radical possibilities. Here, I write about the interlocking pedagogies of love and hope.

In autoethnography, disclosure is an action done with much reflection. This project is an analysis of the data of subjective experiences interpreted to provide a glimpse into world construction.[4] I struggled to write this, for reasons that will become clear. However, one thing I kept returning to was the power of autoethnography and the ways that writing can help educators unpack the ways they have reified systems of oppression and how they have resisted: "In writing [...] we further develop our understandings and actions toward people who have suffered colonizing forces or who have been constructed as colonizers."[5] This personal reflection on pedagogy offers a pedagogical activity designed to decolonize visions of the future as separate and distinct from the past while offering an actionable path toward envisioning concrete articulations of hope through writing at the elementary school level.

Feminist scholarship often "fails to interrogate the location from which they speak."[6] In attempts to decolonize, we must resist an effort to homogenize or brush away lived experiences. bell hooks describes this work as "simply trying to change the way we went about our everyday lives so that our values and habits of being would reflect our commitment to freedom."[7] Teachers shape the future alongside students, not on behalf of them, and we can only hope when we are gone that seeds of hope will bloom.[8] This is why I not only incorporated Africana and Chicana feminisms in building my lessons, but consider them as fundamental to the delivery of curriculum writ large.

I am the first in my family to graduate college. My life could have turned out very differently, but I was given the privileges and opportunities to build on my teaching career and pursue an advanced degree in curriculum and instruction. Shortly after I finished my dissertation, I sought to tether myself to a respectable writing or teaching gig. When I landed the program director role, I celebrated the idea that I'd be in a position to effect such needed change. I wanted to prove to myself and my family that all the work I did to get a doctorate would be put to good use, helping the community. I didn't take into account how hard it would be to get pushback from people I admired and how easily I would fall into the very things I'd railed against in my dissertation.

I learned about bell hooks in an introductory feminism class at the University of New Mexico. In *Teaching to Transgress*, hooks discusses the need for learning to be a space of fun.[9] At 826, the whimsy of the pirate-themed storefront and the reading nooks in the writing lab's tree house made me feel as though fun was infinitely possible. One of the major challenges I faced was translating that whimsy from the third space of our writing center to the often noisy, chaotic classrooms at the neighboring Tenderloin Community School (TCS), where our in-school programs served all the third, fourth, and fifth-grade classrooms. Because a significant portion of these students not only got our services in their classrooms at schools but also came once a week to our After School Program, I felt a need to keep things novel.

However, working in the nonprofit industrial complex, I soon learned that the capacity to dream came at a cost. I was frequently given advice from my supervisors that I should rely on the work of my predecessors and use resources from years past, rather than inventing new lessons for the students. Sometimes that work veered into advice to use scripted curriculum, something that bothered me because as I gathered readings for my dissertation I learned that "schools in high-poverty, low-income communities, adopt scripted curriculum more often than those in more affluent communities."[10] Scripted curriculum felt like a mirror of what bell hooks describes as the "institutionalization and commercialization" of the church that ultimately undermines our ability to "transform souls, to intervene politically."[11] It felt like a further injustice and barrier to acting in true service to my students.

I struggled along until halfway through the spring semester when our nonprofit began preparing to celebrate its twentieth anniversary. My supervisors challenged the program's staff to create lessons that engaged with the concept of the future, and at last, I felt as though I had a chance to try something new. An eighth grader who was preparing to graduate and move on to high school told me that working with our tutors had opened so many doors, and it sparked an idea.

When I was in school, staring out the window was one of my few escapes from the conservative, anti-queer, and often racist and classist school environment. When my classmates would sing about Jesus and talk about George W. Bush's abortion politics, I could lose my thoughts by looking out at the Bradley pears that dotted our campus. I was usually the first out the door when the bell rang, sometimes even before. As I began to brainstorm about lessons, I thought not only of my own childhood at school but also of my mother's spiritual practices. She taught me that when smudging or cleaning one must leave a window or door open, or you'll chase spirits and negative energy around in circles in the room. Together, these inspired me to continue thinking about doors and windows as an escape, which was a sign that I had not yet moved beyond what bell hooks describes as love supplanted by an "intensity of longing and lack."[12]

School windows drew more of our attention in the thick of the Covid-19 pandemic, especially when the Air Quality Index indicated that it was not healthy to crack them open. With increasingly frequent wildfires and smog, San Francisco has a troubled relationship with air, and it is a significant mandate that every occupied, livable apartment in the city must have at least one window. I began to notice the doors on my walks around the Tenderloin and other neighborhoods. Sometimes, the chaos of police presence and sneering passersby was heavy, and the doors to the school and the classrooms concealed tender, magical oases. But, it was a contradictory experience because often, the doors would need to be locked and shut to prevent distraction from student behavior in the hallways and street activity outside. As I prepared the curriculum, I wanted to incorporate the reality that I'd heard from students again and again. They asked me and my colleagues to not ignore their experiences as we coached them on writing. Their poems, short stories, and letters incorporated the sights and sounds of the Tenderloin, including things that were traumatizing or uncomfortable, but also things that inspired hope and admiration.

In order to inspire further thought and discussion, I printed illustrations and art pieces from Afrofuturism and Chicanafuturism and hid them behind paper doors. These pieces of art included portraits of Black, Indigenous, and POC profiles, collages that interrogated the meaning of creation versus replication, and imaginative scenes that dared students to expand their idea of reality. While the students engaged in the activity, there was temporary conflict from a white tutor who expressed discomfort with explaining a particular art piece to her students. In the attempt to make the curriculum culturally relevant and accessible to students, I also needed to prepare the adults who were working closely with them.[13] This meant addressing the students' desire for adults to practice compassion and insight unflinchingly, cultivating the awareness that bell hooks describes as essential to "the process of love as the practice of freedom."[14] Preparing the tutors involved sharing our goals for the lesson, giving adults the framework to work with students instead of on them, and committing to being involved in the conversations that arose.

Through the selection, sculpting, and crafting of doors filled with symbolic ties to one's past, students connected their roots to futurism, engaging in conversations about the challenges that face Black, Indigenous, and POC futurists, including racist policies and practices at school but also a wider climate of purposeful limitations through policy and inaction that continue to bar students from transformative and antiracist education.

Time passed, and we curated some of the pieces the students produced so that we could put them in a printed book. Tutors worked closely with students on the revision process, rather than editing or dissecting their work. When we distributed it, students smiled and shared pride in their work. But, I became aware that other program managers and directors across the city at our Mission Bay center were also using the curriculum. While all of the organization's programming was modeled off a desire to serve communities of Black, Indigenous, and POC students, those who attended our Mission Bay programming were often directly connected to the writing laboratory because it was housed in the ground level of their residential building. The symbolic nature of doors and windows takes on a new meaning in that context, so it felt like decontextualizing the curriculum and applying it without additional place-based awareness was appropriative and careless.

Since I hadn't spoken with them or prepared them to deliver the nuances around the selected art, it felt upsetting. It was at that time that I chose to reach out to 826 Digital, an arm of 826 National, which is affiliated with but distinct from my organization at the time. At that moment, I felt like the most liberatory action would be to provide this curriculum with all of my notes and details online, for free, to everyone who wanted to access it. My hope was that rather than copying and applying my curriculum exactly as it was presented, the notes and metacognitive context-setting would provide a model for other educators to shape their own lessons without a fidelious replication.

I continue to reflect on my time with this nonprofit and the students I served. I wonder if they have found their own way to open the doors and windows to their futures.

> You realize you will be gone when the questions of the future arise like wildflowers on the plains of this earth. You want to be a part of a legacy and so you write and write, questioning and exploring, not knowing if what you write will become a part of America's freedom song, not knowing if there is a rainbow.
>
> —Nellie Wong[15]

Notes

1   https://826digital.com/resources/doors-to-the-future/.

2   Asif Wilson, "Exclusion and Extraction: Situating Spirit Murdering in Community Colleges," *Educational Foundations* 34, no. 1 (2021): 47–67.

3   Bettina L. Love, "Anti-Black State Violence, Classroom Edition: The Spirit Murdering of Black Children," *Journal of Curriculum and Pedagogy* 13, no. 1 (2016): 22–5.

4   Sharan B. Merriam, *Qualitative Research: A Guide to Design and Implementation* (San Francisco, CA: Jossey-Bass, 2009).

5   Felecia Briscoe and Muhammad Khalifa, *Becoming Critical: The Emergence of Social Justice Scholars* (Albany, NY: State University of New York Press, 2015).

6   bell hooks, *Teaching to Transgress: Education as the Practice of Freedom* (London: Routledge, 1994).

7   Ibid.
8   Nellie Wong, "In Search of the Self as Hero: Confetti of Voices on New Year's Night," in *This Bridge Called My Back: Writings by Radical Women of Color*, eds. Gloria Anzaldúa and Toni Cade Bambara (New York: Kitchen Table, Women of Color Press, 1983), 180–1. (Original work published 1983).
9   hooks, *Teaching to Transgress*, 7.
10   Anita Ede, "Scripted Curriculum: A Prescription for Success?" *Childhood Education* 86, no. 1 (2006): 29–32.
11   bell hooks, "Love as the Practice of Freedom," in *Outlaw Culture: Resisting Representations* (New York: Routledge, 1994), 247.
12   bell hooks, *Feminism Is for Everybody: Passionate Politics* (Strand, London, United Kingdom: Pluto Press, 2000).
13   Gloria Ladson-Billings and William Tate, "Toward a Critical Race Theory of Education," *Teachers College Record* 97, no. 1 (1995): 47.
14   hooks, *Teaching to Transgress*, 9.
15   Wong, "In Search of the Self as Hero," 180–1.

10

Connecting through Emotional Solidarity: Learning from Youths' Stories of Hope and Sorrow

Katie B. Peachey, Caitlin M. Donovan, Jennifer C. Mann,
María Heysha Carrillo Carrasquillo, and Crystal Chen Lee

Our understanding of ourselves and others grows through the connections we make with stories, particularly intimate stories of emotional resonance[1]. With multiply marginalized youth, whose feelings and experiences are systematically undervalued in traditional education settings,[2] classroom intimacy frequently takes the form of stories of hope and sorrow[3]. hooks notes these emotions are frequently not embraced within the traditional classroom because of their perceived lack of academic objectivity. The sharing of these subjective experiences provides a vulnerable space for students to express their own feelings and learn from others.[1.] hooks reminds us that "emotional awareness can serve as a force to bind us together in community and enable us to transcend difference."[4] It is from this positioning that we situate our work with youth writers.

Who We Are

The Literacy and Community Initiative (LCI) is a partnership between North Carolina State University and multiple community-based organizations that work with youth (ages 12–22) who have been marginalized through structural inequities, systemic racism, adverse childhood experiences, and/or discrimination. Through collaboration between these distinct organizations and LCI, students write about pivotal experiences and social issues impacting them and their communities in order to engage and lead their communities.

This process can be especially transformative for marginalized youth whose voices are often silenced in formal institutions.[5] Although the writing materials for each organization align, the curriculum is intentionally crafted with collaborative input from each community organization. Through our longitudinal study, we have evidence that these critical literacy practices in out-of-school contexts can offer transformative outcomes when youth write, engage, and lead their communities through increased self-awareness, advocacy, and leadership and thus provide powerful pedagogical lessons for educators and community leaders.[6] These lessons are pivotal to the co-creation of educational spaces that promote healing and collective liberation, which are cornerstones of hooks's teachings.

As former English teachers and current writing facilitators, we have a unique opportunity to cultivate spaces where students feel free to share their truths. Hearing their stories of hope and sorrow builds connections among learning communities by clarifying misunderstandings, bridging gaps, and building emotional solidarity[7]. These stories are the "liberating tales"[8] that hooks describes, as they allow writers to share their stories in a more engaged, equitable community.

What We Do

To structure these writing communities, members from the LCI team meet with each community organization to co-develop a nine-month writing curriculum based on the organization's interests and goals. Each curriculum is designed to support participants as they write across a variety of multimodal genres and culminates in a published book and public reading event (see Appendix 1.1 for sample student-designed book cover). Each writing curriculum (see Appendix 1.2 for a sample of a curriculum) includes the use of guiding questions, mentor texts, facilitated discussions of power, genre writing, and sharing. Some common guiding questions that are explored across organizations include: *Who am I?* and *What makes my community beautiful/strong/important?*. Exploring various genres and diverse mentor texts in this writing program allows youth to see the multifaceted ways stories can hold and challenge existing power structures. An example of a mentor text we utilized at Refugee Hope Partners, a nonprofit organization that works with refugee communities, is Andrew Lam's "Letter to a Young Refugee from Another." After reading and discussing this text, participants were provided with an optional template (see Appendix 1.3) based on the mentor text and encouraged to use their own valuable experiences to write advice to a young refugee in the form of a letter. Reading and discussing mentor texts before writing provides adolescent writers with opportunities to engage with past and present writers to reflect on their own experiences in new ways and name barriers they are facing to reimagine their futures.[9]

On a week-to-week basis, an LCI supported workshop might involve the following steps: community building between the facilitator and writers, introduction of the mentor text, reading and analysis of the text, writing, time for supportive peer feedback, and space for final revisions (see Appendix 1.2 for an example of these steps). Through these practices, we seek to improve youth literacy skills, promote youth social-emotional development, and enhance youth advocacy and leadership skills. Our mission is to amplify student voices through their engagement in a critical literacy writing curriculum that culminates in the publication and sharing of student-authored books.

What We've Learned

In this teaching, we provide a brief portrait of each community partner and an important lesson we've learned from youth in each of these four contexts. The wisdom we have gained from these communities is valuable, because storytellers can leverage these knowledges to reframe stereotypes regarding their communities.[10] It is our hope that our students' stories of hope and sorrow can provide educators and researchers alike with important insights into how we can foster educational spaces that allow us "to learn both to engage our differences, celebrating them when we can, and also rigorously confronting tensions as they arise,"[11] which is key to establishing empathy and solidarity. Some strategies we use to foster these educational spaces include guided journaling with critical literacy prompts, facilitated group discussions, and community reading events (see Appendix 1.2 for an example curriculum). Each of these tools provides youth with opportunities to voice their perspectives while also learning from and engaging with others' perspectives.

Lesson One: Bull City Youthbuild—*Strengthening Relationships through Vulnerability*

While working with Bull City Youthbuild, an organization that helps youth earn their high school diplomas while providing on-the-job skills training, we saw that *sharing moments of vulnerability strengthened relationships between writers* and illustrated the richness of complex lived experiences through future sharing[12]. At Youthbuild, we examined Martin Luther King Jr.'s "Your Life's Blueprint" and wrote our own plans for the future; we saw that writing the future involved acknowledging and accepting the past. Writing grounded community conversations that reflected writers' experiences across contexts. Sharing their experiences while incarcerated led to pieces like Jayden's poem, "I wanted to be grown, I knew it all but in reality, I didn't. Of course, life has its way of teaching lessons. I was taught a lesson, where I couldn't control my life." Jayden shared how he had grown and changed, while remaining true to himself. He noted, "My support system around me kept me going, with constant advice [...] I've gotten plenty of advice from plenty of people but keeping my head up is forever my go to thought when times get tough. I also advise others to do the same." Alvaro also noted that he got "caught up with the wrong people," but that now he wanted to "be top of my game/ Try my best in anything/ Put my mind to things/ And get them done" in order to "make my family proud" and "give back to my people and the community." Both Alvaro and Jayden emphasized the role of their past experiences on future planning, while also affirming the directions they were going. In collaborative discussion with his fellow writers, Deonte wrote that his past wouldn't change the trajectory of his future, but acknowledged that "in my next five years/ for me to reach my goals/ I have to be on my shit/ I can't stop, have to keep going./ I'm the only person that can hold me back." Sharing these vulnerable moments in a community that withholds judgment facilitated authentic connection and positive future orientation that can only grow through the hope they created together and the sorrow they processed. While each approach to helping youth process their trauma is unique to each student's needs and circumstances, across our curricula, we center holistic care, sense of belonging, role models and networks, funds of knowledge, individual and collective goal setting, and self and community advocacy.[6] This emphasis on the community context in connection to healing is vital when considering youth social-emotional well-being.

Lesson Two: CORRAL Riding Academy—*Creating Space without Judgment or Trivialization*

While working with CORRAL Riding Academy, a holistic program that provides equine-assisted psychotherapy and educational support to youth in high-risk situations, the student writers taught us *the importance of creating space for expression of emotions without judgment or trivialization of their experiences.* Just as the cover of her memoir, *Bone Black,* captures a younger version of hooks holding a childhood toy and "looking intensely at the object in her hands,"[13] we asked students to critically analyze a significant object in their own lives. In this session, CORRAL participants considered and wrote about the tangible and intangible qualities that this item carried in their lives. In her poem, Jemma reflected on a cherished necklace that was passed down to her from her abuela before she left Mexico. She wrote, "When I imagine you, I imagine you and me together forever. When others see you, they see whatever necklace. When I see you, I see my world. When I feel bad, I remember when you tell me you love me." Even though others see her necklace as meaningless, Jemma repositioned it to a place of honor and connected it back to her familial and cultural connections in a way that added richness and emotional resonance to her story[14]. This writing supported Jemma in pushing back against the negative comments and stereotypes that others hold to reclaim her own identity. Similarly, Lexie wrote that "when I hear others say you are a ring, I say that you are way more to me. When others see you, they think of you as just jewelry, I see a new mom. When others say that I'm that girl that was in foster care and then got adopted, you say that I'm that girl that is safe now." Lexie challenged labels placed on her due to her experiences in the foster care system. Both students remind us of the importance of providing youth the opportunity to express the entirety of their emotional and physical experiences without trivialization to create space for them to reclaim their identities and bring healing. As hooks reminds us, creating space for students to share and listen intently to each other's stories can be an invaluable "ritual of communion that opens our minds and hearts."

Lesson Three: Refugee Hope Partners—*Student-constructed Community and Belonging*

While collaborating with Refugee Hope Partners (RHP), a nonprofit organization that works with refugee communities through a whole family approach that supports academic learning, community involvement, and social/medical services, we saw *students collectively construct a deep sense of community and forge a space of belonging amongst themselves* through conversations that contended with the discrimination and hardships the students face[15]. Refugee students, in particular, often face exclusion and othering,[16] thus making it significant that they engaged in conversation regarding their experiences and worked to cultivate belonging amongst themselves. The majority of the students at RHP live in the same apartment complex and this sense of community spilled over into a sense of hope in their daily lives. In their writing, students frequently expressed emotions that would typically be perceived as at odds with one another, just as hope and sorrow appear to be opposite emotions. Dani, whose family fled Syria and relocated first to Jordan and then the United States wrote that she is "from good memories/ And loving people/ From a bad president who kills people/ But a country of good people." Similarly, Shamshi, a young Somali woman from South Africa, wrote that she is from "loving and caring neighbors [...] from being scared to get kidnapped but running around with friends." Aina, a young woman from Afghanistan, wrote that "I'm from a place with beautiful and smart women./ I'm from a place with a lot of bloodshed." The students freely shared their experiences and sought to understand one another. Saida, from Tanzania, wrote simply, "I am from a very good and bad place." Noella, from Rwanda, wrote of the community at RHP: "The beauty of my community [...] [is] people come together as one [...] even with different stories [...] we get to hear and learn [...] the similarity we have makes us feel like we are home because we are all refugees." So even though they come from vastly different countries and varied life experiences, they constructed a sense of community that fostered what Sheba, from Burundi, called "a familiar thread as human beings and refugees [...] a sense of belonging." It was perhaps due to the shared experience of holding simultaneously conflicting emotions and the experience of displacement that helped forge a more intimate community among the students.[17] hooks teaches us that "like many writers [...] who have stayed away from their native place, who live in a state of mental exile, the condition of feeling split was damaging [...] Healing [...] meant [...] taking bits of my life and putting them together again."[18] Similarly, through LCI, the students at RHP put bits of their old lives and new lives together and formed a new community with others who understand and provide a nurturing space of belonging.

Lesson Four: Juntos—*Centering Students'*
Cultural and Linguistic Repertoires

Working with Juntos, a program that aims to provide Latino/a/e students and their families with the necessary knowledge, skills, and resources for educational sustainability and post-secondary opportunities, revealed *the transformative power of centering cultural and linguistic repertoires in student writing*. By embracing their cultural and linguistic identities through translanguaging, students authentically expressed their emotions and experiences, resulting in impactful narratives. Translanguaging empowers multilinguals to fluidly leverage their native and acquired languages for enhanced expression and connectivity.[19] Mónica explained that her "family has faced many hardships, y gracias a Dios, we have been able to get through them," acknowledging the challenges immigrant families face in the United States. Mónica reflected on her journey as an immigrant youth, highlighting the profound connection between her cultural heritage and personal experiences. Freely translating across languages provides students with a liberating means to process these challenges. Native language phrases hold deep meaning for students by bridging personal narratives, cultures, and broader experiences. Minerva's reflection on her parents' insistence that "vinimos a darles una mejor vida" (we came to give you a better life) exemplified this connection. Minerva saw this phrase not only as representative of her family's immigration story but also as a reminder of her responsibility as a first-generation American. Minerva found solace in the interconnectedness of her journey with her family, united in their pursuit of a better life. Allowing students to express themselves and reflect on their cultural wisdom enables them to weave powerful and meaningful narratives encompassing their unique experiences and heritages.[20] Her words reflected the emotional and cultural wealth she carries. The lessons we've learned from centering cultural and linguistic repertoires can empower students to authentically explore their identities and share narratives that resonate with their journeys and the collective experiences of their communities. hooks[21] advocates for occupying the margin as a space that fosters creativity, solidarity, and new visions. Similarly, by embracing identities and experiences typically marginalized in mainstream educational spaces, Juntos students drew from their unique backgrounds to author narratives that nourish collective resistance.

Moving Forward

hooks so powerfully reminds us that we "are called to renew our minds if we are to transform educational institutions—and society—so that the way we live, teach, and work can reflect our joy in cultural diversity, our passion for justice, and our love of freedom."[22] Our student authors in the LCI program taught us to renew our minds and to reflect the very joy in our work both inside and outside the classroom. To simultaneously hold both joy and sorrow is to not only reflect

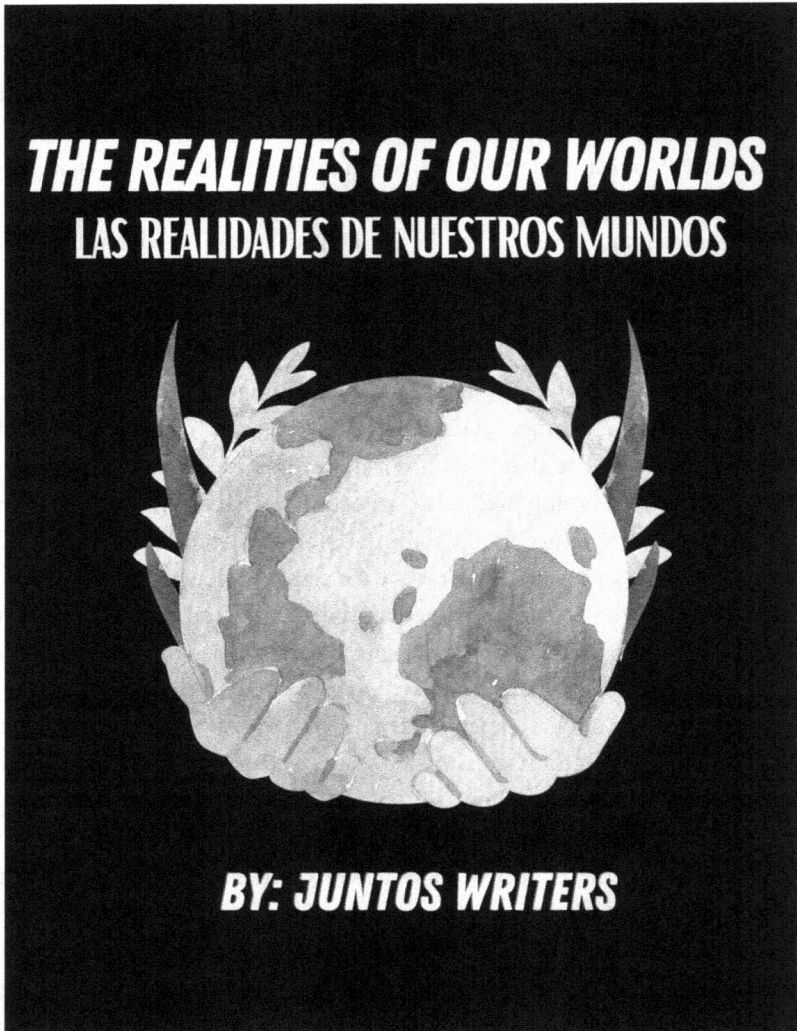

Appendix 1.1 Sample student-designed book cover

the joy in our cultural diversity but also demonstrate the hard and oftentimes difficult work in the pursuit and passion for justice and freedom. Such love and pursuit are often complex endeavors that give way to strength in vulnerability and courage in writing.

In our pedagogical journey, we leaned on hooks's notion that we ought to also share our own lives and complexity with our students as a whole writing

Genre/Text	Objectives	Procedures

Session 1: Show & Tell Poetry
 	
Guiding Question: What physical item holds specific importance to you?
	1. Students will identify LCI writing routines and expectations.
	2. Students will differentiate between tangible and intangible descriptions of items.
	3. Students will compose a poem about an important item and connect it to their identities and personal histories.
		1. **Show and Tell Activity**
		  a. Students will share an item or a picture of an item to the group and discuss its importance
		  b. Discuss the differences between tangible and intangible qualities of objects
		2. **Brainstorm:**
		  a. Students will complete a brainstorm sheet and write a poem about their chosen items.
		  b. Students will think about why their item is important to them and what important memories this item holds.

Session 3: Found Poetry
 	
Guiding Question: What inspires you?
	1. Students will evaluate different vocabulary to determine the impact that these words have on a writing piece.
	2. Students will plan their found poems with a focus on theme and diction.
		1. **Sharing**
		  a. Students will have the option to share their Show & Tell poems
		2. **Warm-up:**
		  a. Explore the Word Mover application
		3. **Introduction to Found Poetry:**
		  a. Discuss the format of found poems, including blackout poems
		  b. Look at examples of powerful found poems
		  c. Read through and select source texts
		  d. Begin constructing found poems using source texts

Session 5: Flash Photo Narrative
 	
Guiding Question: What makes you feel empowered?
	1. Students will construct a narrative about their lives at the farm, at school, at home, or in the community.
	2. Students will strategically select photos that correspond with their written narratives.
	3. Students will create a presentation that synthesizes the two modes.
		1. **Share:**
		  a. Share and submit Show and Tell and Found poems
		2. **Warm-up Activity:** Random photo challenge
		  a. Print pictures of horses/farms and create stories with partners
		  b. Discuss the role of images in telling our stories
		3. **Brainstorm:**
		  a. Complete a brainstorm handout to create their story structures.
		  b. Read through several mentor texts to understand the structure of
		  c. Begin writing narratives and think about photo(s) that they may want to include

Appendix 1.2 Sample of an LCI curriculum for CORRAL Riding Academy

community. We, too, have learned to write alongside our students, sharing our own personal stories of "where we are from," what foods we like to eat, and what experiences we have learned and grown from. We are learning to lean on engaged pedagogy, one in which we adopt a posture to grow and be empowered by the process. In writing this chapter and reflecting on our students' stories of joy and sorrow, hooks reminds us that the collective sharing and writing

Letter to a Young Refugee From Another

	Instructions:
On the news last night I saw you _____	-describe what you saw him doing
and afterward I couldn't get the image out of my mind. You with your wide eyes and shy smile, your	
hand gripping your mother's as if it were a life saver, you are repeating my story of _____ years	-the number of years since you left your country
ago.	
Listen, even if I know so little about your country's tumultuous history, even if I don't know	-age when you left your country
your name, I think I know what you are going through. When I was _____ about your age, I too	-family members who left with you
fled from my homeland with my _____ and _____ and _____	-what happened
when _____ we ended up in _____ and	-name of country you moved to
_____ was left behind.	-family who didn't leave
Back then I couldn't make any sense out of what had happened to me or my family.	
History, after all, is always baffling to the young. One day I was _____	-telling what you were doing when you were told you had to flee your country
_____.	
For the first few days in _____ I walked about as if _____	-new country
_____. Only years later, _____	-how you felt when you first arrived in your new country
_____	-what you learned later that you didn't know then
_____	
My young friend, there are so many things I want to tell you, so many experiences I want	
to share with you, but, most of all, I want to warn you that the road ahead is a very	
_____ one, and you must be _____ and _____ and	-word to describe how life will feel
_____. There are crucial things you should learn and learn quickly, and then there are	-3 words to tell what type of person you must be
things you must mull over for the rest of your life.	
The immediate thing is to learn to _____	-important lesson to learn immediately when moving to a new country
_____	
_____	
_____	
_____	
_____	
_____	

Appendix 1.3 Mentor text integration example

also includes us, as writers and teachers, in order to construct a deep sense of community and forge a space of belonging:

> When education is the practice of freedom, students are not the only ones who are asked to share, to confess. Engaged pedagogy does not seek simply to empower students. Any classroom that employs a holistic model of learning will also be a place where teachers grow, and are empowered by the process.[22]

Therefore, in developing emotional solidarity, it is even more important to be empowered by the writing process as a whole, not only to listen, but to participate, act, and love as student-teachers and teacher-students.[23]

Notes

1   Kimberely Holmes and Kara Sealock, "Storytelling as a Portal to Deeper Wisdom in the Curriculum Studies of Education and Nursing," *Qualitative Research Journal* 19, no. 2 (2019): 93–103.

2   Enid M. Rosario-Ramos and Laura Ruth Johnson, "Communities as Counter-storytelling(Con)texts: The Role of Community-based Educational Institutions in the Development of Critical Literacy and Transformative Action," in *Moving Critical Literacies Forward*, eds. Jessica Pandya and JuliAnna Ávila (New York: Routledge, 2014), 113–25.

3   bell hooks, *Teaching Critical Thinking: Practical Wisdom* (New York: Routledge, 2010).

4   bell hooks, *Teaching Community: A Pedagogy of Hope* (New York: Routledge, 2003), 114.

5   Gholdy E. Muhammad, "Searching for Full Vision: Writing Representations of African American Adolescent Girls," *Research in the Teaching of English* 49, no. 3 (2015): 224–47.

6   Andrea Cervantes, Briza Cruz, Kelsey Dufresne, Kevin Garcia-Galindo, Aldo Galvan Hernandez, Crystal Chen Lee, Nina Schoonover, and Luis Zavala, "Justice Poets and Proponents: Creating Safe Spaces for Minorities," *Fringes: North Carolina English Language Arts Teachers' Association Journal* 2, no. 1 (2020): 37–47; Ernest Morrell, *Critical Literacy and Urban Youth: Pedagogies of Access, Dissent, and Liberation* (New York: Routledge, 2008); Crystal Chen Lee, Jose Picart, and Jennifer C. Mann, *Amplifying Youth Voices through Critical Literacy and Positive Youth Development: The Potential of University-Community Partnerships* (New York: Routledge, 2025).

7   Jamie Zepeda, "Stories in the Classroom: Building Community Using Storytelling and Storyacting," *Journal of Childhood Studies* 39, no. 2 (2014): 21–6.

8   hooks, *Teaching Critical Thinking*, 51.

9   Crystal Chen Lee, Laura Jacobs, and Jennifer C. Mann, "Writing with Dignity among Youth in Urban Communities: Using Mentor Texts as a Reflective Tool for Transformation." *Urban Education*, OnlineFirst publication, 2022, 1–31.

10 Patricia Enciso, "Storytelling in Critical Literacy Pedagogy: Removing the Walls between Immigrant and Non-immigrant Youth," *English Teaching: Practice & Critique* 10, no. 1 (2011): 21–40; Maria P. Ghiso and Gerald Campano, "Coloniality and Education: Negotiating Discourses of Immigration in Schools and Communities through Border Thinking," *Equity & Excellence in Education* 46, no. 2 (2013): 252–69.

11 hooks, *Teaching Community*, 109.

12 Jennifer D. Turner and Autumn A. Griffin, "Brown Girls Dreaming: Adolescent Black Girls Futuremaking through Multimodal Representations of Race, Gender, and Career Aspirations," *Research in the Teaching of English* 55, no. 2 (2020): 109–33.

13 hooks, *Teaching Critical Thinking*, 7.

14 April Brannon, "Emphasizing the Sensuous: Writing for a Richer Life," *English Journal* 107, no. 3 (2018): 26–31.

15 Jennifer C. Mann and Crystal C. Lee, "'They Just Go by Making Their Own Hate Story': Interrogating Stereotypes with Refugee Students in Community-based Spaces," *Language Arts* 99, no. 6 (2022): 417–20.

16 Jessca Sierk, "Religious Literacy in the New Latino Diaspora: Combating the 'Othering' of Muslim Refugee Students in Nebraska," *Journal of Inquiry and Action in Education* 7, no. 1 (2016): 1–3 and 6–7.

17 Gerald Campano, *Immigrant Students and Literacy: Reading, Writing, and Remembering* (New York: Teachers College Press, 2007).

18 bell hooks, *Belonging: A Culture of Place* (New York: Routledge, 2009), 15.

19 Ofelia García and Jo Anne Kleifgen, *Educating Emergent Bilinguals: Policies, Programs, and Practices for English Language Learners* (New York: Teachers College Press, 2010).

20 Candice Powell and Juan F. Carrillo, "Border Pedagogy in the New Latinx South," *Equity & Excellence in Education* 52, no. 4 (2019): 435–47.

21 bell hooks, "Choosing the Margin as a Space of Radical Openness," *Framework: The Journal of Cinema and Media* no. 36 (1989): 15–23.

22 bell hooks, *Teaching to Transgress* (New York: Routledge, 1994), 34.

23 Paulo Freire, *The Pedagogy of the Oppressed* (New York: Continuum, 1985).

11

Rethinking the Classroom as a Hub for Intellectual Joy and Scholastic Passion: A Dialogue

Laiba Rizwan, Melanie Taddeo, and Kosha D. Bramesfeld

Over the last year, I acquired a new role in academia. In addition to being a graduate student, I became a teaching assistant. Standing at the intersection of these two roles, I was able to appraise pedagogy in a unique way. Though I was well-versed in the dilemmas and concerns that students face, the ones that plagued teachers were new territory. As a student, I was aware and critical of how our educational systems and pedagogical approaches seem intent on stripping away the joy, excitement, and curiosity that should underlie every educational endeavor. bell hooks highlights these tensions in *Teaching to Transgress*[1] when she notes, "excitement could not be generated without a full recognition of the fact that there could never be an absolute set agenda governing teaching practices. Agendas had to flexible, had to allow for spontaneous shifts in direction." As a budding scholar, I was determined to rectify this problem for my students by creating a classroom that fostered critical thinking and self-discovery. My aim, however, was met with two fierce contenders: competition and the pressure to perform among students. While observing my students' desperation for grades and their evaluation anxiety, which governed almost every aspect of their behavior and motivation, I was left grappling with a frightening thought: am I complicit in stripping education of joy and excitement?

In a way similar to bell hooks's dialog with Ron Scapp in *Teaching to Transgress*,[2] I engaged in a conversation with two members of the epistemic community I deeply respect and admire: Melanie Taddeo (MT), a passionate advocate for disability rights and first legally blind teacher to graduate in Ontario, and Prof. Kosha Bramesfeld (KB), a teaching stream faculty member, who centers classroom discussions on students' voices and lived experiences while teaching courses in community psychology. Together, we rethink our classrooms as spaces of passion and excitement while taking a critical look at educational praxes and reforms that can help facilitate critical thought in the classroom.

Laiba: First of all, thanks so much for sitting down to chat with me. My first question to you two would be: in your classrooms, what makes learning intellectually stimulating and joyful and in what contexts?

Melanie: It starts off with creating a certain environment or culture in your classroom from day one. You set the stage with the expectations and create a safe space where students can be themselves and show up as they need to. Being open and creating a supportive environment that allows people to be who they are makes the fun come naturally. Adding humor and levity to a situation is important in the teaching style. In my role as a teacher for students with special needs, for example, during broadcast training, I like to share relevant anecdotes with some humor in them to add the extra fun. But, really, truly, it's allowing people to be who they are in the classroom and creating safe, supportive environments for them. This allows people to bring in and share their sense of humor as well—within reason, of course. As bell hooks notes, "[A]s a classroom community, our capacity to generate excitement is deeply impacted by our interest in one another, in hearing one another's voices, in recognizing one another's presence."[3]

Kosha: I agree with everything that Melanie just said. I certainly have had a lot of professors who were funny. But not all effective instructors are funny. I like the term "engaging" more than fun because I think there are many ways to be engaged in the learning process and sometimes that engagement can be light, fun, and silly and that's wonderful. But sometimes, it can be serious, dark, and deep. bell hooks highlights this distinction when she notes, "I have always believed that students should enjoy learning. Yet I found that there was much more tension in the diverse classroom setting where the philosophy of teaching is rooted in critical pedagogy (and in my case) in feminist critical pedagogy. The presence of tension—and at times even conflict—often meant that students did not enjoy my classes or love me, their professor, as I secretly wanted them to do."[4] I can relate to this sentiment, as some of the lessons that I want my students to learn are painful, and they require introspection and self-reflection, which can be uncomfortable. One of the ways that I have sought to navigate this tension is to view teachers and students as partners in the learning process. Like bell hooks, I believe that "excitement is generated through collective effort," which comes from building a learning community in which students and teachers have an opportunity to learn from one another. To create this type of collaborative learning environment, I strive to create opportunities for students to bring in their own voices and experiences into the learning process. In doing so, I adopt bell hooks's perspectives on feminist standpoint and embrace the idea that students come into the classroom with unique vantage points rooted in their experiences as gendered and racialized beings who have been impacted by their social contexts. Students need spaces to explore these life experiences and opportunities to use these experiences as a platform for growth and opportunity. After all, if you are learning something and you can't make the connection to why it is personally important to you, you're not going to be very motivated to learn it. But if you can develop that deep relevance to the content, then it "sticks." Everybody is unique and each individual has their own background and experience. Therefore, in each of my courses I create opportunities for students to explore course topics in ways that are rooted in their own lived experiences and points of reference.

Laiba: In my experience, finding something that students can relate to, whether it's with some kind of joke or by narrating a personal experience, humanizes you and the instructor enhances the joy within the classroom. Talking about the difficulties and challenges encountered as an undergraduate student makes me more relatable to the students. In addition, I find cracking jokes and lightening the mood are useful. I try to make it a dialog, as opposed to a lecture. As a student, the classes that I looked forward to attending were always taught by professors who could add levity to the topic and make it a discussion where the students could chime in with their thoughts. With respect to engagement, I find that sometimes it's hard to create that space for dialog in my role as a TA. Since I am not the one designing the course, I have to follow the structure that is given to me as well as the other TAs by the professor. For example, I recently taught a tutorial for a first-year undergraduate Introduction to Psychology course at the university. The TAs, including myself, were responsible for holding these one-hour tutorial sessions where we were essentially trying to make sure that students are actually keeping up with the lectures, as it was being presented online, asynchronously. To this end, we distributed questions made by the instructor to our students a week before the tutorial. We would then ask them to provide their answers to these questions within the tutorials session and assign them a grade based on the quality of their input. During the tutorials, I noticed many of my students were basically reading answers off the textbook or their notes verbatim without any understanding of what they were saying. While the answers were technically correct and could get them at least partial credit, the tutorials weren't really helpful in enhancing their understanding of the subject material or their ability to apply these concepts beyond the four walls of a classroom.

Melanie: I have a question on that: within the structure that you have described— where you gave these questions ahead of time—would it be possible to make it into an open dialog, a conversation as opposed to, here are the questions ahead of time and I am looking for a specific answer?

Laiba: I would have loved it to be the case, but the grading pressured students to come up with the ideal answer instead of actually engaging with the topic. The criterion for an excellent answer worth full points was kept stringent by the instructors. And, as a TA, I had little to no control over these logistical pieces. It was disappointing to witness a loss of joy and intellectual curiosity amongst my students. It became that much more challenging to keep them engaged and interested. bell hooks talks a lot about engaged pedagogy in her work, to the extent that it is a fundamental tenet of her teaching philosophy. In *Teaching to Transgress*, she says, "Engaged pedagogy begins with the assumption that we learn best when there is an interactive relationship between student and teacher."[5] She further expands on it and writes, "When students are fully engaged, professors no longer assume the sole leadership role in the classroom. Instead, the classroom functions more like a cooperative where everyone contributes to make sure all resources are being used, to ensure the optimal learning well-being of everyone."[6] Considering what we have touched on so far, how do you try to create joy and engagement in your classrooms?

Kosha: Coming back to the realities of teaching in terms of the structures of the university, and the structures of a classroom, and the grading requirements [...] Many years back, when preparing to write my very first statement for a teaching portfolio, I went to a workshop where they were helping the attendees articulate their teaching philosophy. As I thought about my teaching philosophy, I kept thinking about my kids who were toddlers at the time. They were about to be at that age where they were going to go to school and have all the fun sucked out of learning. However, as toddlers, learning for them was like, look there's a puddle, let's jump in it! Or let's experiment with what the water does! Oh, here's a bug, let's watch it! During this glorious time, children learn by doing. They're super engaged, and they're not being formally tested, per se. But you know that learning is happening because they won't touch something that stung at one point, or they continue rubbing something that feels soft, for example. One of the things that I love about bell hooks is how eloquently she captures those moments when teaching and learning are a "sheer joy." For example, when discussing her childhood, hooks writes, "I loved being a student. I loved learning. School was the place of ecstasy—pleasure and danger."[7] Later, hooks discusses her times teaching in community settings and how engaging these exchanges were, writing about how rewarding it was to witness community members' "hunger to learn new ways of knowing"[8] and "their desire to use this knowledge in meaningful ways to enrich their daily lives."[9] These anecdotes illustrate that children and adults alike are capable of genuine curiosity and excitement around learning. When reflecting on my own teaching, I keep asking myself: how can I try to recreate that curiosity and love of learning we have as children before we add the grades, stress, and memorization to the mix. I haven't quite figured out the perfect recipe for it. But over the years I have worked hard to find ways to add more curiosity and wonderment into my courses. This is particularly challenging when teaching courses like undergraduate research methods, which students perceive as boring and challenging. Learning about research methods and statistics can be really challenging, but it can also be very exciting and fun. So, I thought to myself, what can I do to get people interested in learning about research methods? And the answer came to me in the form of these really overexaggerated media claims that I would occasionally read, such as "Sugar rush to prison? Study says candy could lead to violence." The researcher in me knows that the evidence is not going to support this claim. Yet, the newspaper has selected this headline because it knows that it will grab the reader's attention. This is a win-win for me. Because the headline is attention grabbing, I can use it to pique my students' curiosity. But because it is clearly exaggerated, I can also use headlines like these to challenge my students to dig deeper into their understanding of research methods. So, over the years, I have just started using little things like this to start building curiosity. Maybe as a whole, the course can still be boring at times, but bringing in those moments of curiosity can be quite rewarding.

Melanie: Well said! I agree. Obviously, each student learns differently. Therefore, I try to ensure that I have different activities or styles of lessons because, again, not all content is exciting. In order to meet everyone's needs and let everybody truly participate fully, just as they are, we need to have different options. It could be a quiz, games like Jeopardy, or roleplay with people. That way, I can meet people where they are the most comfortable by identifying fun and engaging ways to bring knowledge to the forefront. This way, I notice that desire to learn more or go that extra mile comes through because now they're feeling joy.

Laiba: I have a good friend who was homeschooled as a child. Spending time with her, I have come to notice that we approach and appraise education and learning in fundamentally different ways. For starters, she doesn't get stressed out at each assignment and evaluation that comes along. For me, a mistake on a math test determined my rank in class and how I fared compared to my peers. Naturally, I grew quite scared of making mistakes. I have noticed the same amongst my students. Mistakes at school mean a lot more than what they should. That fear of evaluation certainly takes the fun out of learning. It has been true to me and is sadly true for most, if not all, of my students. I have also noticed that learning for her isn't a matter of knowing enough to ace a test. The whole world is her classroom. She enjoys getting to know things that are not relevant to her field of study. I find that holds the childlike enthusiasm that Kosha alluded to: she collects rocks, takes pictures of plants, and insects to later Google their habitats and attributes. Learning is experiential for her in a lot of ways. Therefore, to bring the concepts I teach to life and make them more relevant, I often ask my students to reflect on why we should care about a topic, or why it should matter to us. One way of doing that is to think about examples from daily life that demonstrate whatever concept is at play. For example, when teaching behavioral modification techniques, I like to take particular scenarios and think about what makes them fit into category A vs. category B. Let's say positive vs negative reinforcement and what would have to be different about the scenario for it to fall into the second and not the first category. Another thing that I am curious about is whether or not the structure of academia helps or prevents intellectual joy or as bell hooks might call it, engaged pedagogy. The fear of assessment and getting low grades definitely takes the joy out of learning. I find that for my students and me, the focus is on not necessarily learning for the sake of learning, but on getting the best grades and standing out amongst the crowd. The competition that academia fosters is another thing that makes it stressful and joyless. It also makes it that much harder to learn from your colleagues and be partners in learning. It's quite a missed opportunity, I think.

Kosha: An issue I struggle with a lot is that I want school to reflect the real world so I understand why universities have grades. As adults, we are constantly judged and assessed on a regular basis and these judgments have consequences. On the other hand, I dislike this assumption that we necessarily need to have winners and losers in education (or even in society, more generally). To me, anybody who is learning is a winner. I'm intrigued by the idea of competency-based learning. The challenge is that competency-based learning doesn't work well within our existing, university structures. Competency-based learning is the idea that you need to meet a set of learning outcomes—like when you go to get a driver's license, you must reach a certain level of confidence in driving before they give you the license. It's all or none. You either get the driver's license, or you don't. In the real world though, if you fail your driver's test, you can go back in and take your test again. For some people, it may take a couple of months. For others, it might take a couple of years. And we just accept that there's this range of variability. In a university setting, we don't allow for that variability. If a student can't understand research methods in twelve weeks to the level that they're expected to understand it, then they fail. So, in essence, students are getting graded based on the speed at which they learn things, as much as how well they've learned it. These time pressures create opportunities, but also real stressors and tensions. Indeed, as hooks explains, "[T]he classroom is one of the most dynamic work settings precisely because we are given such a short amount of time to do so much."[10] But, as hooks points out, when distractions, unrealistic academic expectations, and classroom dynamics become too much, everyone feels burned out.[11] Along these lines, there are many things that I want to try in my classrooms to make learning more authentic, but I just don't know how to do these things within the confines and rules of our academic structures. So, I think there's a lot in our structures that prevent learning from happening, but I don't necessarily know that competition, in and of itself, is bad. Rather, I would want people to compete with themselves more than with others.

Laiba: I always have a hard time with that concept because there are only so many spaces in different graduate programs, such as clinical psychology. Let's say I try to be the best version of myself, academically speaking. What if it's still not as good as someone's "okay" self? I can compete with myself as much as I want, but I still won't make the cut into my desired program. Ultimately, when it comes to concrete, substantial life altering opportunities, we compete against others.

Kosha: There's a more significant why behind this: why do you want to get into graduate school? I bring this up because scholars like bell hooks have motivated me to start pushing back on the use of "schooling to reinforce dominator values."[12] We tend to place a lot of importance on status and labels, but we rarely think about what those labels and status positions represent. Do you want to get into graduate school because you want to earn a big income or because you want to help people? There are many ways to make money if that's your goal, and there are a lot of ways to help people if that is your goal. Neither of these paths has to involve getting a medical degree or getting a Ph.D. in clinical psychology. But as a society, we've done this huge disservice to people by defining success along fairly narrow paths by weighing some occupations higher than others and by rewarding some career paths with greater prestige and higher wages. I would love to see a society that values people's work and contributions more than their specific labels or status.

Melanie: I agree. As a society, we've created barriers by creating a hierarchy of prestige. These biases are drilled into us. We grow up hearing statements like, if you're not a lawyer or a doctor, you're not going to have a successful life. You're never gonna make it in this world. This can be quite challenging for individuals with disabilities, which is where much of my experience comes from. Whether it's a learning disability or simply a different speed of learning, we're doing such a disservice by allowing labels to have that much power. They make it hard for individuals with disabilities to feel accomplished compared to others if they don't stand up to the ideals our society has created. I try to mitigate this concern as much as I can by having honest conversations with my students and generally trying to shift the focus from disability to ability. Focusing on how their unique contributions and perspectives enrich the overall landscape of the places they go. Reminding them of how far they have come and how much they have accomplished!

Kosha: Well, Laiba, let me ask you a question. As a graduate TA at the moment, you are at the mercy of faculty. So, first, what could faculty do to make TA appointments more rewarding for TAs? And my second question is what will you do differently if you get a chance to teach your own course?

Laiba: First, I'd take feedback from my TAs and provide them with clarity about what is expected of them. Unfortunately, in my experience as a TA, my peers and I felt unappreciated in more than one way. Unrealistic expectations regarding time commitment, pay structure, and support as well as face time with course instructors is a concern. When creating my own courses, I'll try to have assessments that focus heavily on tapping into understanding of the course material. I would want my students to know and understand the material well enough to be able to apply it to real-world scenarios and to solve novel problems. Moreover, I would foster that scholastic passion by conveying my deep appreciation for the relevance and importance of the content that I am imparting as well as a genuine concern for my students. Because "when we teach with love we are far more likely to have an enhanced understanding of our students' capabilities and their limitations"[13] Lastly, encouraging a growth mindset. With respect to the value of psychological growth, bell hooks says, "I became accepting of the need to assist my students with their psychological growth when I began to see this work as enriching my teaching rather than diminishing it."[14] For me, this would include teaching my students to view their skills and abilities as plastic and buildable. It'll help them persist despite challenges by appraising failure as a successful learning attempt. Without the fear of evaluation and an intense focus of avoiding mistakes, they could be genuinely motivated to learn and be better. This reminds me something bell hooks said about mistakes, "If we fear mistakes, doing things wrongly, constantly evaluating ourselves, we will never make the academy a culturally diverse place where scholars and the curricula address every dimension of that difference."[15] After all, "whenever genuine learning is happening the conditions for self-actualization are in place, even when that is not a goal of our teaching process.[16]

Notes

1   bell hooks, Introduction to *Teaching to Transgress: Education as the Practice of Freedom* (New York: Routledge, 1994), 7.

2   bell hooks, "Building a Teaching Community: A Dialogue," in *Teaching to Transgress: Education as the Practice of Freedom* (New York: Routledge, 1994), 129–66.

3   hooks, introduction to *Teaching to Transgress*, 7.

4   bell hooks, "Embracing Change: Teaching in a Multicultural World," in *Teaching to Transgress: Education as the Practice of Freedom* (New York: Routledge, 1994), 41.

5   bell hooks, "Engaged Pedagogy," in *Teaching to Transgress: Education as the Practice of Freedom* (New York: Routledge, 1994), 19.

6   Ibid. 22.

7   hooks, introduction to *Teaching to Transgress*, 3.

8   bell hooks, Preface to *Teaching Community: A Pedagogy of Hope* (New York: Routledge, 2003), xi.

9   Ibid.

10 bell hooks, "Time Out: Classrooms without Boundaries," in *Teaching Community: A Pedagogy of Hope* (New York: Routledge, 2003), 14.

11 Ibid.

12 bell hooks, "The Will to Learn: The World as Classroom," in *Teaching Community: A Pedagogy of Hope* (New York: Routledge, 2003), 1.

13 bell hooks, "To Love Again," in *Teaching Critical Thinking: Practical Wisdom* (New York: Routledge, 2009), 161.

14 bell hooks, "Self-Esteem," in *Teaching Critical Thinking: Practical Wisdom* (New York: Routledge, 2009), 125.

15 bell hooks, "A Revolution of Values: The Promise of Multicultural Change," in *Teaching to Transgress: Education as the Practice of Freedom* (New York: Routledge, 1994), 33.

16 bell hooks, "Engaged Pedagogy," in *Teaching Critical Thinking: Practical Wisdom* (New York: Routledge, 2009), 21.

Part Three

Pedagogies of the Bodymindspirit

The chapters in this part recognize that our whole beings—both educators and students—are comprised of our physical, intellectual, emotional, and spiritual selves; a truly engaged pedagogy must embrace opportunities for collective acknowledgment and fortification of our inner lives, as well as meaningful engagement with the social and natural worlds with which we are intimately connected. Marlaina Martin's reflection, "Flirting with Self-exile," addresses limitations to belonging in academia for Black woman teacher-scholars. Foregrounding experiences in graduate school that singled her out and tasked her with undue burdens of representation of her community and education of her faculty, Martin explains how she learned to bring her full self into her own classrooms, building trust with students, honoring their well-being, and modeling and encouraging radical truth telling. Operating with a baseline of compassion that stands in resistance to the hypocrisies of academic culture, Martin offers ways to make room for embodied and affective engagement with course content where flexibility and inclusion of students' own expertise are prioritized. In "Soul of the Syllabus," Dr. Rev. Natalie Coe models the restructuring of her syllabus in order to ensure that her course is not only academic, but also a spiritual endeavor that promotes and lifts the voices of all students. Foregrounding hooks's own array of spiritual influences, education, and investments in Christianity, Buddhism, African Traditional Religions (ATRs), and their syncretic hemispheric American beliefs and practices, Coe underscores the need to fortify our own spirits as essential preparation for modeling and encouraging wholeness among our student body. Coe's actionable bulleted items in the form of "syllabus suggestion snapshots" support educators' efforts to treat the syllabus like a covenant that underscores communal respect, challenge dominator culture socialization, prioritize accessibility of materials and content, and provide growth opportunities toward increased harmony between mind, body, and spirit for students on an educational journey.

Deepening the framework of hooks's pedagogical commitments through her spiritual path, in "Freedom Teaching: Black Feminist Ethic and the Death of the Ego," Nicole A. Spigner examines how hooks's contemplative Buddhism informs her pedagogical philosophy and lifelong commitment to self-actualization. Having already taught in a variety of environments, Spigner's graduate school introduction to hooks's freedom pedagogy illuminated the ways that she and hooks incorporated multiple schools of thought and avenues of practice into their pedagogical praxis and spiritual journeys. Given that hooks modeled the impact that personal work toward self-actualization can have for the creation of a pedagogy that can be healing, Spigner's classroom vignettes show how wellness—as integral to education—becomes a strong pathway toward reflective, adaptive, and liberatory strategies. Similarly organized around fostering trust and transparency, honoring humanity and exigent circumstances, and grounded in the five pieces of hooks's practical wisdom informing her pedagogical commitments over two decades of university teaching, Joanna Davis-McElligatt's "Practical Wisdom: Praxis and the Urgency of the Moment" provides actionable strategies for honoring students' full humanity and cultivating an atmosphere in which they can see and hear each other. In this way, their learning community becomes one in which rich connections engender dialog and growth in an otherwise impersonal and detached educational atmosphere exacerbated by years of Covid-19 social distance and collective exhaustion.

In "Spiritually Engaged Writing and Community Pedagogy: Honoring bell hooks's Legacy," Rachel Panton's students create bridges from the classroom to the environment beyond by embracing values inherent in African diasporic religions in their developing eco-justice writing practices. In the midst of climate and pandemic crises, Panton discusses privileging the writing process in her public health rhetorics course, and conceptualizing writing as a sacred act. Panton's amalgamation of hooks's ecofeminism as a touchstone in conversation with her own Africana womanist pedagogy guided students through ways of conceptualizing their interbeing with the Earth as a way to explore conservation rhetoric, and participate in World Oceans Day in 2022. Overall, the chapters in this part attend to the essential recognition that transformative education must necessarily invoke that which animates our inner lives. By creating space for students to share and be recognized for who they are as individuals and to practice who they can be in community, educators can open up avenues for engaging with work in a way that values the fullness of our interconnectedness with the world outside of classroom walls.

12

Flirting with Self-exile: The Contentious and Curious Commonsense of Academic "Belonging"

Marlaina Martin

If we examine critically the traditional role of the university in the pursuit of truth and the sharing of knowledge and information, it is painfully clear that biases that uphold and maintain white supremacy, imperialism, sexism and racism have distorted education so that it is no longer about the practice of freedom.

—bell hooks

I am a US-born Black cisgender woman, and I have long been associated with academics. Early on, my teachers labeled me "gifted," motivating me to take Honors and Advanced Placement courses throughout grade school. Admittedly, I came to identify success—and even myself, to a degree—with high grades and whatever I could include on my CV. However, in moving through the "ranks" of attaining a Ph.D. and multiple postdoctoral fellowships thereafter, I have grown increasingly aware of and disillusioned by the race, gender, class, and other hierarchies (and hypocrisies) that scaffold contemporary academic and academia-adjacent spaces. For me, graduate and postgraduate experiences unveiled systems that claimed to promote diversity but instead perpetuated "a single norm of thoughts and experience, which we were encouraged to believe were universal." I have felt overextended yet overlooked, shocked at being openly labeled hypersensitive and intense, and disheartened severely and frequently enough to question whether I do or can ever belong. In *Teaching to Transgress: Education as the Practice of Freedom*,[1] bell hooks describes this conundrum thusly: "As a black woman, I have always been acutely aware of the presence of my body in those settings that, in fact, invite us to invest so deeply in a mind/

body split so that, in a sense, you're almost always at odds with the existing structure."[2] If I belong, on what terms? If I don't belong, is it worth trying to?

Like hooks, I had several unnerving graduate school encounters that led me to confront my intellectual, personal, and social relationships to feminism specifically; and identity more broadly. For example, without warning during one seminar, a white peer recounted our out-of-class chats and called on me by name—also involuntarily—to back up her feminist critique of Freud. In that moment, I felt singled out and offered up as evidence for her argument's sake. Another semester, an international student who would be racialized as white in the United States announced to the class that I had given more than the class's two assigned presentations. I, in fact, had not. Nonetheless, my existence and contributions in that Feminist Thought seminar seemed to overwhelm her memory to the point where it just had to be declared and addressed aloud.

I have also been (t)asked to remedy lacking racial diversity issues I did not create. After a first-day class session spent skimming over the syllabus of a course on memory's social and cultural imprints on and across generations, I mustered up the courage to mention to the professor (one-on-one) that, while there were several warranted and thought-provoking readings on collective Jewish memory, there was not even one assigned to assist us in examining legacies of US slavery. In response, he asked what pieces I might suggest. While I could not quite grasp why this felt unsettling back then, I have since realized that, as hooks prophetically explains, "this [...] places an unfair burden on a student. It also makes it seem that it is only important to address a bias if there is someone complaining."[3] Indeed, I was startled that, in interpreting my critique, the professor seemed to pin my identifying the omission—not the omission itself—as the problem. Furthermore, it was put to me to fix. Disenchanted, my takeaway from this interaction haunted me for years; the absence of a group's current relationship to centuries of violence and perseverance could be morphed into and reframed as a specialized cultural interest left for individual members of said group—in this case, me—to resolve.

Bringing Self into Learning Spaces

Now, as an educator myself, I see learning not as a unidirectional information dump, but as a series of holistic experiences in and from which everyone present stands to add, learn, and gain something. I aim to embolden class atmospheres by treating students as unique individuals participating in a learning community built on pillars of self-reflexivity, active listening, intellectual bravery, collaborative knowledge production, and mutual respect. Sincere about this goal, I intentionally work to set a course's tone, both in terms of content and norms of interaction, from the start. First-day syllabus review session may be a convention, but it is not mere formality for me. To the contrary, it is a chance and opportunity to outline course themes and expectations, explain writing assignments (and reasons for each), and introduce myself. Realistically, many students born and raised in the United States have endured an educational system that demanded that they conform, appease, and satisfy whichever institutional representative controlled each space just to "get through" school unscathed. Therefore, liberatory pedagogy must begin with rattling and recalibrating such arrangements, removing punitive notions of reading and writing assignments and class participation to alternatively characterize them as productive exercises in critical thought and application of cultivated knowledge.

Some examples of how I facilitate this transition—which is notably not just one of technique, but also of expectation and mindset—are to foreground transparency, explicitly informing students of my reasons for asking them to engage in certain course requirements (i.e., restrictions or assignments). If a course has AI restrictions, for instance, I explain that the developing, reflecting on, and curating their original voice is a crucial course goal, hence positioning the use of AI as a deterrent to a particular and ongoing objective. Regarding assignments, I typically try to provide ample verbal description of a course's different assignment types and intentions ("The purpose of this assignment is X, and what you are meant to get from this that is different from other assignments is Y.") as early as possible. This helps to put students in the figurative driver's seat of their own education and situate all readings, writings, and discussions—along with any guidance I offer—as being in service to their development as critical, civically, and globally aware interpreters and creators of knowledge. A third way that I champion so-called radically transgressive approaches to conventional classroom norms is to incorporate elements of assignments into lesson planning and protocol themselves. One way I do this is through an assignment type I alliteratively call "Discussion of the Day" (DOD). As the shortest but most frequent among my three assignment types, a DOD is a 250-to-450-word response that demonstrates understanding, critical reflection, and curiosity about texts assigned for a single course day. As part of this, students must end their submission with a lingering question posed to the rest of the class, whether that concerns confusing moments within the piece(s) or attempts to further clarify, cross-read, or broaden their arguments. I would then create a slide at the top of every class that listed their various questions in a compiled list, which not only helped me to add more content on especially confounding or inspiring points but let their individual inquiries and investments guide the direction of class discussion before a single word had been spoken out loud.

Self-introductions, too, are not hollow acts. They can help to humanize the instructor as an active and accountable party within the larger class dynamic. On the first class each semester, I share an overview of my personal and academic trajectories to render myself more relatable (i.e., "I once sat where you are") to students and lay groundwork for them to know and ideally grow to trust my training, rigor, and intentions. Among the tidbits I mention are change from Chemical Engineering to Anthropology during college (sparked by an elective course); research questions that have long had roots within but intersectional interests that reached beyond the field's traditionally conceived "turf"; and at-times conflicting relationship with the field's past and present as a Black woman. As hooks suggests, "When professors bring narratives of their experiences into classroom discussions it eliminates the possibility that we can function as all-knowing, silent interrogators."[4] This move goes beyond admitting that an instructor's experiences inform—and, hence, implicate them in—the design and dynamics of any class they teach. It celebrates responsible navigation of such experience/education overlaps as a strength. In practice, this approach turns the tables on the very idea of an all-knowing, silent interrogator: a dangerous fallacy that shrouds norms of power and privilege in cloaks of "objectivity," "data," and "fact."

Fittingly, I also cite anthropologist Bianca Williams's "Radical Honesty: Truth-telling as Pedagogy for Working through Shame in Academic Spaces" quite often as inspiration for my own expressed commitment to pedagogical sincerity and nuance. In a tradition shaped by hooks and many other Black feminist scholars, she expounds, "Early on in my career, I decided that, rather than finding ways to strategically draw attention away from my body, my experiences, and others' assumptions about me, I would embrace them and use them as a starting point for teaching about power, privilege, and inequality."[5] Like Williams, I believe that the crucial liberatory move to undercut the "all-knowing" educator trope involves consciously making sure not to preach let alone monopolize claims to knowledge based on one's title alone. However hard earned, it is not sufficient nor is it responsible to lean on one's degree all-access pass to complete, continuous, and unconditional authority over what is "right." This practice is not only vapid but dangerous to our alleged aims as instructors. Relevantly, hooks argues that this kind of shallow reliance on so-called hierarchies of authority can actually diminish the efficiency or effectiveness of work accomplished in its name "One of the things blocking a lot of professors from interrogating their own pedagogical practices is that fear that '*this is my identity and I can't question that identity.*'"[6]

My identity is so much longer, broader, and deeper than my Ph.D. In not-to-distant memories of graduate school, I can recall experiences of being the unwilling recipient of academic egos whose defensive maneuvering around my critiques unnecessarily caused a lasting sense of self-doubt that I had to do prolonged, intentional work to undo. Therefore, from the first session of each and every class, I openly acknowledge and then position my degree not as a stamp of superiority but a tool to help anchor and guide productive group conversations. In line with yet another tenet of Black feminist pedagogical tradition—experience as a valid influence in intellectual spaces—introducing myself models for and invites students to question what "normative" power looks like in and beyond schooling contexts, and to reflect on the explicit and also subtle ways that they have come to understand their own and others' lives in relation, conflict, or resistance to it.

Compassionate Flexibility

It is not always bad when plans derail. While I strive to diligently arrange syllabi with diversity across social categories (e.g., race, gender, class, age, religion, geographic origin) and media genres (e.g., articles, book chapters, films, pop culture videos, music) in mind, I believe that astute real-time adaptability is crucial to liberatory pedagogy. Unpredictability scares some professors, inciting them to recoil into conventions for comfort. However, it is not inherently bad— and sometimes immensely advantageous—for things to not go as planned. Turning again to our muse for thought, I agree that while "excellence must be valued, […] standards cannot be absolute and fixed."[7] I believe that some of my main jobs as teacher are to follow along with, assess, and when promising, take heed from conversational shifts that suggest students are particularly excited, troubled, or otherwise moved by a surfacing topic or line of argumentation. Reiterating the freeing impetus "to disrupt the notion of professor as omnipotent, all-knowing mind,"[8] I made student-centered adjustments during class time not only to incorporate their questions and concerns into our discussion in crucial rather than shallow ways but also to signal to them that their thoughts and critiques matter. In these situations, I do my best to pivot when I think students could benefit from a different focus, direction, or amount of time allotted to certain issues.

Here, I describe two examples of such flexibility, both from a Media Anthropology course I taught in Fall 2020. Enrollees ranged from freshman undergraduates to graduate students nearing Ph.D. candidacy. Some were anthropology majors and minors, while others were housed in other programs— pre-medicine, performance studies, political science, and journalism—with no previous exposure to the discipline. Even two British exchange students registered. If my confidence had depended on some presumed need to maintain ultimate control over content or minds, I would have instated prerequisites to narrow enrollment. However, I felt galvanized by prospects of continual learning and productive spontaneity and welcomed the intermixture.

Example #1: I asked students to read an article about depictions of post-Hurricane Maria Puerto Rico in mainstream US media versus those created by domestic and diasporic Puerto Rican communities. At one point in our discussion, a few journalism majors objected to the author's constant denunciation of "the press." To them, the term lumped all US media outlets into one bucket. The term was too generalized and not sophisticated enough to hold the variegated foci, ethics, political biases, and levels of depth that exist across different outlets. Their interjections on these grounds were extremely generative, both for the journalism students articulating their views in a community that could only benefit from the clarification and for those students less familiar with and ready to learn from the introduced complexities. Affirmed by their outspokenness, I let them complicate the conversation. They broadened our terms for engaging the works on our syllabus. Additionally, my willingness to follow their lead demonstrated respect for their burgeoning expertise. This session was invigorating because it made room for students to try out and refine their active listening and public speaking skills. In voicing their ideas, they were also honing confidence. This happens most when students feel comfortable and valued enough to skillfully reroute conversation without fear of judgment, scolding, or retribution. Oscillating between roles of lecturer, conversant, facilitator, and listener, my flexibility to student needs let students know that just because conflicting attitudes or viewpoints arise does not mean that a discussion is fruitless. In fact, conflict could lead to better outcomes if oriented around group pledges of dialog, respect, and open-mindedness.

Example #2: For a week organized to interrogate dominant media representations of Africa, I assigned two readings—one for each of our class periods. One was an article that theorized the film *Black Panther* as a historically revisionist commentary on extractive colonialism. The other was Kennedy Odede's "Slumdog Tourism," an op-ed that openly lambasted the phenomenon referenced in its title. Our conversations that first day turned over colonialism's violent theft of Africa's resources and people, but with the cushion of a majestically imagined otherwise. The second pulled an emotional about-face, daring us to dig into and digest the problematic racial, political, and classed undercurrents of international tourism and volunteerism. Especially coming off the uplifting fantasy of the Marvel blockbuster, the second class brought about a foreseeable yet still visceral frustration into our space. This shift indicated a need to be flexible in the face of students' uneasiness—a state that some instructors might strive to dodge or skip over at the risk of losing claims to a control they arguably never held. This article was useful for our ongoing deliberations not only for its meta-reference to the "Hollywoodification" of global imaginaries (a titular ode to the 2008 film *Slumdog Millionaire*), but also for its move to openly oppose common, flattening media depictions that cast Westerners as altruistic givers and people "native" to a place as objectifiable, forlorn, and "in need." Of great but twisted importance is the fact that historically, such voices have been notoriously overshadowed by those same Western mainstream media channels.

As is typical of my pedagogy, I also leaned on multimedia to help ground this session. Specifically, I incorporated a virtual exploration of Odede's biography and his co-founded organization *Shining Hope for Communities* (SHOFCO for short) into the lesson. Throughout, I stayed alert to students' widening eyes. Several even quietly queried where hyperlinks on the webpages I was showing might lead. I not only stayed attuned to the room's energies, but also sought fit to react to them. Taking what some teachers—and likely, those uttering students— might have considered futile suggestions, I clicked some of the hyperlinks. I then asked for volunteers to read blurbs aloud before prompting the larger class to relate those points to the day's assigned reading(s). This energized students by spiking both their curiosity and investment in what they were learning. As hooks encourages, I acted upon my conviction that "the simple act of recognizing a mood and asking 'What's this about?' can awaken an exciting learning process."[9]

Centering Compassion

Before going into what has made me feel alienated, I would first like to spotlight the compassion and concern for students' well-being that drove me despite that feeling. In conversations with other women-of-color educators, I often heard the mantra, "We are here for our students. Who would they have if we weren't here?" Understanding how much of a respite my classes and mentorship have given some students, I understood how appreciated my attention to active student participation and if theme-appropriate, joy in class was—and also how uncommon. A few weeks into the semester, one of three graduate students taking the course shared that, at that point, ours had the most student engagement out of all their classes. More than one professor remarked on the laughter they heard coming from my class—with varying degrees of commendation or suspicion. This comment, though passive-aggressively telling of its normative classroom expectations, did not shake me. After all, "Pleasure in the classroom is feared. If there is laughter, a reciprocal exchange may be taking place [...] To prove your academic seriousness, students should be almost dead, quiet, asleep, not up, excited, and buzzing, lingering around the classroom."[10]

In fact, I was pleased with comments about students' remarkable levels of in-class interactions because I, too, see laughter and excitement as engagement. To avoid potential doubt in the power and legitimacy of this approach, especially in light of its general unpopularity, I have also worked for years to cultivate networks of support with like-minded colleagues in other departments and even universities. This community has helped me better hold and when appropriate, critique whatever skepticism (or potentially, envy) my approach to and conduct in classes might stir in others. Focused on my students' experiences and gains, I am often flattered by their merry and conversant participation. Ultimately, I work to challenge the misconception that joy and intellectualism are mutually exclusive and insist that emotions can be an outward display of students' embodied connections to knowledge being co-produced with and around them. Emotions can communicate interest and involvement, especially where words may fail. As hooks forwards, "If we focus not just on whether the emotions produce pleasure or pain, but on how they keep us aware or alert, we are reminded that they enhance classrooms."[11] However, while I am flattered by students' willingness to engage in class so wholeheartedly, I am disappointed in something; the undeniable reality that these same students could not expect all of their other classrooms to be similarly involved and inviting.

Besides laughter, pain can also come from critically reflecting on our realities. I would be remiss if I did not stress that "students taught me, too, that it is necessary to practice compassion in these new learning settings."[12] Shifts necessitated by the pandemic were exceptionally enlightening. I will forever remember the Spring 2020 semester because it corroborated my belief that we must consider emotions as part of, rather than tangential or damaging to, liberatory education. Amidst the chaos, professors' different priorities were exposed. Panicked, many doubled down on the status quo, making only whatever changes were necessary to phase from analog to digital. While I would never deny the hefty amount of labor it took to quickly make everything online-compatible, hearing professors commiserate about students having their cameras off or not participating "enough" upset me. Among *my* first thoughts were, "How can I adjust lessons, reading loads, or deadlines to make school as useful for students—most still coming of age—in these turbulent times?" In addition to scheduling one-on-one meetings with students to discuss final paper ideas (as a burst of momentum and direction), I tried to relieve them by saying things that some teachers appeared to leave unsaid: "This is scary stuff." "Many of you have moved into homes—domestic or abroad (for exchange students)—where you may have familial, financial, or other responsibilities you are trying to balance with academics." "Some of you may be trying to figure out why and how school fits in." Following Ahmaud Arbery's murder in February 2020, not long after we transitioned online, I carved out fifteen minutes at the beginning of our next class in which students could opt to share how they were entering the space, and anything that our work with and around media anthropology might offer them to even start grappling with all the tragedies going on. Being in community with myself and their classmates was one thing I could provide—and I took that seriously.

Ultimately, it is not a class's content, difficulty, or pace that determines its impact but how graciously it is taught, how much trust is fostered among participants, and how firmly it privileges and contributes to students' growth. Some of my greatest gifts have come in the form of student appreciation, whether in the form of one student who thanked me for smiling during a Zoom meeting he was logged into from a cold basement because Wi-Fi was most reliable there or a former student reaching out years later to ask about graduate school because my course had stayed with her.

Academia's Hubris Problem

So, in the face of these pockets of care and trust, why would I ever consider leaving? Many US higher education institutions run on and even pressure educators to put themselves above the collective. Having one's name on publications—as sole author, or the first and most lauded in a string of co-authors—heavily informs hiring and tenure processes. Universities search out and pay individual scholars to deliver talks as experts on what largely are community- if not world-sweeping phenomena. But at what costs?

As a postdoctoral fellow, I remember logging into a virtual Diversity Equity, and Inclusion (DEI)-themed workshop as an audience member. After witnessing many white faculty members confess uncertainties around breaching class topics or dynamics around which they might lack their usual level of expertise, I felt compelled to write in the chat. I knew some graduate students were also present and likely similarly frustrated by the number and tone of these comments. Collectively, such questions could breed student disaffection by inferring that academic hubris could legitimately outweigh concern for a diverse student body's need to feel listened to, represented, and respected. Also, upholding the status quo is not without consequence. Even when differences in race, gender, religion, geographic origin, or ability are not explicitly addressed, that does not mean students are not constantly affected by them. My impulse to add context through that workshop's chat forum exemplified hooks's observation, "Again and again, it was necessary to remind everyone that no education is politically neutral."[13] Through direct messages shielded from public view, several students immediately messaged their thanks. Such secretive solidarity spoke to the survivalist tendencies that students develop to sense out which institutional actors might listen to and value their perspectives, and which professors would expect and even institutionalize acquiescence too.

Reflecting on a multiculturalism seminar that she boldly co-led as a junior scholar, hooks recalls an analogous situation: "Many folks found that as they tried to respect 'cultural diversity' they had to confront the limitations of their training and knowledge, as well as a possible loss of 'authority'. Indeed, exposing certain truths and biases in the classroom often created chaos and confusion."[14] Indeed, fear of conceding expertise or worse, conceding to one's complicity in or potential gains from structures of domination can result in contradictory claims and ends. While some may default to the comfort of norms, others might pursue change, but in ways that undermine their purpose. For instance, even when they have not had official DEI training, many of the people most affected by social, class, racial, gendered, and institutional orders (myself included) know the feeling of being asked—typically in the form of "volunteered" (read: assumed) unpaid labor—to lead workshops on whiteness, diversifying access, or social justice. This conflation of professional training with identity can be reductive and extractive. It taps on victims of structural violence to revisit and publicly perform their pain for others to consume and maybe, just maybe believe. Furthermore, this trend drips with irony because the volunteered party is usually one of the few *non*white people in a program. Effectively, these asks leverage an already marginalized person's earnest dedication to students and justice to place additional duties on them without due recognition of the power wielded in making, or labor involved in fulfilling such requests.

On top of diversity asks on this smaller, more sporadic scale, talks on diversity and inclusion are now annual events across various campuses along with numerous other DEI-related initiatives purposely on public display. Here, I must question the ethics of charging the most structurally precarious—and to some, disposable—faculty to lead training sessions on inclusive student-centered pedagogy, write public statements condemning hate crimes and other incidents, curate panel discussions with baselines that never seem to progress, and disproportionately advise students—all while limiting how much institutional impact, reward, or permanence they actually have. To me, one-off workshops, service on strategizing committees, running "student-of-color advisee" tallies, and itemized checklists used to externally document "diversity work" (an umbrella terms that subsumes DEI, DEIJ, IDEA, and similar acronyms) tend to draw vital attention away from the widespread "unwillingness to approach teaching from a standpoint that includes awareness of race, sex and [...] often rooted in the fear that classrooms will be uncontrollable that emotions and passions will not be contained"[15] practiced in many of these very organizations.

Making space for emotions, bias deconstruction, and attention to well-being in academia challenges what we are taught to hold in the utmost regard. Significantly, many faculty from marginalized communities—especially those invested in liberatory, transformative pedagogy—can detail instances of administrative and bureaucratic confrontation. I would even argue that such faculty members are widely perceived as conduits and mouthpieces for the feared 'uncontrollable' elements mentioned above, which can lead to their treatment and at times, targeting as threats. However, I have learned that tuning into my feelings during uncomfortable institutional encounters—shock at a professor's request to buttress their syllabus or annoyance when professors attribute low student-of-color counts in their courses to *the latter*'s deficient ability or ambition—is to accept and find ways to deal with the reality that "as the classroom becomes more diverse, teachers are faced with the way the politics of domination are often reproduced in the educational setting."[16] If "education as the practice of freedom" is truly our goal (which is still in question for some), we must be willing to admit when our words do not align with our actions, and acknowledge the far-reaching consequences that such mismatches can have on faculty and students not only institutionally and intellectually, but also emotionally and psychologically.

Yes, I have flirted with academic self-exile. By saying this, I am not saying one must commit once and for all to being only inside or outside of higher education. Of course, creative programs and hybrid options are options too. However, this flirtation has revealed other avenues of possibility to me. At this point in my journey, I have managed to disentangle myself from common ivory-tower rhetoric that suggests one just be grateful for whatever job may come along— at whatever detriment to one's spirit and soul. I can and will no longer allow the prestige of job titles or aspirations of academic belonging to monopolize my vision of success. Whether or not I work *in* universities, I am not *of* them. My wholeness requires thorough reckoning with whatever compromises and oversights might be expected in certain spaces, and complete commitment to hold onto self-confidence as a person equipped not only with expertise but versatility and empathy as well.

My joy does not come from academic prefixes or conditional invitations to meetings or committees. Rather, it spurs from those transformative interactions I have with students, research interlocutors, and community members that keep us all talking, learning, growing, emoting, and reimagining our world(s). My loyalty is to my personhood and principles. Career memories of cautiously offering or withholding comments in graduate school, performing allyship vis-à-vis chat comments, and delivering responsive and flexible pedagogy have fortified my conviction in the power of "the engaged voice." As hooks insists, "[T]he engaged voice must never be fixed and absolute but always changing, always evolving in dialogue with a world beyond itself."[17] For me, this voice—alert and strategic yet always bold—has become a tether, tenet, and throughline that kindles my self-realization and community-building efforts more than a diploma ever could.

Notes

1   bell hooks, *Teaching to Transgress: Education as the Practice of Freedom* (New York: Routledge, 1994), 35.
2   Ibid.,135.
3   Ibid., 44.
4   Ibid., 21.
5   Bianca C. Williams, "Radical Honesty: Truth-telling as Pedagogy for Working through Shame in Academic Spaces," in *Race, Equity, and the Learning Environment: The Global Relevance of Critical and Inclusive Pedagogies in Higher Education*, eds. Frank Tuitt, Chayla Haynes, Saran Stewart (New York: Routledge, 2016), 71–82; 75.

6   hooks, *Teaching to Transgress*, 134–5.

7   Ibid., 157.

8   Ibid., 138.

9   Ibid., 156.

10   Ibid., 145.

11   Ibid., 155.

12   Ibid., 42.

13   Ibid., 36.

14   Ibid., 30.

15   Ibid., 39.

16   Ibid.

17   Ibid., 11.

Soul of the Syllabus

Dr. Rev. Natalie Coe.

bell hooks invites us to experience a new vision that allows us to step into who we are fully, and to be part of an expansive and inclusive community of learners. As educators, we are given the privilege to create a syllabus, a sacred pact, to take a journey alongside our students. We can encourage our students to share their stories, to allow the invisible to become visible in the classroom. Creating an engaged community of active learners takes conscious effort; the curriculum lies within us. Immersion requires unrequited, bold imagination.

Nurturing Self-development and Self-actualization of Ourselves and Our Students

There is a unification yet spaciousness in the realm of body, mind, and spirit that leaves room for ancient wisdom and wild imagination to accompany us. hooks draws us to the words of the Dalai Lama, who understands spirituality "to be concerned with those qualities of the human spirit—such as love and compassion, patience, tolerance, contentment, a sense of responsibility, a sense of harmony—which brings happiness to both self and others."[1] hooks was inspired by Martin Luther King Jr., Thich Nhat Hanh, Julian of Norwich, and Rainer Maria Rilke among others.[2] She learned of African folk traditions, hoodoo, and Indigenous wisdom from her maternal grandmother, Saru. Her paternal grandfather, Daddy Gus, an animist, encouraged her to tell stories and listen to her dreams.[3] hooks drew from prayer and meditation as a Buddhist and Christian, acknowledging both the realities of suffering and the ways in which love, *as an action,* can alleviate suffering.[4] Her personal and professional lives were informed and embraced by her spirituality. hook observes, "Honestly naming spirituality as a force strengthening my capacity to resist enabled me to stand within centers of dominator culture and courageously offer alternatives."[5] Her spiritual lens is all encompassing; spiritual strength sustains spiritual resistance to the status quo.

As a force, spirituality can surely be fierce—educators must take the time to nurture our full selves to have the patience and creativity essential to our profession. Our personal practices can be secular, religious, or some weaving of both, taking on any form that promotes qualities such as love, gratitude, and compassion. Preparation can utilize diverse approaches including positive affirmations, gratitude meditations, nature walks, formal or informal prayers, mantras, rituals, or special gatherings. We can continue to explore and experiment, to find a spiritual routine that works for us and brings us back to a focus on our human spirit, without denying the body or mind. It is critical to find a process that will renew us daily, bringing us back to the learners we are. As we become more spiritually centered, we will bring this energy and light into the classroom naturally.

A spiritually focused classroom becomes a connected community, building trust over time that begins on the first day of class. One way to be in relation with others safely and positively is to develop a covenant, or set of agreed-upon guidelines, on how one wants to show up and be treated. This practice is communal and becomes a physical part of the syllabus. The same strategy is effective in developing rubrics for major assignments. Encouraging students to be part of creating the framework by which they will be assessed helps to clarify expectations and nurture investment in their learning.

Standard university syllabi require a non-discrimination statement and a statement regarding violence or harassment that will direct students to the university's Title IX office and campus police. Consider how we might also show how being aware of the subtle and overt ways discrimination works, we can help to consciously push back against it. Develop your own equanimity, kindness, or diplomacy statement. My colleague, Nina de Gramont, borrows from the Sufi mystic Hafiz, for her statement:

The small man
Builds cages for everyone
He knows.
While the sage,
Who has to duck his head.
When the moon is low,
Keeps dropping keys all night long
For the beautiful

Rowdy

Prisoners.

We're here to drop keys. Not build cages.

Let it be clear to all that we have expectations that include how we will treat each other.

My colleagues are often surprised how respectfully my students offer critical, on-point feedback to each other. Covenant and community building are essential to lay the groundwork to make this type of positive interaction possible. If we cannot trust each other, how can we share work that is personally meaningful with others? Why would we risk being vulnerable? I often use the "rose-bud-thorn" approach to provide feedback both verbally and in writing. I model this early for my students, so they then can try it. A rose offers someone an explanation of what is working well, whether it is inside a short story or within an experimental design. Buds come in many forms allowing the reader to share what they would like to see more of (character development, conversation, research findings, etc.). Thorns come last and often organically flow from those buds.

Where does an argument feel soft? What inadvertent bias is in diction or examples? By workshopping and allowing a student's writing to become the focal point of a class discussion, each student feels that we take them and their work seriously.

Syllabus suggestions snapshot:

- Treat the first day of class as a welcome to a new learning community
- Develop course/class guidelines (covenant) with students (see appendix for example)
- Utilize student-input to create assessment rubrics and grading parameters
- Include an equanimity statement (see appendix for example)
- Model positive critical feedback orally and in writing for students
- Provide opportunities for students to engage with peers directly

Undermining Socialization That Leads Us to Behave in Ways That Perpetuate Domination

bell hooks took on a daunting role as one of the few Black women in predominantly white academia, and this stress cannot be underestimated.[6] Systemic racism requires systemic antiracism. Let us not stand aside and allow this work to fall to those already marginalized, ignored, or fighting for a place in the workspace. This charge can be buried under other responsibilities for faculty jockeying for tenure. hooks struggled with the ethics of working from the inside, trying to be an effective advocate within a patriarchal system designed to otherize. Haunted by dreams of running away, in the weeks leading up to her tenure approval, hooks recognized them as a response to the fear that with tenure she would "be trapped in the academy forever."[7]

Self-reflection can take many forms: personal, professional, spiritual, intellectual—but at its core lies equanimity, the emotional wherewithal to overcome challenges.

To nurture equanimity takes willingness to look at ourselves objectively, always with loving kindness. If we are to "teach to transgress," we will need to break down the cultural constructs of the "isms" to promote the self-actualization of ourselves (first and foremost) and our students. It is not possible to foster this type of freedom if we are still bound up inside a narrow perspective. This willingness to explore our shadow sides and take responsibility for our conscious and subconscious choices can allow a joyous beginning to this humble work of a lifetime.

As faculty, we can support each other by providing spaces to discuss diversity and inclusion from our lived experience. Affinity groups can increase visibility and provide opportunities to meet regularly to empower individuals and groups. As teachers we also must focus on neurodiversity, ableism, and ageism, as well as demographic discrimination. We must openly discuss where we are if we hope to make strides as individuals and institutions. This will aid us in looking at our implicit biases so that we can learn from each other while learning more about ourselves.

hooks speaks of some "white people in [her] life being divested of their racism" and that she does not "believe that one has to be racist in some essentialist way."[8] As uncomfortable as it can be to consider the "isms" we may carry within ourselves, it is essential to examine them. hooks believed that white people can choose to be antiracist.[9] Professor Ibram X. Kendi defines an antiracist as "one who is supporting an antiracist policy through their actions or expressing an antiracist idea."[10]

I have asked my students to take implicit biases tests from Harvard University.[11] They choose from fifteen topics, including gender, skin tone, weapons, age, weight, sexuality, and religion. We then discuss what surprised us or didn't, and how this information can help us individually. It can be argued that this is a critical part of one's self-actualization and eventual freedom. It would be difficult if not impossible to recognize biases in one's syllabus without this critical self-examination. We need to make ourselves the object of inquiry. We must examine ourselves in the context of our culture (patriarchal, colonial) to actively move toward appreciation and learning from diverse vantage points. At its root, a syllabus will embrace and celebrate diversity as the foundation from which it is created. The highest learning for all is rooted in diversity.[12] As faculty members, if we do not feel equanimity in our bones, we will create only a superficial attempt at this.

Inclusivity starts with intentional decisions. When teaching Genetics of Human Behavior, I allow the students to choose the behaviors we study—we brainstorm, and then we vote—and each student will write and present their research paper on whatever behavior most interests them. Of course, this approach is more complicated than using a standard textbook with three or four multiple-choice exams for assessment. Since the cost of a standard science textbook is beyond the means of many students, I have stopped using textbooks when I can utilize the plethora of online and free library sources.

It is essential to employ multiple forms of assessment (rubrics designed with students for major assignments, short in-class responses, papers [varied lengths] on student-selected topics, no- or low-stake checking in assignments) and create ample and creative opportunities for students to show mastery of content, skills, and ultimately of their growth in the course both orally (through workshops, discussions) and in writing (with built-in scaffolding assignments). Growth is the goal in all of my classes, so students can take great pride in the final tangible form of expression of their learning whether it is through an exam (generally open-book with ample time that stresses application not memorization) or a portfolio of revised works. These efforts can overcome slow starts or difficult hurdles earlier in the course and are designed as celebratory opportunities to showcase progress, not to overwhelm and demoralize. The last day of class is a cause for celebration for the growth of our collective community and this day is as powerfully important as the first meeting.

Syllabus suggestions snapshot:

- Share sources of your personal spiritual strength with your students
- Provide information on campus wellness initiatives
- Take implicit bias tests
- Ask for and provide feedback on inclusivity aspects from colleagues
- Include multiple voices/perspectives

- Use multiple forms/types of assessments
- Consider final class or "exam" a day of celebration.

Opportunities for Students to Move between the Mind Space and the Heart Space

Admittedly faculty and students have become comfortable with the formal lecture even though it is only *one* method of dissemination and can often be lackluster. hooks suggests that faculty are afraid of losing the respect of their students if they try new approaches to teaching. Each student comes with certain expectations and may not want, for example, to sit in a circle, because sitting in a circle means being a participant, which has been devalued in our classrooms. Understandably we are again working against a false dichotomy that insists that the heart needs to be kept in check to allow the mind to learn best, when in actuality, as hooks explains, "It is the failure to achieve harmony of mind, body and spirit that has furthered anti-intellectualism in our culture and made our schools mere factories."[13]

Consider that not only can we cover the content and have the conversations, but that doing *both* is imperative. hooks understood this dynamic and continuous struggle, acknowledging the effort we must put forth to pull this all together successfully, day after day, semester after semester.

> The classroom is one of the most dynamic work settings precisely because we are given such a short amount of time to do so much. To perform with excellence and grace teachers must be totally present in the moment, totally concentrated and focused.[14]

We must repeatedly ask ourselves what it is we hope our students will gain. *Who* is in our classroom matters. If semester to semester, students are more or less *interchangeable*, then so are faculty, regardless of the order of things, regardless of tenure. Who is here now, together, makes all the difference.

As a Writer in Action in the Wilmington public schools, I always invite my students to breathe with me before we start our class. Quickly it becomes a habit, with students raising their hands eagerly to grab the honor of being that day's "breath counter." There is something spiritual in twenty-six sixth graders closing their eyes and breathing in deeply and breathing out slowly *together*. I admit to them that the breathing is for me, too, to help me arrive here in the middle of a busy day and focus—because we have important work to do, writing that is worthy of all of us! Once they have written their first poems, I call them poets. We learn to finger-snap and to be silent while someone else is reading—that this is a sign of respect for them and their work. Consider how you arrive each day for your students. Consider how you support their arrival.

While teaching in Vermont, I would bring my environmental science students to reclaim farmland by planting trees to increase forest habitat. One year I joined David sitting on a cooler, trying to find some shade and water. As I sat with him, he put his face into his hands and softly cried. He was from Boston, a true city kid and he had never been to a farm, planted a tree, or even touched soil. This experience connected his life to the land in ways I could never do. As teachers, we are merely conduits. By bringing our students to the land, the land will speak for herself—in a language that all can understand if given the space, time, and permission to be still. This connection, which David had not fully realized until that day, allowed those tears to flow. hooks warns us, "Schooling that does not honor the needs of the spirit intensifies that feeling of being lost, of being unable to connect" and likewise denies these critical opportunities for growth.[15] Neither David nor I knew beforehand the true transformation that would happen that day. This was only possible by aligning course content (ecological restoration, riparian buffers, nutrient management, soil science) with course intention (working with others to connect with and nurture the land). In developing course objectives, consider qualities that will be developed throughout the semester alongside specific content.

Envisage how activities and assignments we have already created can be further enriched with a sense of place. How can the very place where we have come to teach and, where we and our students have come to learn, be part of the work itself? Consider coupling a reflective writing response with a walking meditation in a natural campus setting. Develop assignments that encourage/ require students to visit particular places nearby that are of historical, social, or ecological interest.

I am surprised by how little my students know about Wilmington, NC, and the people who once lived on the land that our homes and university now inhabit. Including a land acknowledgment in our syllabus is an immediate entry way. Due to colonization this acknowledgment will name the massacred Indigenous peoples of our regions. I am no longer surprised that this is something students have little awareness of. As current inhabitants, we must take the time to commune with our environment and with the land itself while acknowledging our collective past. Discipline-specific assignments can ask students to research and learn of Indigenous wisdom and culture—this can be then applied to where students have been raised. From a pragmatic standpoint, consider the complexity of the research this would require and how students will gain skills to access databases, and come to know the library staff and use the resources available to them, including exploring your institution's archival collections. I regularly introduce students to the infinite possibilities of the interlibrary loan. From a spiritual standpoint, we can support connections to our collective past as new arrivals in this place.

Syllabus suggestions snapshot:

- Challenge ourselves to try something brand new
- Consider alternatives to lecture (or transition to mini-lectures or flipped classrooms)
- Choose readings from multiple, diverse authors
- Avoid expensive standard textbooks (especially with additional on-line testing subscriptions)
- Incorporate a spiritual practice (breathing/ walking meditation/ yoga) into daily meetings
- Bring students outdoors during class
- Create assignments that are connected to exploring the campus/town/region
- Discuss the land acknowledgment
- Design an assignment connected to the ancestry of campus lands

Conclusion

"To teach in a manner that respects and cares for the souls of our students is essential if we are to provide the necessary conditions where learning can most deeply and intimately begin."[16] As teachers, we will always be learners. We must have our own oxygen masks securely fastened before we can help another in this often turbulent world. By nurturing self-development and self-actualization of our students through our own modeling, we can let the work we have done shine through our syllabi and truly set us and our students free. We can be active in our antiracism by consciously undermining unhealthy socialization, and continue to foster opportunities to help our students to navigate between the intellect and the heart.

Appendix

Example of a Covenant

Each class can create a covenant (a collectively generated and agreed upon set of "rules") that can be added directly to the syllabus. Students can most easily generate a list of words or phrases that represent ideas that they value: listening, asking questions, respect, working together, open minds, communication. By creating a covenant together that is based on how we want participants in the class to treat each other, I find that I do not need rules about the minutiae (like cell phone use and being on time). I also have students include how they want late work to be handled and if it will be accepted or not. As work outside the class always informs work inside the class, students set high expectations on themselves for getting assignments done on time. A covenant focuses on community and community action, not mandated policies.

1. *I will arrive at class ready to actively participate.*
2. *I will ask questions and respond to thoughtful questions raised by my peers.*
3. *I will engage in discussions deeply having prepared the work assigned.*
4. *I will learn the names of all of my peers in our learning community.*
5. *I will bring all necessary assignments and readings to class—I want to positively impact my own learning and the learning of others who have depended on me.*
6. *I will discuss any concerns that arise during our class with (Professor) Natalie to help resolve the issue.*

Example of an Equanimity Statement

Merriam-Webster defines equanimity as "evenness of mind especially under stress"—from the Latin *aequanimitas*, or *aequo animo*, "even mind." Each week we will bring our full selves to class, knowing that each of us have many other commitments and ongoing concerns that can easily distract us. We will consciously leave these outside the classroom door (they can wait outside for just an hour!). While we are together we will be attentive, respectful, and kind. We will allow space for each other's ideas and respect a diversity of viewpoints. We will encourage each other to share openly. Equanimity does not mean we do not feel a wide range of emotions, but it allows us to avoid reacting from a place of fear, knowing we are all speaking from right intention.

Notes

1   bell hooks, *Teaching Critical Thinking: Practical Wisdom* (New York: Routledge, 2010), 148.

2   Nadra Nittle, *bell hooks' Spiritual Vision Buddhist, Christian, and Feminist* (Minneapolis, MN: Fortress Press, 2023).

3   Ibid.

4   Ibid.

5   bell hooks, *Teaching Community: A Pedagogy of Hope* (New York: Routledge, 2003), 181.

6   Corliss D. Heath, "A Womanist Approach to Understanding and Assessing the Relationship between Spirituality and Mental Health," *Mental Health, Religion & Culture* 9, no. 2 (2006): 155–70.

7   bell hooks, *Teaching to Transgress: Education as the Practice of Freedom* (New York: Routledge, 1994), 1.

8   Stuart Hall and bell hooks, *Uncut Funk—A Contemplative Dialogue* (New York: Taylor & Francis, 2017), 42.

9   hooks, *Teaching Community*, 61.

10 Ibram X. Kendi, *How to Be an Anti-racist* (New York: Routledge, 2003).

11 https://implicit.harvard.edu/implicit/selectatest.html.

12 Heather McGhee, *The Sum of Us, What Racism Costs Everyone and How We Can Prosper Together* (New York: One World, 2021).

13 hooks, *Teaching Community*, 181.

14 Ibid., 14.

15 Ibid., 180.

16 hooks, *Teaching to Transgress*, 13.

Freedom Teaching: Black Feminist Ethic and the Death of the Ego

Nicole A. Spigner

In preparation for teaching during my graduate program, mentors had us read standard texts for English composition pedagogues, *They Say, I Say* and *Elements of Style*. However, our pedagogy teacher and coach, the now Senior Associate Dean and Director of Undergraduate Education at Vanderbilt University, the wondrous Dr. Roger Moore, also added to our reading list perhaps the best known of hooks's pedagogy trilogy. *Teaching to Transgress* added a political and critical dimension to our weekly discussions about teaching our required literature and composition classes. Unlike the other teaching texts, hooks's first book of pedagogical philosophy offered not only methodology for teaching but also a person behind the words. hooks introduces her deep spiritual practice as a critical foundation for ethics and teaching. This was mind-blowing to me. Before grad school, I'd known hooks as a Black feminist theorist and critic; however, I did not understand that she was also a practicing Buddhist. Moreover, I didn't realize how much her Buddhism influenced her academic philosophies. Through *Teaching to Transgress*, I learned the practical application of a Black feminist pedagogical ethic built from Buddhist teachings: bringing oneself into the room, modeling vulnerability, and committing to a deep exploration of the self outside of the classroom to foster a trustworthy process and experience for one and her students inside of the classroom. For hooks, the classroom could be a place of healing and the teacher could be a healer.

Teaching to Transgress was unlike anything else I would ever read—apart from Freire, of course—and through it I could see the classroom as a space for activism. By the time I reached Vanderbilt's Ph.D. program in English, I had taught English GED exam prep courses for Temple University's Pan-African Studies Community Education Program, jewelry-making and beading workshops with an Africanist historical framework in classrooms of school children, and hatha yoga in studios. I began the first yoga program at the West Philadelphia YMCA and was proud to make accessible to a mostly Black, underserved population this tool through which I'd found some physical and psychological ease. In these classrooms, I always hoped to connect with my community and deepen my own intellectual, artistic, and psycho-spiritual-bodily practices. I understood, even then, that the classroom was not a space of one-way informational flow and that my most powerful classroom experiences happened when I, too, learned something new about the material at the center of the class or about myself.

So, when I first encountered hooks's idea of "freedom pedagogy," I was heartened by the possibilities it provided me as a future instructor in higher education. This multifaceted pedagogical philosophy, explored throughout hooks's teaching trilogy, requires an openness to multi-directional teaching. More fundamentally, hooks outlines that the teacher must be on the path toward "self-actualization." I'd never read such language from a Black feminist theorist before, but I recognized it from other parts of my life. Self-actualization was language that I encountered in yoga communities and studios across the Philadelphia area, most often tripping from lips of white, pencil thin, woowoo teachers who showed little patience for my larger brown body and lack of flexibility. I'd also experienced this notion the few times I'd meditated with the Shambhala Center of Philadelphia or went to one of their speaker events (most memorably from the voice of the famous Buddhist nun, Pema Chödrön). And while I didn't always find myself comfortable in those spaces, by the time I'd encountered *Teaching to Transgress*, I'd begun to walk my own spiritual path that I must admit was jump-started in those first yoga and meditation classrooms.

hooks's words hit home deep within my spirit. My own spiritual and psychological path toward what I understood as self-actualization—a combination of talk therapy, yoga philosophy study and asana practice, and meditation—had already encouraged my investment in knowing myself and trying to identify who I felt myself to be. Really *be*. I understood the idea of self-actualization as the oft-spoken "enlightenment," waking up to a reality beyond the material world in which we usually concentrated and connecting to a deeper self, unattached to ego or personality. I had no real expectations for attaining enlightenment. It seemed like something only sages and gurus could obtain. However, I did know that the teachings and practices helped me with my anxiety, depression, and focus, and had ultimately enabled me to realize my dream of graduate school. I knew that I grew more and more comfortable in my own skin, and if that wasn't the process of self-actualization, I'm not quite sure what is.

And yet, I compartmentalized my graduate school work from my psycho-spiritual life, a habit I began while working a 9-to-5 in the insurance industry before returning to academia. I countered the experience of the greedy, inhumane industry in which I was working with my spiritual practice, all the while attempting to find some kind of balance in my life. I found more motivation to attend morning yoga class than to wake up for work, every day. So, I'd thought of my asana and philosophy study as not just apart from my "work life," but a remedy for the harm that work caused my spirit.

As I read hooks, I felt the truth in the text. Her connection to Buddhism reminded me of my own connection to Vedic practices. Her insistence that a teacher could be healer made complete sense to me, in that I'd found healing through various teachers in the nontraditional classroom. Even more, when I researched Thich Nhat Hanh's teachings, I read words I'd heard my own yoga Teacher express: "A teacher has to give birth to the teacher within his student."[1] The role of the teacher is much like the role of the parent, to prepare the student/child to take over as their own teacher. In the words of Dr. Vijayendra Pratap: "The guru is inside."[2]

I found myself agreeing out loud and talking back with a "mmm hmmm" or a "yes!" when hooks said something particularly meaningful. The idea of the classroom as a "liberatory" space was one such powerful concept. *How could I participate or organize liberatory pedagogy if I were not also invested in my own personal liberation or if I thought of my true self, my deepest interiority, as separate from my work life? Wasn't it the sterile, profit-driven, unsatisfying corporate world which had driven me to seek more fulfilling practices, in the first place?* I'd not before considered how my own personal and spiritual progress directly affected my teaching. Moreover, it just *made sense* that a better and more realized me would make a stronger and more effective teacher. Coming into oneself, what I understood about self-actualization would be for me also coming into my teacherly self.

Fundamentally, self-actualization includes practicing what one preaches. Because self-actualization relies upon truth—perhaps some of the deepest truth—it demands practice. Truth is a roving subject, even within ourselves. Therefore, in order to *stay true*, one must engage with the ongoing practice of self-actualization. In fact, bell hooks would likely agree that self-actualization is about process far more than it is about an endpoint. There may or may not be a place called "self-actualized." But, again in the words of Dr. Pratap: "The endpoint is not your concern."[3] Instead, self-actualization is action-based: the uncovering, remembering, or in literal terms the "realization of the self."[4]

Connecting this practice—which hooks does not overtly map for her readers—to Thich Nhat Hanh gives the reader some grounding about hooks's approach. It is important that hooks practices contemplative Buddhism— Buddhism as taught and practiced by nuns and monks rather than the secular or, in hooks's words, "get-what-you-want-Buddhism."[5] hooks vehemently rejected the Buddhism made popular to Black folk through Tina Turner and others during the 1970s and 80s and instead asserted that "the kind of Buddhism that engages me most is about how you're going to live simply."[6] She was interested in a type of austerity that monastic Buddhism touted, and found Thich Nhat Hanh's teachings attractive because, as a survivor of the Vietnam War, he combined his contemplative practice with politics. In fact, it was politics that brought her to Nhat Hanh:

> My seeking led me to the work of a Buddhist monk Martin Luther King had met and been touched by—Thich Nhat Hanh. The first work I read by this new teacher in my life was a conversation book between him and Daniel Berrigan, *The Raft Is Not the Shore.*
> At last[,] I had found a world where spirituality and politics could meet, where there was no separation. Indeed, in this world all efforts to end domination, to bring peace and justice, were spiritual practice. I was no longer torn between political struggle and spiritual practice. And here was the radical teacher—a Vietnamese monk living in exile—courageously declaring that "if you have to choose between Buddhism and peace, then you must choose peace."[7]

Thich Nhat Hanh, hooks's "radical teacher," did not separate his politics from his spiritual practice, as is often the case in secular Buddhist communities. There feels like an organic connection between King and Nhat Hanh, especially their insistence on peace even and especially in the face of violence. Each figure comes from a religious tradition with a violent past.[8] Each figure witnessed and was subject to extreme individual and institutional violence. Each chose peace despite and as an antidote to these violences. While so often the ideas of "enlightenment" and self-actualization are cast as transcendent and therefore somehow in excess of the material (read: the human), both King and Nhat Hanh lived in both material and spiritual worlds and maintained that, in the words attributed to King: "We must pursue peaceful end through peaceful means."[9]

Nhat Hanh's teachings helped hooks navigate the political and intellectual "pullings" with which she wrestled. Furthermore, and perhaps most importantly, those teachings also supported her need for spiritual healing. In hooks's own words:

> I had felt pulled in all directions by anti-racist struggle, by the feminist movement, sexual liberation, by the fundamentalist Christianity of my upbringing. I wanted to embrace radical politics and still know god. I wanted to resist and be redeemed. *The Raft Is Not the Shore* helped strengthen my spiritual journey. [...] As all became well with my soul, I began to talk about the work of Thich Nhat Hanh in my books, quoting from his work. He helped me bring together theories of political recovery and spiritual recovery.[10]

By talking about Nhat Hanh's influence on her thinking, she also demonstrates the vast field upon which she and all scholars draw to reach their conclusions. She also reminds us that political and professional healing requires spiritual healing. She shows us a more holistic roadmap to her thinking by including Nhat Hanh and simultaneously establishes how her own spiritual healing is inextricable from her professional trajectory. More than that, she found that her own existing philosophies, in particular her engagement with "radical politics," did not conflict with her Buddhism. The political education available in Black Christian churches surely primed her for this combination of politics and spiritualism, as Black American history will tell you that Civil Rights was nurtured through the Black Church and that Black liberation movements have always been deeply supported by collective spiritual engagement. In fact, through Buddhism she found a place for seemingly disparate parts of herself: where feminism, less-fettered sexuality, rebellion, and antiracism could meet without self-sacrifice. This seemingly confounding set of self-expressions opened hooks's eyes to the healing potential of her Buddhist practices. It was her own healing that made her realize that the classroom could also be a space of healing.

However, I must confess: I've hesitated to call my classroom a healing space. There are many reasons for my hesitance. First and foremost, I hear this little judgmental voice when I contemplate this label for my classroom—any classroom—especially within the walls of a PWI, the site of all my experience in higher education.[11] *Who am I to call my space healing? Who am I to suggest my guiding students through Black literature leads to healing? Are activism and healing even possible in an educational institution created for white, wealthy men?* If we believe Audre Lorde—and how many of us would be foolish enough not to—then it is impossible to extricate a classroom from the institution in which it sits. If we are not invested in the project of "dismant[ling] the master's house," so to speak, and are rather invested in another project of exploring the interior expressions made by underserved and underrecognized BIPOC peoples and primarily Black folk, we can shift the focus away from the institution and instead find models for our own expressions of interiority.

The fortunate by-product of this process, accepting the institution as limited and ultimately not the place for our reformist efforts, actually works against the institution as there is no room for interior expression from people who are not supposed to *be* in the institution. In other words, the creative and intellectual products and expressions by Black people are not meant for formal classrooms in the United States. Some might say that they aren't even *meant* for anywhere in US culture, regardless of how much US culture depends on this output. Instead, Black folk have had to fight and elbow our ways in, and have likely only been allowed in higher education because our study and conversations initially focused on our relationships with whiteness and white people—a logical step in the evolution of Black studies scholarship, which became formally introduced to the academy in the 1970s, as the Civil Rights Movement was quieting and Black Power was on the rise.[12] While surely the institutionality of whiteness and white supremacy, and many other factors that make Black oppression possible, come up in class discussions.

However, by centering Black expression in the classroom, by making it a space to intellectually and emotionally sit with the lessons left for us by Black artists, we begin to practice a type of healing—we recognize human existence that is not always in response to material conditions but rather investigates the interior self, places left untouched by the constraints and limitations of the material plane.[13] However, like the process of self-actualization, healing is an ongoing and complicated set of practices and changes. It is, after all, heal*ing* not heal*ed*. Ultimately, I am not interested in some goal or place called "healed," as I'm not even sure that place exists. Instead, my pedagogical practice, influenced by hooks, engages with methods of healing and looks to Black artists and authors for models of this process. For instance, as a result of her teachings, I have opened my own personal history to scrutiny and criticism by students as a means of modeling the Black feminist and Buddhist self-reflexivity and -analysis that critical studies nurtures. I have also extended my academic lens to my spiritual world, which helped me uncover a tradition of literature that I call "Black Mindfulness Literature." I designed first a graduate course and then an undergraduate class which surveys mostly US literature written by

Black authors who have been influenced by contemplative religious practices, including Buddhism, Vedic philosophy, Transcendentalism, Christianity, and syncretic African religions. In the spirit of study and practice, each version of the course includes mindfulness practices introduced by class participants at the beginning of each meeting. I encourage students to look to these texts as well as the practices we share and develop as strategies and philosophies to support their intellectual lives and with the hopes that the course reaches even further. I know that some of these classroom formats challenge students' expectations for a typical college course; however, by encouraging students to examine their own affective and embodied experiences of Jean Toomer's vision of a race-less world in his poem "Blue Meridian" or the ecstatic healing experienced by the main character of Paule Marshall's *Praisesong for the Widow*, I expose students to a more capacious application for critical methodology.

At the very least, and as hooks reminds us in *Teaching Critical Thinking: Practical Wisdom*, a critical practice undermines notions of conformity. It is unsurprising that when articulating her motivations for revolutionary pedagogy, bell hooks looks to Thich Nhat Hanh's emphasis of, in hooks's words, "the teacher as a healer."[14] This claim feels like it is not mine to make for my students. I can, however, say that I have experienced healing as student and teacher in various classrooms and I hope to access healing through my own pedagogy. I have also experienced the magic of teaching. As Nhat Hanh explains to hooks in their conversation published in *Lion's Roar*:

> In fact, the true teacher is within us. A good teacher is someone who can help you to go back and touch the true teacher within, because you already have the insight within you. In Buddhism we call it buddhanature. You don't need someone to transfer buddhanature to you, but maybe you need a friend who can help you touch that nature of awakening and understanding working in you.

So a good teacher is someone who can help you to get back to a teacher within.

This does not mean that every class meeting is an experience of profound transformation. Instead, I plant seeds of healing by providing models of and routes toward healing. I ask students to ponder the discipline and love it took Harriet Jacobs to remain in a crawlspace for seven years in order to liberate her children. We talk about what it means to have a "healed" body after that confinement, and the amount of disability created through Atlantic slavery. I also ask them to map out the ways that Jacobs psychologically freed herself even when her body was bound. For example, I ask them to consider how she resolved to buy her body even though she never accepted that she was a commodity. In this, I hope for students to reflect on the limitations within their own lives and the legacy of great interiority and self-motivation in which we all live as Black folk in the United States. More than that, I hope that students can see an example of someone who held fast her own sense of hope and futurity even when she was told she was owed none. As hooks has made plain, I must also be active in the healing process. I must teach material that sows those seeds. I must teach students how to ask questions of that material in ways that also teach them to ask questions of themselves, their environments, and their investments in current political configurations.

What I have also learned from hooks is the way that I must practice my classroom ethics to also account for *my* humanity.[15] And now, to say something seemingly conflicting: at no point am I my complete self in the classroom. If we are honest, there is almost no time that we are our complete selves in any public context. Instead, we edit ourselves when interacting with other people, are in different spaces, and expect particular outcomes. As part of that editing practice, we expose parts of the self that are true, that adhere to an ethic of peace for ourselves and our students. We can actually be vulnerable and real and authentic in ways that do not confuse our students by obscuring the systemic power dynamics in which the classroom participates. Furthermore, we can counter these dynamics through transparency and by creating courses that encourage student success rather than "weeding out" students. We can use the inevitable and cyclical campus crises moments to teach students about the very system in which they are navigating, which includes making clear our own positions as simultaneous challengers and agents of the institution. I can be honest about my own investments in institution as a university professor—from direct resources like pay and benefits to the cultural capital enabled by my association with an R1 university—to demonstrate the complexity of these relationships and how we might use them to carve out spaces and resources that defy the very systems in which we traverse.

Our appropriate and strategic personal offerings, what I call "editing" ourselves above, do not mean that we are purposely hiding ourselves from others. I am referring to a much more subtle process of self-regulation that we often do in a rote fashion. I bring this up because I do not want to overly romanticize my experiences, and I don't want to pretend as if I come before my students and lay my whole self out in front of them. That would not only be inappropriate; it would be exhausting. The point is to bring the relevant portions of myself into the room: my compassion, humor, and personal history framed by boundaries necessary to do my job. I do not pretend to be my students' friends, because to imply that I am their friend would be dishonest considering the power differential in the classroom. Moreover, clear boundaries make the space safest for my students and me. However, I offer myself as a complex person and see my role as more dimensional than classic instructor-student hierarchies suggest. *How can I see their humanity if I cannot see my own in the same space? How can I ask them to be open and vulnerable in the classroom if I do not model the same?* Just like when I come in late for a class *one time*, and then students begin to roll in when they feel like it, what I do in the classroom creates a precedent and I am primarily responsible for setting the standards for the classroom culture and habits.

At the same time, the more I can "be myself" in my classroom, the more effective I am as a teacher. The more I can consciously, thoughtfully, and mindfully bring myself into the classroom, the more I can trust that my personality supports my teaching praxis, the more likely my students will see my humanity. I must admit when I have made a mistake. I must also make proper amends for that mistake. To this end, I do not ever add work to a syllabus. Instead, if the class needs to linger on a particular text or if I have over-assigned work and the majority of students find it difficult to keep up, I will take things off of the syllabus to adjust for the particularities of that group. When my ADHD becomes difficult to manage and affects my classroom, I admit to the students what is going on without giving them inappropriate details. I've had to cultivate a type of comfort with my own limitations in order to express them to others. Perhaps even more, I must be comfortable with my own humanity if I want my students to be able to recognize it without risking the professional teacher-student relationship. Just like hooks, I tell relevant and appropriate personal anecdotes. Actively making connections with my personal history helps me remember what it was like to be a college student and see that history within the context of my study, my desired classroom outcomes, and my own changing self.

As hooks identifies, any practice of "self-actualization" is already a practice of one's humanity, an investigation of one's interiority. hooks leaves this language undefined and, therefore, ripe for interpretation. If you consult the *ur-texts*[16] that hooks studies, you will find the concepts of enlightenment, self-acceptance, and compassion, but the literal language of "self-actualization" seems more hooks than Thich Nhat Hanh.[17] In the words of philosopher George Yancy, hooks's idea of self-actualization "suggests working toward a form of wholeness, a concept that also connotes restoration, integrity, and processes of overcoming/

transcendence."[18] While Yancy concentrates more on healing and wholeness, Gretchen Givens Generett sees hooks's idea as one of transformation. I do not disagree with either and want to push these ideas a bit further.[19]

Self-reflexivity has long been a Black feminist tenet—in part, because of hooks. It is exactly that kind of framework that we witness in current Black feminist conversations. For instance, we can consider how, years after writing about hooks's "homeplace," scholar Jennifer Nash calls us to rethink the tendency for self-defensiveness in the face of white appropriation of Black feminist frameworks and knowledge production.[20] *How else do we keep evolving our thinking if we cannot be honest about our soft spots? How can I teach material that I do not know? How can one teach yoga if one does not practice it? How can one teach reading comprehension without knowing how to read? How can I ask my students to be self-reflective, vulnerable, and deeply engaged if I am not?* If I want to create a place of transformation, one must consider, first and foremost, oneself, one's ability to transform, one's dedication to her healing.

Consider, for instance, the ways that we poo-poo student evaluations. We know that student evaluations are a symptom of the corporatization of higher ed. Academic institutions' most influential leadership tends to come from monied, corporate-oriented trustee boards that focus on the productivity and profitability of their investments. In other words, many trustees want academic institutions to resemble the for-profit world since it is through that world that they amassed or retained their wealth. Moreover, it is through academic institutions upon whose boards they sit that these capitalists further their gains, formally and informally. Adopting the corporate notion of "the customer is always right," administrations look to student evaluations of instructors with little concern for students' understanding of the art of teaching—and it is an art. I am a harsh critic of these assessments, much like many of my colleagues offended by the implicit and overt biases that show up (racism, homophobia, transphobia, misogyny, classism, ableism), the unfair assessment of our value and talent, and the ways we feel beholden to these evaluations. For many of us, especially those in Black bodies, these evaluations lead students to consider how much they liked and respected us.

Largely, student feedback often critiques our styles and personalities more than any thoughtful engagement with teaching efficacy or how much students changed/learned through their classroom experiences. I have been labeled a host of things that do not directly reflect my teaching style: nice and approachable; mean and unapproachable; knowledgeable but too concerned with things like race, gender, and class; strict; easy; intimidating; caring; concerned, the list goes on and on and on, and largely reflects whether the student critic liked or disliked me. The ones that I tend to remember are in the latter category. Harsh criticisms of my personality particularly send me reeling, worming their way into my brain for weeks after reading them. Because I do want to be liked. I do not need to be, but I will admit I want to be.

As a result, I have often gone for long periods without reading my evaluations. I struggle with dismissing them in the context of my own experience, particularly because the most important feedback I've received about my teaching came from a generous student from my second year of teaching on the tenure-track. I began my postgrad teaching career at Columbia College Chicago, where I carried a 3–3 teaching load and was among the few Black professors on campus. It is something else to cut your professional teeth in an art school, given that it is not the typically liberal arts-centered environment of research and public colleges and universities.

The students were so open and hungry for Black literature and history, and they showed up and showed out in nearly every class. They adapted the stories and poems from the syllabus into countless media and changed how I see literature forever. Gayl Jones's *Corregidora* inspired a music student to write and perform a live, complicated, and affecting blues song about love, loss, and impossible persistence. Seeing and hearing this song performed brought the main character Ursa directly into our midst and filled out dimensions written words could not capture. Another student created a stop motion short film adaptation of "A Wall of Fire Rising"—a story by Edwidge Danticat—that pushed the class to confront the text's emotional resonance more deeply. The film student eliminated typical human figures and instead gave us abstracted, somewhat-amorphous red clay bodies as the characters. Through this abstraction, the film offered us some distance from historical experiences of human violence. Moreover, the project encouraged us to explore our various complicated feelings around the story and its ending by inspiring a complex critical conversation around suicide and freedom-through-death, issues explored both in the story and in Black life.

As successful as I felt in my CCC classrooms, at least once a year, a student revolted against the ideas in the classroom, my style of teaching and classroom management, or some combination of both. At the time, the English Department was a service department that supported students pursuing artistic concentrations: film, theater, music, dance, installation, and a host of other visual arts. English classes were part of the core curriculum, but we did not have a major. Most classes began with a discussion about why a liberal arts curriculum would support and enhance an art practice and career. I spent this time trying to justify the value of my course to my students—to sell it to them (talk about corporatizing). In some ways, it was important to my ego because I was in a school that did not privilege English. I never imagined I would have to convince students that literature was worthy of study. During one spring semester, I had a particularly difficult student who, from the first day, approached me and the classroom in a way that I found disruptive, insulting, and disrespectful.

I took student behavior very personally, early in my teaching career. I struggled all semester to regain what I thought was control of the class. The student's consistent moments of rebellion included turning his back to me in the classroom, talking while others were talking, picking fights with other students, sitting behind a pillar in the room so he could do something other than participating and paying attention, entering the classroom late and in a disruptive way, making faces at my statements and laughing inappropriately, and more. I may not have been my most graceful self and often let his distractions take over the classroom. Although I wanted him to drop my class, after several private meetings, the student and I agreed to behavior changes on both parts, and the last third of the course was mostly incident-free. I found out that he was craving my attention and approval and, ultimately, didn't know how to do that in a positive way. I left that class believing I had done a good job sorting through this challenge. I was proud of myself that I never came fully out of my face in front of the class, although I've been told my expressions may have told the whole story despite my best efforts to conceal my frustration. I left the class feeling like I recruited a troubled and troubling student with an appreciation of literature and respect for me.

At the end of the semester, I opened my student evaluations and expected to see a reinforcement of my wonderful job. Many comments were positive, and most of the students who completed the evaluations seemed satisfied with their experience. However, one comment stopped me in my tracks: "The syllabus for this class was really interesting, but Professor Spigner spends too much time concentrating on problem students and ignores the rest of us." I was stunned. This comment brought into sharp focus how much I missed in my classroom and how much my ego took over the experience. I realized that I was centering myself, my personality, and my desires for approval, far more than I'd realized. The evaluation comment made me realize that while the student I described in detail was difficult, he was not the problem. I had a classroom full of students who *wanted* what I offered, and I had failed them because I was too distracted by my desire to be liked and "successful" in the classroom. The person I needed to recruit, heal, and transform in this case was me—but not in a way that reinforced my ego and desire. I was and am grateful that one student cared enough about herself to tell me that she had been forgotten in my class. I have tried to remember my students ever since, especially those who want to learn from me.

I had to be open to this criticism and not be distracted (again) by my own biases against the course evaluation process. I had to resist the urge to dismiss this critique as unfound or amateur. I had to be honest about my shortcomings and sit in that discomfort. I had to be in a self-evaluation process—an ongoing practice with no end—to get closer to being the teacher I wanted to be. I had to kill my ego—essential to the process of self-actualization—to get closer to freedom that the Black literature I teach and the pedagogical philosophy that hooks left to guide us.

Notes

1   Thich Nhat Hanh, *Peace Is Every Step: The Path of Mindfulness in Everyday Life* (New York: Random House Publishing Group, 1992), 55.

2   I quote my Classical Yoga Teacher, Dr. Pratap, not from published text but from my notes from years of class. Those quotes I use in this chapters are repeated lessons from Vedic practical (yoga/asana) and philosophy classes that I took with Dr. Pratap in Philadelphia, PA, between the years of 2003 and 2009. I understand that my experience with Dr. Pratap and yoga/Vedic philosophy as different than hooks's with Nhat Hanh and Buddhism; however, Dr. Pratap often draws from various traditions including Buddhism and Christianity. Moreover, it was my experience with Dr. Pratap that helped make hooks's Buddhism more legible for me.

3   Ibid.

4   According to the Oxford English Dictionary Online, actualization means: "The action of making real or actual; realization in action or fact." The "action" in the definition supports the idea of self-actualization as a process or set of practices. The OED defines self-actualization as: "Realization or fulfilment of one's true nature or ideal self, esp. regarded as a human need." Of course, in order to understand this definition, one must define "true nature" and "ideal self"; however, this is language that circulates in Vedic and Buddhist literature (in English) as well as the popular culture that has been influenced by this literature. For me, ultimately one's "true nature" can only be defined or discovered by the one doing the searching. In Buddhism there is the idea of the "no self" which is the self beyond the ego, personality, and materiality. "Actualization, n. Meanings, Etymology and More | Oxford English Dictionary," accessed March 9, 2024, https://www.oed.com/ dictionary/actualization_n.

5   Helen Tworkov, "Agent of Change," *Tricycle: The Buddhist Review*, January 9, 2017, https://tricycle.org/magazine/bell-hooks-buddhism/.

6   Ibid.

7   bell hooks, "Building a Community of Love: Bell Hooks and Thich Nhat Hanh," Lion's Roar, accessed March 20, 2024, https://www.lionsroar.com/bell-hooks/.

8   I cannot rehearse or catalog the violence in both Christian and Buddhist histories, as it is far outside of the scope of this chapter. However, one can look at each tradition and see war and empire built in the name of or under the pennant of religion. Yes, even Buddhism. And despite these religions being misused for greed, there are and always have been messages of peace and love in each.

9   This is often served as a quote from King; however, the original reference has been difficult to track. I use this quote, here, because it re-articulates Nhat Hanh's quote, above, and because of the popularity and, perhaps, familiarity to readers.

10   hooks, "Building a Community of Love: Bell Hooks and Thich Nhat Hanh."

11   This is not to suggest that this does not also apply to HBCUs or other kinds of institutions. Instead, I am writing from my own experience which has been only studying and teaching in PWIs.

12   I am not suggesting that Black scholarship begins in the 1970s. After all, I am a scholar of the nineteenth century. Instead, I'm thinking about when Black studies departments were formed as a result of the political activism of Black students and scholars. Moreover, in the logical deployment of thought and the politics of institutions, it would make perfect sense that we would first have to confront and perhaps center white supremacy before being able to make room to centralize Blackness in Black thought, creative production, and interiority within institutions and in the academy.

13   My favorite academic references concerning Black interiority are, at least: Audre Lorde's "Uses of the Erotic" (1978); Hortense J. Spillers's "An Order of Constancy" (1985); Kevin Quashie's *The Sovereignty of Quiet* (2012); and, Tara Bynum's *Reading Pleasures* (2023).

14   bell hooks, *Teaching Critical Thinking: Practical Wisdom* (New York: Routledge, 2013), 14.

15   This was also taught to me during graduate school by the poet, my friend, colleague, and mentor, Dr. Donika Kelly. Dr. Kelly taught me that in the world proposing "safe spaces" for our students, she needed the classroom also to be safe for her. She insists on asserting her full humanity not just through personality, but through the ethics she practices in class that [attempt to] protect her from harm.

16   hooks references many works and often quotes Thich Nhat Hanh when discussing Buddhism and Buddhist influences on her work, although she doesn't always identify the texts in which she is referencing. However, in interview she has particularly mentioned the following texts as having influenced her Buddhist

study, some of which I quote from in this chapter: Joanna Macy, *World as Lover, World as Self* (Ypsilanti, MI: Parallax, 1991); Chogyam Trungpa, *Shambhala: Path of the Warrior* (Boulder, CO: Shambhala Publications, 1984); Gloria Steinem, *Revolution from Within* (Boston, MA: Little Brown, 1991); M. Scott Peck, *The Road Less Traveled* (Ypsiolanti, MI: Simon and Schuster, 1978); Erich Fromm, *The Art of Loving* (New York: Bantam Books, 1963); Thich Nhat Hanh and Daniel Berrigan, *The Raft Is Not the Shore* (Boston, MA: Beacon Press, 1975); Sister Chan Khong, *Learning True Love: Practicing Buddhism in a Time of War* (Ypsilanti, MI: Parallax Press, 1993).

17 Rather than "self-actualization," Nhat Hanh and many other Buddhists use the frameworks of "nonself" or "non-Atma" to identify a deeper and some would say true version of ourselves that can become accessible through contemplative Buddhist practice. In *The Raft Is Not the Shore,* Nhat Hanh says: "[Buddha's] reaction to the Veda traditions was total; He denied the whole thing. The idea of Atma or self is the center, the kernel, of the Veda and of the Upanishads. But the teaching of the Buddha was based on the idea of non-Atma." Nhat Hanh understands Buddhist practice as a decentering of the personality, the ego, which is bound by social and material conditions. Instead, the nonself is boundless and is endlessly connected to everything (and even nothings). One can think of hooks's spelling of her name as an extension of this particular framework, as pointed out by Maria Quintana and Carolyn M. Jones Medine. See: Maria Quintana, "Bell Hooks/Gloria Jean Watkins (1952–2021)," January 11, 2010, https://www.blackpast.org/african-american-history/hooks-bell-gloria-jean-watkins-1952/ and Carolyn M. Jones Medine, "Bell Hooks, Black Feminist Thought, and Black Buddhism: A Tribute," *Journal of World Philosophies* 7, no. 1 (July 18, 2022): 187–96.

18 George Yancy, "Engaging Whiteness and the Practice of Freedom: The Creation of Subversive Academic Spaces," Maria del Guadalupe Davidson and George Yancy, *Critical Perspectives on Bell Hooks* (New York: Routledge, 2009), 36.

19 Gretchen Givens Generett, "Engaging bell hooks: How Teacher Educators Can Work to Sustain Themselves and Their Work," Maria del Guadalupe Davidson and George Yancy, *Critical Perspectives on Bell Hooks* (New York: Routledge, 2009), 84.

20 Jennifer Nash refers to hooks's concept of "homeplace" in many places in her work, but particularly, see: Jennifer C. Nash, "Home Truths on Intersectionality," *Yale Journal of Law and Feminism* 23, no. 2 (2011): 445–70 and *Black Feminism Reimagined: After Intersectionality* Next Wave: New Directions in Women's Studies (Durham, NC: Duke University Press, 2019).

15

Practical Wisdom: Praxis and the Urgency of the Moment

Joanna Davis-McElligatt

Not long ago, a colleague mentioned to me that he was having difficulty connecting with his students. He'd written the requisite lectures, delivered them faithfully, and marched his students through the necessary materials—but they seemed disinterested, bored, maybe even depressed. He admitted eventually that his lectures were very long, sometimes running for the entire class, during which time he alone spoke. When he occasionally—and somewhat randomly—asked questions of the class, only three or four students would speak; the rest seemed disengaged, lost, or miserable. He'd mentioned the problems he'd been having to his chair, who'd described to him how engaged her students were by a game show she had devised for them, a bit of fun and silliness to help them learn and remove some of the pressure associated from memorizing and retaining ideas and information. She suggested that he work to find ways to break up the structure of the class, to interrupt the lectures and find entry points that would allow his students to share knowledge with him and one another. I encouraged him to rethink the lecture format entirely, and to consider a flipped classroom, where students would be responsible for reading primary and secondary sources at home, and come to class prepared to dig into them. When I suggested that he might also call on students directly to draw them out, or, even better, arrange them into groups to begin to communicate with one another and build community, he laughed, and said, "Well, that would require learning my student's names!" The conversation ended there, but I was struck by two things: my colleague's seeming total confusion about what to do in the classroom space to improve student learning and experience, and his unwillingness to do what seems to me the most fundamental and essential parts of our work—connect with, encourage, and instruct our students.

Over the more than twenty years I have been teaching in higher education classrooms, I have repeatedly returned to bell hooks's practical wisdom, and her strategies for meaningful engagement, mutual uplift, and critical care for the learning community's bodymindspirits, or what hooks (and others) describes as the total enmeshment of physical, mental, and intellectual domains of living being. I use this teaching as an opportunity to highlight some of bell hooks's most salient and urgent ideas about our responsibility to our students and to one another. I offer this teaching as a companion guide to instructors who are, like my colleague, struggling to connect, remember what our function and purpose is, or sustain community in the classroom. Among the many things I appreciate about hooks's insights in her work on pedagogy is her consistent attention to the intermingling of the mundane and the spiritual, of her refusal to dismiss or ignore the very real demands of our work in a heteropatriarchal white supremacist settler state, but of her incredible hope that we can make the world otherwise through our engagements with one another. For that reason, I want to highlight both her more abstract thinking about pedagogy—her considerations of hope, the Now, well-being, and love—and more applied ideas about what can be done on a material level. I offer five brief excerpts from *Teaching Community: A Pedagogy of Hope* and *Teaching to Transgress: Education as the Practice of Freedom*, alongside my own meditation on her words, explanations of my experiences, and suggestions for developing a critical praxis. These quotes embody the deepest parts of what I have learned from hooks, and form a critical foundation for my own pedagogical work in the classroom.

1 "Commitment to teaching well is a commitment to service. Teachers who do the best work are always willing to serve the needs of their students. In an imperialist white-supremacist capitalist patriarchal culture, service is devalued."[1]

As a Black queer academic, I find myself performing vital—though almost entirely uncompensated—service to the institution. I often teach unpaid independent studies, direct undergraduate honors projects, Master's theses, and doctoral dissertations, labor which is undervalued and disregarded by my institution. More importantly, as one of the only nonwhite professors my BIPOC students encounter in the classroom, I am routinely called on to provide them with mentoring, help them navigate the hostile microsystems of academia, or find solutions to the many difficulties they encounter in other classrooms. In an era of increased adjunctification and the disappearance of tenure, when universities are continuously imperiled both politically and financially, it is very easy to see our work in the classroom as a direct extension of those systems of exploitation and neglect, and resist them by refusing to give the institution any greater part of ourselves than is absolutely required to do our work. But it is critical that we remember that our function as teachers necessarily exists beyond and outside the institution which, in its current structure, is unable to provide care for us or love us back. hooks reminds us that our commitments remain to one another—ourselves and our students—not to the "imperialist white-supremacist capitalist patriarchal culture" in which we meet. Our critical work in the classroom is to reprioritize our relationship to pedagogical community beyond the constraints of the dysfunctional institution, remembering all the while that our service to our students is part of the function of teaching well, and that our best work should persist in critical resistance of the neoliberal logics of devaluation.

2 "In *All About Love: New Visions* I defined love as a combination of care, commitment, knowledge, responsibility, respect, and trust. All these factors work interdependently. They are a core foundation of love irrespective of the relational context. Even though there is a difference between romantic love and the love between teacher and pupil, these core aspects must be present for love to be love. When these basic principles of love form the basis of teacher-pupil interaction the mutual pursuit of knowledge creates the conditions for optimal learning."[2]
I believe that teaching is not only an act of service, and, when done effectively, is also a demonstration of love. But, like hooks, I have also been "told again and again that emotional feelings impede one's capacity to be objective."[3] Both the tacit and implicit expectations for professors are that they, as hooks notes, love their subjects, but not their students—that we remain devoted to our profession as academic researchers and writers, but not as committed pedagogues in critical relation with others. To many extents, my colleague had internalized the idea that so-called objectivity and delivery of information is all that is required for teaching and learning to take place—and yet, his perception that his students' negative affect was an indication that something profound was amiss is important. I believe that even the most resistant and narcissistic professors understand that the principles of love—"care, commitment, knowledge, responsibility, respect, and trust"—are essential to effective pedagogy. I work hard to foster a community of love in my classroom by learning each student's chosen name and pronouns, and using them in our conversations together. At the very beginning of the semester, I insist that we all engage in this activity, learning to respect the essence of one another. I prioritize listening to students

and respecting their voices and opinions, encouraging students to offer feedback on the course readings and our schedule in real time. I treat the classroom as a collaborative space, a place of mutuality and reciprocity. I make space for students to express affect, both positive and negative. I acknowledge the burden of the system that does not make space for students with disabilities, students who are grieving, students who are undocumented, student who are parenting, or students who are poor. I gain from instituting this structure, as well—as I develop real, positive relationships with my students, operating as professor, friend, and mentor in equal measure, I am changed, challenged, and made new. By prioritizing our feelings about the work, ourselves, and the world around us, and by encouraging mutual affection, respect, and care among the community members, the classroom space becomes a reflection of this ethos.

3 "Progressive, holistic education, 'engaged pedagogy' is more demanding than conventional critical or feminist pedagogy. For, unlike these two teaching practices, it emphasizes wellbeing. That means that teachers must be actively committed to a process of self-actualization that promotes their own wellbeing if they are to teach in a manner that empowers students."[4]

In my colleague's defense, he was exhausted, depleted, and at the very end of his emotional and intellectual energy. Teaching together at our university has arguably never been more difficult—at my institution in Texas, for example, the state legislature recently banned all DEI offices and university activities, stripping students of access to funding for affinity groups, graduations, and spaces. The closure of the university's Pride Alliance and Multicultural Center have had long-standing ripple effects for our students, placing more pressure on BIPOC faculty and staff than ever before to find ways to fill in the critical gaps in experience, knowledge, and community. The most important thing I have learned from hooks is that I have to prioritize my own well-being—physical, emotional, intellectual, and interpersonal. It can be exhausting and enervating to navigate the antiblack institution, racist and queerphobic colleagues, and the general violence of the state. I have to remember that Black people in the United States are more likely to sicken and die from the stress of antiblackness and discrimination, and that we are also less likely to receive adequate medical care when we are unwell. Within our power and however we are able, we must make certain to care for our bodymindspirits. This means paying close attention to the ways we negotiate space on campus and beyond, to protecting our peace whenever and however we can, and making time to rest. We cannot teach our students well if we cannot show up for ourselves, if we cannot be well enough to grow and accept change, if we cannot cherish and love our own bodymindspirits.

4 "To engage in dialogue is one of the simplest ways we can begin as teachers, scholars, and critical thinkers to cross boundaries, the barriers that may or may not be erected by race, gender, class, professional standing, and a host of other differences."[5]

Among hooks's most critical pedagogical interventions is her rejection of what Paolo Freire describes as the banking model of education, in which professor think of their function as "depositing" information in their students heads, treating the sacred classroom space as a neoliberal transaction.[6] In this model of education, professors are seen as unequivocal experts, students as passive receivers of their beneficent knowledge, and the system as the facilitator of space for the transaction. And yet, as Freire and hooks note, this model is profoundly alienating for teachers and students alike, given that it denies each an opportunity to be in community with one another. The notion that professors are eternally wise and have nothing to learn or gain from interacting with students is dangerous and inaccurate. Education requires communication, and communication requires a willingness to learn and be changed by an encounter with another person. hooks's engaged pedagogy centralizes the need to engage in critical exchange, to be in dialog with one another in ways that work to bridge misrepresentations, misunderstanding, and gaps in empathy and experience. Rather than calling on students to perform the role of native informant, dialog allows for teachers and students to approach one another as they are, to have an emotional and loving interchange. As my colleague noted, having a dialog requires a certain amount of intimacy and trust. As he rightly intimated, in order to have a critical dialog he would have to learn his students' names and pronouns, address them and engage them one-on-one, listen to them, and respect their perspectives—he would also have to be vulnerable, self-critical, and humble. I operate my classes, to a one, by modeling respectful and loving dialogue. I actively listen to my students, making direct eye contact with them— and I ask others in the classroom to do the same. When my students speak to one another, I insist that they use one another's names and pronouns. I always respond to my student's statements, confirming what they have said, and I either respond myself or link their statement to the course themes, another student's comment, or to something in the world. I encourage students to talk back, critique, interrupt, or get excited (or angry or sad or jubilant, as the case may be).

Establishing the parameters for conversation is why most of my students signal in-class discussion as the most helpful and transformative tool for their learning.

5 "Any professor who teaches the work of black women writers is struck by the fact that the vast majority of these books will have been written by females who did not live long enough, who died young. Teaching this work, I am called, both in reflections on the past and by our present existence, to contemplate the meaning of dying as I ponder the quality of life in the classroom. [...] Teaching students to be fully present, enjoying the moment, the Now in the classroom without fearing that this places the future in jeopardy: that is essential mindfulness practice for a true teacher. Without a focus on the 'Now' we can do the work of educating in such a way that we draw out all that is exquisite in our classroom, not just now and then, or at special moments, but always. Teaching mindfulness about the quality of life in the classroom—that it must be nurturing, life sustaining—brings us into greater community within the classroom."[7]

I write this Teaching at the end of the spring semester in 2024. In the waning weeks of the term, my students and I bore witness to the emergence of multiple anti-genocide and pro-Palestinian protests, including one on our campus—though it was entirely peaceful, and, unlike on other campuses, did not conclude in the setting up of encampments, the university nevertheless responded by sending in a large police presence, including two low-flying helicopters. As students presented their final papers in my graduate seminar, we could hear the thrum of the helicopter's wings, the distant chanting of students pleading with the state to end its complicity in the murder of innocent civilians, and calling for an end to the ongoing violence of settler occupation. During the breaks in presentations, we spoke about the way our being in the classroom space, as generative as it was and needed to be, coincided with and was also the site of terrible pain and despair. At the same time, my students had worked very hard on their papers, and were eager to present them and learn from one another. Our being in the classroom together had been an expression of the Now, a way for us to connect with and learn from and with community. I wanted to honor both my students' feelings and trepidation about the ongoing genocide and the increasing brutality against faculty and student protestors on campuses around the world, and our collective feeling that our intellectual work in the moment mattered very much. It is becoming harder to keep the pain of the world from my students—and, indeed, I do my very best to make sure that they know what is happening in the world around them (many of my undergraduate students, for example, did not know about the protests until we discussed them in class). At the same time, our course materials matter—as hooks notes, it is vitally important that we keep the thought, literature, and hope of our intellectual ancestors in play in our classroom spaces, and that we continue to ask our students to be shaped and influenced by their work. As we ask our students to meditate on the uncertain future and its promise of death, so too must we ask our students to consider the power of the present—as a critical pivot point, as that which we can experience, as a way of being-in-community together.

I believe that hooks is correct when she argues that "the classroom remains the most radical space of possibility in the academy."[8] But I believe that teachers and students must make that space together, reaching out to one another in love, respect, humility, and compassion. It is my hope that this brief spotlight on hooks's practical wisdom will prompt you into an embrace of the urgency of the moment, to think about your own praxis, and help you as you work to build your own classroom communities, wherever they may be.

Notes

1   bell hooks, *Teaching Community: A Pedagogy of Hope* (New York: Routledge, 2003), 83.
2   Ibid., 131.
3   Ibid., 128.
4   bell hooks, *Teaching to Transgress: Education as the Practice of Freedom* (New York: Routledge, 1994), 15.
5   Ibid., 130.
6   Paulo Freire, *Pedagogy of the Oppressed* (New York: Herder and Herder, 1970), 58.
7   hooks, *Teaching Community*, 173.
8   hooks, *Teaching to Transgress*, 12.

16

Spiritually Engaged Writing and Community Pedagogy: Honoring bell hooks's Legacy

Rachel Panton

For more than twenty-four years in the writing classroom, I have attempted to lead my students with new possibilities that rest in the hopefulness of change.[1] No time was this more challenging than during the onset of the Covid-19 pandemic. As an "othermother,"[2] my concern was for the whole student, not just their academic well-being. After the initial semester ended, I created a new syllabus based on our current sociohistorical circumstances, focusing on the writing processes, not production. Our study on the rhetoric of health and wellness extended to ocean conservation, public health, mental health, and women's maternal health. Within each subtopic, particularly as they concerned social media and scientific literacy, I centered the voices of Black women scientists as well as the role of POC LGBTQIA+ scientists in public health initiatives. I hoped to provide a nurturing environment where my students felt empowered through writing assignments and discourse that allowed for mindfulness, compassion, and empathy that they could take out into the world. This "engaged pedagogy"[3] and approach to writing and teaching as sacred acts[4] also empowered me to "talk back"[5]—outside of the classroom and into the community[6]—to the dominant narratives on ocean conservation, which often suggests that Black and Brown ocean advocates are a recent phenomenon and have been relatively absent from blue spaces.

hooks is known for her trailblazing approaches to intersectional feminism and dismantling barriers to education, but many may not know about her contributions to eco-feminist writing and teachings, especially as they relate to Black spiritual and practical connections to the earth.[7] I drew on all these facets of her work to move my teaching forward with the knowledge of ancestral "blue consciousness" rooted in African indigenous and diasporic religions that have maintained a hydro-feminist, embodied connection with water through water spirit veneration, primarily through female and nonbinary deities, for generations. Hydro-feminism is "solidarity across watery bodies" and suggests that given our bodily makeup of 60–90 percent water, there is no separation between humans and water as "water flows through bodies, species, and materialities, connecting them."[8] What grew out of my new course, then, was a three-day weekend community event celebrating World Oceans Day in 2022, underscoring the centrality and reverence for water in the rituals and practice of African indigenous and diasporic religions that are not often acknowledged in the dominant narratives of blue care. Along with Dr. Charlene Désir, and the generous donations of Green Space Miami, she and I hosted: *Ancestors, Orishas, and Ocean Conservation: The Rhetoric of (Mami) Water in Afro Diasporic Environmentalist Education in Florida* at multiple locations throughout South Florida. We sought to educate our local communities on the praxis of ocean conservation within the rituals and beliefs of African Diasporic Religions (ADR, including but not limited to Lucumi, Candomblé, and Vodun) and African Traditional Religions (ATR, including Ifa, Akan, Vodou, and others), which are all highly prevalent in the South Florida area. In the spirit of bell hooks, this project resisted existing dominant narratives of ocean conservation by centering the hydro-feminist and transmaterial approaches to ocean conservation embedded within ADR and ATR communities, as well as their intersections of environmental, social, and political justice.

Rooted in these ancestral ways of knowing, hooks lovingly reminds us not only of our interdependence with the earth but that "to tend the earth is always then to tend our destiny, our freedom and our hope."[9] For Black Americans in particular, her work guides us back to the embodied wisdom of our "ancestral legacy"[10] in the agrarian South—before the Great Migration to the industrial North—where the concept of "interbeing" with the natural environment meant having reverence for and surrendering to the "divine spirit" of nature for survival and sustainability.[11] Likewise, issues surrounding micro-biopolitics and "oceans within"[12] that have emerged in hydro-feminist literature are already rooted in the ontological blue consciousness of ADRs and ATRs. The embodied spiritual connection of ADRs and ATRs that are "trans-material [and] interspecies"[13] offers ways to center current discourses on hydro-feminism and eco-feminism through an Africana lens.

Spiritually Engaged Pedagogy: Sacred Teaching, Sacred Writing, and Risk

Historically, for many Black women teachers, care has become an act of preservation for "selves, communities, and social worlds."[14] Drawing from the works of hooks and Audre Lorde, Beauboeuf-Lafontant outlined three pedagogical characteristics of Africana womanist teaching, including embracing the maternal, political clarity, and ethic of risk.[15] Through an amalgamation of these three characteristics, Black women historically view "caring and mothering in [a] larger socio-historical [realm] [...] [...] [and] in sharing knowledge we can also share power."[16] hooks described this ethic of care and "othermothering" through her elementary school teachers, all of whom were Black women and who were "committed to nurturing intellect so that we could become scholars, thinkers, and cultural workers."[17] Throughout my career, I had long identified as an Africana womanist, but never had the feeling of care and the need to act feel so visceral than during the onset of Covid-19.

The onset of the pandemic grounded me at a time when everyone and everything around me seemed completely out of control. I was led to sit at the feet of the ancestors of my bloodline, as well as teachers, writers, and scholars who had guided me throughout my career as a writing professor. I was particularly inspired by hooks who invoked her great-grandmother each time she wrote, choosing as her nom de plume to honor Bell Blair Hooks who was "known for her snappy and bold tongue"[18] During this time, I felt a renewed sense of writing and teaching as sacred acts. I anchored myself in my writing, in my role as an othermother to my students, and in a time when so many restrictions were being placed on our movements, our learning, and our workspaces—even our physical bodies—elevating liberatory pedagogy became more important than ever to me. hooks wrote, "To educate as the practice of freedom [...] comes easiest to those of us who teach who also believe that there is an aspect of our vocation that is sacred; who believe that our work is not merely to share information but to share in the intellectual and spiritual growth of our students."[19] This moment in history found me focused on my well-being, which included journaling, grounding myself in my spiritual practice, and questioning how I could use writing instruction as a tool for healing instead of another method of control.

In the mornings, I would sit in the garden, in the stillness of dawn, and practice mindfulness writing. As a practitioner of African diasporic spirituality, connecting with nature is an essential component of my spiritual practice, and in "owning that space [there comes an] understanding that we have this intricate relationship with the divine, [and a partnership] with our brilliant selves [...] "[20] In these moments, I also envisioned my students and what they might be waking up to, what thoughts and scenes they might encounter, and I took a moment to silently acknowledge their circumstances. Although I wanted to be as productive as possible each day, my thoughts kept returning to my students and their well-being. I learned from hooks what she learned from her teacher, Thich Nhat Hanh, that the teacher is a healer and that it is possible to "think [...] about pedagogy [in a way that] emphasize[s] wholeness, mind, body, and spirit."[21] My mind kept wondering about the totality of their current circumstances, as well as their physical, emotional, and inner states of being, so I began writing to each student, seventy-five in total, asking about their well-being. I personalized my notes to inquire about their locations, their clubs, their team sports, etc. I wanted them to know I was thinking about them and their families. To my surprise, every one of my students wrote back to me and most commented on how much they appreciated the personal communication. Their heartfelt responses informed my pedagogical practices moving forward (see Appendix).

After the semester ended, I continued my journaling practice concerning my teaching and spent the entire summer creating an entirely new syllabus. This new course and syllabus on the rhetoric of health and wellness allow students the space to participate in low-stakes mindful journaling and also facilitates documentation of pandemic rhetorics, as well as social justice issues concerning ocean conservation, women's health, LGBTQIA+ concerns, and mental health. hooks discussed the risks involved in changing curriculum and "pedagogical strategies as risky"[22] but progressive and necessary. She argues that we make these changes not to be provocative but to invoke a more engaged pedagogy, which is a mode of instruction that is liberatory because it requires mutual labor by the teacher and the student, one that addresses not only the mind but the whole student: mind, body, and spirit. hooks has argued that intellectual and spiritual guidance comes into play when we are concerned about the inner well-being of our students. Spirituality must not be separate from intellectual inquiry among "writers, thinkers, and scholars."[23]

Keeping in mind the desire of my students to make positive change in the world, the sheer number of students who majored in marine biology at my institution, along with my own ancestral hydro-ontological embodied practices, the first quarter of the revamped syllabus focused on the rhetoric of ocean conservation. I began to center Black women ocean marine biologists like Dr. Ayana Johnson in our discussions. I also invited alumnae who formed the Minorities in Shark Sciences collective (MISS) as guest speakers. Together, my students and I examined the various environmental rhetoric concerning ocean sustainability, particularly when it comes to who is represented in leading these discussions in various mediums. To that end, hooks noted that although she was known for her writings on the intersections of race and gender, as a Black woman who grew up in the rural south, her attempts to speak to issues of ecological activism were most often dismissed: "As a black woman writing about Appalachia, I receive little notice. I can talk race, gender, class, and be heard, but when I speak on environmental issues and all the ways agrarian black folks hold the earth sacred, few listen"[24] In other words, as a Black womanist, it was not her space nor place to contribute to discussions about green and blue spaces.

Hydro-feminism and Eco-feminist Nature of ADR Blue Space Narratives

The dominant narrative that Black folk are new to ocean conservation is, in part, due to the relatively new white imagination that Black American bodies belong to urban, "Black spaces." hooks writes that Black American connections to the land before the Great Migration gave our ancestors power to counter the racial injustices they were exposed to—yet the visual rhetoric of US news media often frames images of Black and Brown people occupying intra-urban enclaves.[25] Despite Black American roots in the rural Southern lowlands, these discourses often suggest that Black bodies "don't belong in nature."[26] Little emphasis, however, is given to the "blue consciousness" and fluid symbiotic relationship with water in African traditional and diasporic spiritual beliefs and practices.[27] Such embodied and spiritual connections to the ocean and collective ecological consciousness of preservation are rooted in ADR and ATR connections and devotion to the ancestors, as well as sea-dwelling Orishas and Lwa. They underscore "microbiopolitics, ocean imaginaries, transcontinental sisterhoods and oceans within," as we seek "blue spaces [...] and blue care as sea-proximal experiences of health" physically, spiritually, and mentally.[28] Our ancestors knew that the ocean depends on us to take care of it, just as we depend on the ocean and other waterways for our total health. hooks offers that if we embrace our connections to the earth—that we are apart and not separate from it—we can all work toward eliminating environmental injustices. Such eco-logics are also present among practitioners of ADRs and ATRs like Ifa among the Yoruba in Nigeria.

Currently, the Osun-Osogbo grove, a UNESCO World Heritage site, is a protected worship location for the goddess Osun and is a living example of the indigenous beliefs and praxis of environmental sustainability in the Yoruba traditional practices of Ifa. The core of attitudes, practice, and knowledge of human behavior with the environment is predicated on animistic beliefs of the interconnectedness of the people and environmental landscapes/waterways. The Earth and its waterways are therefore reactionary and sensitive to the treatment of the humans that inhabit it. In other words, "Yoruba religious perception about the environment and its constituents which includes water depicts relatedness with other entities of life forms like trees, humans, and animals among others for the purpose of enhancing ecosystem balance or order."[29] For example, fishing or the killing of buffalo within Osun Osogbo is prohibited. In certain instances, water-related life-forms are considered "accomplices" to the deities, therefore hunting or fishing of these resources might also be discouraged. Likewise, the role of sea and coast in human health is an intangible cultural heritage (ICH) in African ontology that reveals an ecological consciousness that is preserving ocean health. Life with water is a trans-material and embodied practice. Even recent research on South African and Southeast Indian Ocean islands indicates "reverence for the sea and consideration of sentience beyond humanity."[30] This blue consciousness centers on spiritual and interspecies connections with the ocean.

Ocean Conservation and Liberatory Pedagogy in Praxis

As the threat of climate change puts pressure on South Floridians to make major changes in how we interact with nature, I sought to educate our local communities on the connections between ADRs and environmentalism, specifically ocean conservation. Partnering with Dr. Charlene Désir of T.E.N. Global for the weekend of World Oceans Day, we highlighted and celebrated Afro-Caribbean, Afro-Brazilian, and African American traditions that have always been proactive in their fight for ocean conservation, as well as other environmental, social, and political justice movements through their connections and devotion to the Orishas and Lwa. These deities represent the natural elements and forces of nature. The relationship and reverence of water deities such as Yemonja (also known as Yemaya, Yemanja), Olokun, Oshun, Agwe (Agoue), La Sirene, Simbi, and Mami Wata were of particular interest for this project. These deities are revered for their protection of ancestors and for their mighty powers to create balance even in the wake of natural disasters. In many of the Afro-Caribbean communities, even those situated in South Florida, there is a belief that many of the water deities are wreaking havoc on the land due to our lack of regard for the environment and waterways.

For Dr. Desir and I, as well as the beloved communities[31] we were engaging with, this three-day event was liberatory pedagogy in praxis. hooks teaches us that "beloved community is formed not by the eradication of difference but by its affirmation, by each of us claiming the identities and cultural legacies that shape who we are and how we live in the world."[32] In essence, we were affirming the "subjugated knowledge"[33] embedded in Africana womanist traditions of intersecting spirituality, education, and community through resistance to oppression and colonization of the mind by "breaking with the ways our reality is defined and shaped by dominant culture and asserting our understanding of reality, of our own experiences."[34] This project was meant to embolden these communities to persist in their traditional pathways and as a means to educate non-practitioners that Black and Brown people are not new to blue spaces and blue care.

For those who practice African and African diasporic ancestral ways of knowing, there are no binaries, no separation between human experiences and nature, and no separation of spirit from either. They are all interconnected. hooks also believed that our acceptance of our connections to nature and the power that lies within the natural world would liberate us into a higher consciousness for ourselves and the whole Earth. Her lessons on how we educate one another were also nonbinary; not only is teaching a sacred act and accounts for students' well-being, but students also instruct the teachers, and education is not relegated to the classroom. Deconstructing notions that the instructor is the only one who contributes is the starting point of access for engaged pedagogy. Likewise, accessibility beyond the ivory towers is a necessary component of liberatory pedagogy that applies to "the real world," as hooks reminds us that movements against and beyond boundaries "make education the practice of freedom."[35] Thus, my work continues how hooks taught me: teaching, writing, "talking back," and examining the rhetoric of Black bodies, blue spaces, and belonging within beloved communities in the writing classroom and beyond.

Appendix

Sample of Emails to Students and Responses during Initial Covid-19 Shutdown

Hello professor,

I made it back okay. UK has just gone into a half lockdown with only being able to leave the house for work or shopping so stuck in the house with no golf. All is good here though. If I have any questions which I probably will, I will definitely send you an email.

It is much appreciated, hope you are well.

Sincerely,

Michael H.

Get Outlook for iOS<https://aka.ms/o0ukef>

_____

From: Rachel Panton <notifications@instructure.com>

Sent: Wednesday, March 25, 2020 3:51:44 PM

To: Michael H

Subject: Rachel Panton (Winter 2020 Advanced College Writing) just sent you a message in Canvas.

How are you?

Hi Michael,

How are you? Did you make it back to the UK? Are you able to practice golf at all through all of this?

Let me know how you're doing and if you have any questions about anything.

Best,

Dr. P

How are you?

Hello Dr. Panton,

I am doing well, how are you?

My family is fine for now, one of my sisters came to join us for the quarantine. My brother is also here, but he lives here, so that is normal. My county is locked down but Pennsylvania is too cold to be outside right now anyways. How is your family?

Thank you for checking in,

Becky B.

––––––––––––––––––––––––––––––

From: Rachel Panton <notifications@instructure.com>

Sent: Tuesday, March 24, 2020 12:58 PM

To: Rebecca B.

Subject: Rachel Panton (Winter 2020 Advanced College Writing) just sent you a message in Canvas.

How are you?

Hi Rebecca,

I'm just checking in with you to see how you're doing. How's your family? Your siblings?

All my best,

Dr. P

Good afternoon!

I am doing as well as I could possibly be doing considering the circumstances. As a procrastinator at heart, online school would never be my first choice but I'm making do. I appreciate you reaching out!

I do not have any questions about the class so far but in the event that any arise I will communicate them to you as best I can.

I hope all is well with you. I know that I have been driving my parents crazy in our circumstantial house arrest, so I'm sending you all the vibes of patience and strength in this time when you have to focus on work as well as a child.

Thank you so much for reaching out! The effort you're making to make this "new normal" as smooth as possible is not lost on me.

Well wishes,

Good afternoon Dr. Panton,

I appreciate your checking in it means a lot. I am feeling great and my family is good as well, although having all 6 of us stuck home 24/7 can be a bit hectic. So far I understood how the scheduling for the rest of classwork will go thus far but if I end up confused I will be sure to contact you. The only thing I am unsure of right now is my motivating move/s, just trying to find what categories fit my research.

Thank you for reaching out.

Kateryna A.

How are you?

Thank I did finally make it back home recently but it was a struggle. Finding out in days notice that I have to pack everything up, move stuff into storage and stuff the rest in my car was pretty stressful. I made it work though and I'm back now tryna get back into the swing of school and trying to find these online assignments to do. I don't have any questions this second, but if I do I'll be sure to reach out. Thank you for taking the time to ask me.

Thank you again,

Chase C.

From: Rachel Panton <notifications@instructure.com>

Sent: Tuesday, March 24, 2020 1:59 PM

How are you?

Hi Loren,

How are you doing? Did you drive your car up north? Did your brother and his girlfriend make it back home?

You've been in my thoughts.

Hope all is well.

Best,

Dr. P

[Rachel Panton]

Rachel Panton

How are you?

Good Evening! I drove back to Pennsylvania on Wednesday so I'm fortunate to be back and able to stay here at home for the time being. My brother and his girlfriend were able to fly home before the travel ban was placed on England. This transition is very tough, but I know that everyone is struggling. I'm hoping we get to come back to Nova one last time. Thank you so much for reaching out, it truly means a lot. I hope you are safe as well, and not too stressed with these course changes.

Get Outlook for iOS<https://aka.ms/o0ukef>

How are you?

Hi Dr. Panton,

Thank you for asking! I'm trying my best to stay calm and collected through all of this. My family is doing the same as well. In fact, to stay positive, we like to think of this whole quarantine as some good 'ol family bonding. As for IMAN, members are continuously texting via WhatsApp with tips on how to stay safe and prayers that should be conducted during times like these. In terms of the class, I wanted to ask if there is anything new that we should include in our introduction aside from the motivating move and thesis? With that being said, I look forward to the rest of the semester online. Although I must admit, I do miss your lectures as I always learn a lot. I hope this situation improves, and I hope you and your family stay safe and sound.

Sending happy and healthy wishes,

Mariya B.

From: Rachel Panton <notifications@instructure.com>

Sent: Friday, March 27, 2020 5:19 PM

To: Mariya B.

Subject: Rachel Panton (Winter 2020 Advanced College Writing) just sent you a message in Canvas.

How are you?

Hi Mariya,

How are you? How's your family? Is IMAN keeping in contact with its members through all of this?

Do you have any questions about the class so far?

All my best,

Dr. P

Notes

1 bell hooks, *Talking Back: Thinking Feminist, Thinking Black* (Boston, MA: South End Press, 1989).
2 bell hooks, *Teaching to Transgress: Education as the Practice of Freedom* (New York: Routledge, 1994).
3 Ibid.
4 Ibid.
5 hooks, *Talking Back*, 5–9
6 bell hooks, *Teaching Community: A Pedagogy of Hope* (New York: Routledge, 2003).
7 bell hooks, *Belonging: A Culture of Place* (New York: Routledge, 2009).
8 Maria Bordoff, "Hydrofeminism Is Solidarity across Watery Bodies: Planetary Thinking Is Feminist Thinking, State the Curators Behind Laboratory for Aesthetics and Ecology as They Publish a Book about Hydrofeminism," *Kunstkritikk Nordic Art Review*, 2018, https://kunstkritikk.com/hydrofeminism-is-solidarity-across-watery-bodies/#:~:text=Elena%20Lundquist%20Ort%C3%ADz%3A%20 Hydrofeminism%20is,mention%20just%20a%20few%20examples.
9 hooks, *Belonging*, 117.
10 Ibid.
11 Ibid., 118.
12 Rosabelle Boswell, "Ocean and Human Health in the Blue Era: Indian Ocean and African Perspectives," *Journal of Indian Ocean World Studies* 6, no. 2 (2022): 21.
13 Ibid., 213.
14 bell hooks, *Ain't I a Woman: Black Women and Feminism* (New York: Routledge, 1993); Hi'ilei Julia Kawehipuaakahaopulani Hobart and Tamara Kneese, "Radical Care: Survival Strategies for Uncertain Times," *Social Text* 38, no. 1 (2020): 1–16, https://doi.org/10.1215/01642472-7971067.

15 Tamara Beauboeuf-Lafontant, "A Womanist Experience of Caring: Understanding the Pedagogy of Exemplary Black Women Teacher," *The Urban Review* 34, no. 1 (2002): 71–86.

16 Ibid., 283.

17 hooks, *Teaching to Transgress*, 2.

18 Nadra Nittle, *Bell hooks' Spiritual Vision: Buddhist, Christian, and Feminist* (Minneapolis, MN: Fortress Press, 2023).

19 Ibid., 4.

20 Lakeesha J. Harris, "Healing through (Re) Membering and (Re) Claiming Ancestral Knowledge about Black Witch Magic," in *Black Women's Liberatory Pedagogies: Resistance, Transformation, and Healing within and beyond the Academy*, eds. Olivia N. Perlow, Durene I. Wheeler, Sharon L. Bethea, and BarBara M. Scott (New York: Palgrave Macmillan, 2018), 245–63, https://doi.org/10.1007/978-3-319-65789-9.

21 Hooks, *Teaching to Transgress*, 12.

22 Ibid., 141.

23 Ibid., 17.

24 bell hooks, "Connecting Appalachia to the World Beyond." bell hooks books, https://bellhooksbooks.com/connecting-appalachia-to-the-world-beyond/ (N.D.).

25 Paul Messaris and Abraham Linus, "The Role of Images in Framing News Stories," in *Framing Public Life: Perspectives on Media and Our Understanding of the Social World*, eds. Stephen D. Reese, Oscar H. Gandy, Jr., and August E. Grant (New York: Routledge, 2001), 231–42.

26 Beshoy Boutros, "Writing the Target on Your Back: A Review of Simone Brown's Dark Matters: On the Surveillance of Blackness," *Somatecnics* 11, no.1 (2021): 112–17; Dianne D. Glave, *Rooted in the Earth: Reclaiming the African American Environmental Heritage* (Chicago, IL: Chicago Review Press, 2010), 5.

27 Boswell, "Ocean and Human Health," 213.

28 Ibid.

29 Adewale O. Owoseni, "Water in Yorùbá Belief and Imperative for Environmental Sustainability," *Religion* 28 (2017): 18.

30 Boswell, "Ocean and Human Health," 214.

31 George Brosi and bell hooks, "The Beloved Community: A Conversation between bell hooks and George Brosi," *Appalachian Heritage* 40, no. 4 (2012): 76–86.

32 bell hooks, "Killing Rage: Ending Racism," *Journal of Leisure Research* 28, no. 4 (1996): 316.

33 Patricia Hill Collins, "On Our Own Terms: Self-defined Standpoints and Curriculum Transformation," *NWSA Journal* 3, no. 3 (1991): 367–81.

34 hooks, *Teaching Community*, xxxii.

35 hooks, *Teaching to Transgress*, 12.

Part Four

Strategies of Resistance and Anticolonial Frameworks

The work we do in the classroom as small communities of purpose can and does lead to impacts that make shifts for our broader communities. The authors in this part continue to disrupt the false dichotomy between classrooms and communities, and underscore the importance for teachers to center cultural and community values, and embrace our own continuing positions as learners. In "Indigenous (Zapotec) Queer Feminist Pedagogy: Accessible, Healing and Transformative Theory," Nancy Morales explores how compassion and reciprocity in her classroom communities become practices that challenge Western educational systems' investment in settler colonialism. Placing bell hooks's conception of theory as liberatory practice in conversation with Indigenous decolonizing praxes, Morales provides her students with opportunities to respond to injustice with care and community labor as opportunities arise on campus and beyond.

In an effort to contend with institutional environments that are growing increasingly hostile to educators' and staff members' work to sustain spaces of liberatory possibility for students in college, in *Reading Circle as a Model of Cultivating Engaged Pedagogical Praxes*" Savannah Geidel and Maia Butler reflect on their experiences developing and facilitating a bell hooks Teaching Trilogy reading circle on UNC Wilmington's campus. Twenty-five faculty and staff came together for a pedagogical development opportunity—a space of compassionate, critical self- and community reflection—to work together through hooks's teaching trilogy, alternating between reading and writing reflections, and convening biweekly for discussion. Geidel and Butler offer a model for strengthening solidarity across disciplines, and ways to consider what goes right in our teaching, where we can grow in our teaching, and how university structures support or undermine truly transformative engaged pedagogies.

The final two chapters construct bridges between college classrooms and pedagogical praxis to K-12 learners who are coming into themselves and their work in their communities. In "Intersectional Latinidad as a Critical Praxis Connecting College to Classroom: Lessons, Lineages, and Legacies of Liberatory Pedagogy from *Teaching to Transgress*," Alyssa Garcia, Margarita Mojica, and Glenview middle school students, explain how several of hooks's core pedagogical tenets hold liberatory possibility for their Latinx and/or LGBTQIA+ identifying students in East Moline, Illinois. A culminating project for Garcia's Latinx Feminisms college course, Mojica's eleven-week after school workshop—sorely needed in a community where the number of Latinx families is steadily rising, but the diversity of the teaching force has not kept pace—offers four modules addressing culture and language, body image and media representation, and wellness in community and activism. The activities and impacts of each module show that critical self-actualization and resistance work are possible where student languages and cultures remain valued building blocks of resistance to dominator values in Western education. Similarly, "Community Writing Programs as Communities of Resistance," by Charles McMartin, Nicole Crevar, Maxwell Irving, and Charisse Iglesias, shows how high school and college teachers and learners come together as Wildcat Writers in Tucson, Arizona, to complete community-based projects. Leveraging university funds to social justice ends, and working in the context of fear mongering by anti-CRT legislators and Department of Education officials, the Wildcats are a collective of marginalized teacher/learners choosing resistance through their work in the realm of possibility and transformation. The collection of individual reflections in this chapter enacts the collective's commitment to polyvocality as a narrative pathway to agency, growth, belonging, and action, whose member projects emerge as models of resistance. It is our hope that this final part of reflections and teachings bears witness to the work of every teacher/learner in *bell hooks's Radical Pedagogy: New Visions of Feminism, Justice, Love, and Resistance in the Classroom*, and demonstrates many different ways to move from theory to practice in our own pedagogical praxis, and in our work with other scholars, teachers, learners, leaders, and home communities both near and far.

17

Indigenous (Zapotec) Queer Feminist Pedagogy: Accessible, Healing, and Transformative Theory

Nancy Morales

Introduction

I am a first-generation Indigenous (Zapotec) feminist scholar-activist. As a second-generation Zapotec, I have roots in San Bartolome Zoogocho, community of origin, which is located in the Sierra Juarez of Oaxaca, Mexico, and a guest on the lands of other Native/Indigenous people.[1] I learned from Black, Indigenous, and women of color scholar-activists the value and challenges of being a teacher in the classroom. In particular, the challenges of teaching and learning in feminist studies (or more commonly known as women and/or gender and sexuality studies) classes at a predominantly white institution, including Hispanic-serving institution.[2] I have a responsibility to students for creating an informative learning environment that allows us to think critically and challenge ourselves on social justice issues around gender, race, class, and sexuality, particularly for underrepresented communities. bell hooks's engaged pedagogy has been pivotal to my training as a teacher who challenges hierarchy within the classroom. Further, my Zapotec feminist pedagogy emerges and engages with the Black feminist scholar, poet, and cultural critic bell hooks and the Michi Saagiig Nishnaabeg scholar, writer and artist Leanne Betamosake Simpson that offers approaches toward anticolonial pedagogies based on a collaborative approach to transform spaces of learning within and outside higher education. In this chapter, I discuss two pedagogical strategies that explain how theory is accessible and can transform our lives. I invited students to join me during a campus sit-in to express solidarity with University of California graduate students' wildcat strikes to link with social movements, which we were learning about. In another strategy, I employed strategic storytelling exercises that built generative discussions and encouraged students to share insights while using validation rather than judgment. I hope readers will see that these pedagogical strategies make it possible for teachers and students to inspire each other beyond the classroom. I aim to transform spaces of learning that animates discussion based on a collaborative approach to learning that makes a positive impact in higher education and future.

Positionality

Following Joteria-Muxerista and feminist teachers, activists, and scholars I share my positionality and further identify myself in relation to my work, place, and Indigeneity.[3] I am a first-generation Zapotec queer feminist scholar-activist and a second-generation Zapotec who has Indigenous roots in San Bartolome Zoogocho, community of origin, located in the Sierra Juarez region of Oaxaca, Mexico. I was born and raised on Tongvaa lands, known as South Central Los Angeles. I am a by-product of the Los Angeles Unified School District's inner-city public schools in a predominately Latinx immigrant community. My mother was a garment worker for over twenty years who worked in the sweatshops in downtown Los Angeles. Growing up, I remember my *apa*, sister, and I picking her up on Saturday afternoons and being so excited to see her and spend time with her as a family by eating fast food as a treat. I grew up as the eldest daughter and would cook, clean, and care for my younger sister during the summers while both of my parents worked. I also practiced strategic distancing of my Zapotec roots as a way of protecting myself from the racism and discrimination by my mestizo Latinx peers at school. At the same time, my critical consciousness emerged as a youth organizer with Concerned Citizens of South Central Los Angeles, a nonprofit organization founded by the late Juanita Tate, Black feminist activist.[4] As a youth organizer, I became aware of environmental racism and the value of raising awareness and using our voices to demand justice. As a result, I developed a passion for social justice issues and I became a student-activist during my higher education journey. Also, I was motivated to pursue higher education, and I am a proud nontraditional student who transferred and a graduate student parent. During my doctoral degree program in feminist studies, I was able to utilize Black, Indigenous, and Chicanx/Latinx feminist and queer activist approaches to reclaim my Indigeneity, which has been relegated to a romantic past. As an Indigenous (Zapotec) queer from a working-class migrant background, I further learned to resist forms of erasure, including developing pedagogical strategies in the classroom to make theory accessible to all that can be a transformative experience.

Radical Compassion in the Classroom

My Indigenous (Zapotec) feminist teaching philosophy—grounded in *Guelaguetza* system—revolves around radical compassion and deep reciprocity.[5] My anticolonial pedagogies aim to create collaborative learning spaces, meaningful relationships, and community within and outside higher education. I embrace students' multifaceted identities and recognize their lived experiences as a form of knowledge production. At the beginning of the semester, I introduce myself and explain that I am also a native Spanish speaker and my parent's native language is Zapoteco. I encourage multilingual students to express themselves in all the languages they feel most comfortable, even though not everyone will understand to build generative discussions. Following hooks's engaged pedagogy on multilingualism (1994), I challenge students, particularly monolingual English speaker students to "learn from spaces of silence and spaces of speech, that in the patient act of listening to another tongue we may subvert that culture of capitalist frenzy and consumption that demands all desire must be satisfied immediately"[6] Our differences need to be embraced in the classroom as much as possible that allows for different ways of expressing ideas and knowledge as a form of self-determination.

Further I employ personal counternarratives to produce generative discussions based on deep radical compassion rather than judgment. For our Women of Color: Race, Ethnicity, and Class course readings, we discussed the "welfare queen" myth, which demonizes Black women and other women of color for using public assistance. I shared how I was a CalFresh (formerly known as food stamps) recipient because I could not afford our basic needs as a graduate student and parent. It took me a long time to feel comfortable to apply for and share with others that I received CalFresh because of the continued stigma regarding welfare recipients, particularly Black women, Indigenous women, and women of color. My personal story rejects the distorted image of the "welfare queen." bell hooks explains that engaged pedagogy is more than empowering students, and includes teachers learning and growing with their students. As a teacher, I need to be the first one to share my story, while enhancing everyone's understanding of the course material, and encouraging students to do the same.

Therefore, students are met with radical compassion rather than judgment in the classroom.

My radical compassion also stems from the *cariño* (critical care), which is one of the three tenets of Chicana/Latina feminist pedagogy that allows a teacher to create positive and meaningful relationships with students from various backgrounds. In Linda Prieto and Sofia Villenas article, "Pedagogies from 'Nepantla': 'Testimonio,' Chicana/Latina Feminisms and Teacher Education Classrooms" they identify cultural dissonance, *conciencia con compromiseo* (conscious with commitment), and cariño as Chicana/Latina feminist pedagogy.[7] As Chicana/Latina educator scholars, they reveal the tensions and contradictions as well as the potential of transformative teaching and learning at predominantly white institutions. Cariño is to recognize the various ways their parents supported them while navigating the education system, such as the everyday acts of nourishment and care (e.g., home-cooked meals). Those moments of cariño shaped their sense of self as well as developed the basis for connection and compassion for others. They enact cariño in their pedagogy with students in order to work across differences. For them, acts of cariño in the classroom include celebrating student's milestones as well as education and advocacy work in local farmworker communities. Linda Prieto and Sofia Villenas, further explain:

> In our praxis, cariño pays attention to the whole person, including the historical and political struggles in which we are embedded. It concerns appreciating and embracing shared and diverse histories.[8]

I share some of my personal experiences as examples in order to help students further analyze course texts, and so they can begin to see me as more than just their instructor. The radical compassion that I embody allows me to see the complexity of students. In addition to many positive student evaluations on my courses, I have received multiple emails and notes of gratitude and appreciation from students of various backgrounds. Their actions affirm my labor and commitment. The classroom transforms into a space that embraces our differences and begins to disrupt the notion of individualism while challenging hierarchical roles.

My personal counternarrative as a recipient of social services further makes visible class differences in the classroom, including myself as the teacher. As bell hooks explains, often the feminist classroom becomes the only place where students and professors from working-class backgrounds could speak from their class positionality to acknowledge "both the impact of class on social status as well as critiquing the class bias of feminist thought."⁹ There remains a great silence on class differences in higher education that makes those from working-class backgrounds invisible. She explains that academia may be hostile to the working class because it aims at upholding bourgeois values and practices. There are challenges to build a sense of belonging in academia. However, this hostility may be an opportunity to subvert and challenge the existing structure of academia. She further states:

> Those of us in the academy from working class backgrounds are empowered when we recognize our own agency, our capacity to be active participants in the pedagogical process. This process is not simple or easy: it takes courage to present a vision of wholeness of being that does not reinforce the capitalist version that suggests that one must always give up something to gain another.¹⁰

Indeed, in the process of developing my own Indigenous (Zapotec) feminist philosophy including pedagogical practices, I have reclaimed my Indigeneity that is relegated to a romantic past under settler colonialism. I have offered my *tequio*, or community labor, to increase Indigenous visibility both on and off campus. I, like many Indigenous youth, experienced discrimination and racism by mestizo Latinx peers who used derogatory terms like *oaxaquita* to dehumanize us. In my own processes of healing from intergenerational trauma, I too have begun to formulate theory and practice based on my lived realities through my research and praxis beyond the classroom. The process of recovering and restoring my wholeness and spirit through language and new tools is at the essence of theorizing.

Deep Reciprocity beyond the Classroom

In my other course Women, Globalization, and Resistance, I also practice a deep reciprocity, which transforms the classroom into a space that embodies various forms of agency, leadership, and decision-making skills. Leanne Betamosake Simpson (2014) explains that one must depart from Western education because it is a system that produces individualism that maintains settler colonialism.¹¹ Simpson explains that theory becomes regenerative by new generations of Indigenous people who are concerned with recovering their knowledge systems that allow them to engage more with their worldviews and less with the nation-state, which is a transformative experience. Furthermore, she explains the meaning of theory for Indigenous people:

"Theory" is generated and regenerated continually through embodied practice and within each family, community, and generation of people. "Theory" isn't just an intellectual pursuit—it is woven within kinetics, spiritual presences and emotion, it is contextual and relational. It is intimate and personal, with individuals themselves holding the responsibilities for finding and generating meaning within their own lives.[12]

Like hooks, Simpson argues that theory is for everyone and must be accessible beyond academia. Moreover, theory must be meaningful to the individuals who are building tools and language derived from their lived realities. In essence, providing context to the ongoing inequalities and self-determination of Indigenous people is critical to effective learning environments both inside and outside the classroom. Indigenous people's self-determination processes grounded within their knowledge systems are concerned with creating

a generation of land based, community based intellectuals and cultural producers who are accountable to our nations and whose life work is concerned with the regeneration of these systems, rather than meeting the overwhelming needs of the western academic industrial complex or attempting to "indigenize the academy" by bringing Indigenous knowledges into the academy on the terms of the academy itself.[13]

Accordingly, we discuss materials on "How to Be an Effective Ally," which requires us to be actively engaged beyond the classroom. In winter 2020, I joined the wildcat strike that began at UC Santa Cruz and was led by Graduate Student Teaching Assistants and allies who were demanding a living wage.[14] There was a profound teachable moment when I invited students to have discussion sections at an organized UC Santa Barbara Chancellor's office sit-in. The purpose of the sit-in was to express solidarity with the graduate students' wildcat strike at UC Santa Cruz. The wildcat strikers demanded increased wages for Graduate Teaching Assistants, who struggle to meet basic needs. At the time, I struggled to access basic needs as a graduate-student-parent. In particular, as a single parent of a young child, I simply could not afford to purchase food under my monthly stipend as a Graduate Student Teaching Assistant. I always encourage students to consider the various ways they can engage with social justice issues, including labor organizing. There was a profound teachable moment when I invited students to join me for our discussion sections at an organized UC Santa Barbara Chancellor's office sit-in to express solidarity with graduate student's wildcat strike at UC Santa Cruz. Many students attended and provided statements, which were published by the campus weekly newspaper. A reporter initially invited me for an interview, however, I encouraged students to provide their own statements because their voices matter as much as my own. I also provided informal presentations at the picket line, during which students learned about labor organizing and the inequalities graduate students experienced. There was large and growing support from undergraduate students. I received an email from a student who, in her junior year, thanked me for the course she took with me when she was a freshman, and expressed her support/solidarity for the wildcat strike. Consequently, she wrote me a letter of recommendation for the UC Santa Barbara 2021 Graduate Teaching Association's Excellence Teaching Award, which I won. In her letter of recommendation she explains more about how taking my course during her freshman year cemented her decision to pursue a degree in feminist studies. This student was proud to be one of my former students when she witnessed my own form of student activism with direct action.

Furthermore, my community-based scholarship and overall struggle for self-determination as an Indigiqueer (Zapotec) feminist includes regenerating the *Guelaguetza*, knowledge system. A Zapotec system of reciprocity that is foundational to Indigenous people's way of being and knowing. Following Kaupapa Māori education scholar Linda Tuhiwai Smith, I see decolonization as part of a daily struggle and commitment to intergenerational healing from historical trauma. To do this, I have offered my *tequio* (community labor) to build meaningful relationships and community by creating spaces for critical reflection and care as the advisor for the Collective of *Pueblos Originarios* in Diaspora (CPOD) and Oaxaqueñx Youth *Encuentro* (OYE) committee member. This work strategically positions me to advocate and amplify the voices of Indigenous Latinx women and queer youth (Zapotec, Mixtec, and Maya) from Latin America living in diaspora. During my doctoral program, I was nominated to be the advisor for Collective of *Pueblos Originarios* in Diaspora (CPOD). CPOD is a student campus group, which I co-founded with a group of Indigenous (Mixtec, Zapotec, and Maya) Latinx students during the onset of the Covid-19 pandemic. As the advisor, I encouraged students to lead discussions on topics about Indigeneity that foster another space for an effective learning environment. I also organized off-campus with Oaxaqueñx Youth Encuentro (OYE), a collective that hosts annual gatherings for Indigenous youth living in diaspora. My scholarship and activism are significantly bound to my commitment to new generations of Indigenous diasporic communities, particularly Indigenous women and Indigiqueer youth.

Healing through Theory *and* Praxis

In the process of learning and teaching, I have come to understand how theory and praxis are both reciprocal and regenerative. In bell hooks's foundational essay, "Theory as Liberatory Practice" (1994), she explains how theory allowed her to heal from systemic violence, including the institution of patriarchal family in her own household.[15] hooks was healing from intergenerational trauma, stemmed from her childhood experiences; for instance, as a child hooks discouraged from asking questions about gendered roles, including being punished for challenging patriarchal heteronormative standards. hooks explains when one can begin to formulate theory and practice from lived experiences—the healing process may begin. For hooks, the process of theorizing becomes meaningful when it is part of collective liberation. In essence, theory and praxis are reciprocal processes— one enables the other. hooks further argues that "theory is not inherently healing, liberatory, or revolutionary. It fulfills this function only when we ask that it do so and direct our theorizing towards this end."[16] In other words, those that call themselves theorists must also be practitioners who aim for collective liberation and self-determination. Indeed, the relationship between theory and practice is what defines the power of liberatory education for critical consciousness to challenge systemic violences. Consequently, theory becomes relevant to students and communities whose lives are at stake, particularly under a rise of white nationalism.

The radical compassion, including cariño that I embody in my classroom, is also to challenge the hierarchy between theory and praxis. As hooks explains, the gap between theory and practice emerges from class elitism, which creates a hierarchy between theory and practice. In other words, theory becomes abstract and inaccessible to the general public. She argues that Black, Indigenous, and people of color (BIPOC) begin to internalize this division and devalue theory. Consequently, many refuse to engage in theorizing which results in an undermining of struggles for liberation and self-determination. Initially, I struggled to understand the relationship between theory and praxis because of the ongoing hierarchy that exists in academia. During college, my undergraduate student activism seemed irrelevant to what I was learning in the classroom. It was after receiving the mentorship by women of color faculty that I began to think about theory in relation to my own lived experiences as an Indigenous (Zapotec) queer person. A radical compassion is necessary to invite those that are in opposition to theory to engage in critical reflection and feminist praxis.

hooks says, "[T]his [feminist] theory emerges from the concrete, from my efforts to make sense of everyday life experiences, from my efforts to intervene critically in my life and the life of others. This to me is what makes feminist transformation possible."[17] Theory must emerge from our lived experiences so that we may heal from the sexism, ableism, racism, classism, homophobia, transphobia and create language. On the first day of class, I share with students that the classroom is a space where we will learn with and from each other. I emphasize that everyone's lived experiences is a form of knowledge production that will allow them to further analyze course readings, which encourages them to engage in critical dialog with each other and across differences.

Consequently, Joteria-Muxerista pedagogical praxis is also rooted in a healing approach to do social justice work. Anita Tijerina Revilla, Joana Nunez, Jose Manuel Santillana Blanco, and Sergio A. Gonzalez (2021) are Joteria-Muxerista educators employ hook's liberatory pedagogies for social transformation.[18] hooks (1994), argues that, as teachers, we must "have a real concern with education as a liberatory practice with pedagogical strategies that may not be just for our students but for ourselves." Indeed, a Joteria-Muxerista pedagogical practice in the classroom is an intervention that uses an intersectional framework as well as a holistic approach to affirm and acknowledge students' multifaceted identities, including gender variance and sexual desires. Moreover, Joteria-Muxerista educators may be the first people in jotx (queer) and trans students' lives who acknowledge that they are not heteronormative or cisnormative due to the compulsory of heteronormativity and rejection by society, family, and friends.[19] Joteria-Muxerista educators explain that healing also stems from the multidimensional fatigue, which is an extension of a "racial battle fatigue" (Smith, Yosso, and Solorzano, 2011) that students of color who are also queer, trans, women, disabled and/or poor experience due to racism, racial microaggressions, and systemic violence that cause harm to people's spirit that may sabotage their dreams, hopes, and desires.[20]

hooks argues that theory and praxis emerge from a place of healing as a result of all the pain and trauma under ongoing systemic violence. Racism, sexism, xenophobia, homophobia, transphobia, and ableism continue to cause so much pain and harm to marginalized communities on a daily basis, including BIPOC educators. Indeed, Sandibel Borges, a queer migrant studies scholar, emphasizes how BIPOC women and femme's important contributions to the academy as teachers and scholars in the fields of ethnic and feminist studies have caused personal health issues and misfortune.[21] In other words, educators in higher education experience multidimensional fatigue as much as their students. One main cause on why Borges's and others alike own health and wellness are at stake is due to the exploitation of their labor in academia. For instance, when she teaches about systemic violence she may become subjected to oppressive discourse as well as triggered by unresolved trauma. She shares her pedagogical strategies, known as "trickle-up pedagogy, " or tools to "challenge the neoliberal university's exploitation of historical trauma to meet its own 'diversity' goals."[22] In other words, neoliberal universities recruit the labor of BIPOC women and femme faculty in the name of "diversity." Under this model, their teaching and research are exploited and challenged by privileged students in predominantly white institutions. Those who teach service courses, known as "diversity" courses, fulfill the general education requirements for all students who are pursuing various majors. For example, feminist and ethnic studies courses fall under a "diversity" course, which are made available to students outside of the feminist and ethnic studies major. As a result, the majority of students enrolled in these courses are in the Science, Technology, Engineering, and Mathematics (STEM) field. The lack of institutional support for BIPOC women and femme educators allows the ongoing extraction of their labor and burnout.

Similarly, Borges's pedagogical strategies aims to challenge power dynamics in the classroom by ensuring that BIPOC women, femmes, queer, trans, and gender-nonconforming students "see the classroom as *their* space instead of being props for other students' learning."[23] In essence, the classroom becomes a healing space that validates their lived experiences and daily acts of resistance. Moreover, Borges employs feminist and queer healing practices outside the classroom as a way to build a community that centers the well-being of BIPOC women and femme educators to prevent burnout and disrupt the demand to produce knowledge under a capitalist ableist model. Borges's feminist and queer healing methods remind me that these practices are necessary to enact an engaged pedagogy because of its emphasis on well-being. hooks's more than twenty years of teaching made her aware of the ways bourgeois academic institutions aim to objectify the teacher through a binary category of mind/body, which devalues wholeness and/or well-being of a teacher. Here, she says:

> This support reinforces the dualistic separation of public and private, encouraging students to see no connection between life practices, habits of being, and the roles of professors. The idea of the intellectual questing for union of mind, body, and spirit had been replaced with notions that being smart meant that one was inherently emotionally unstable and that the best in oneself emerged in one's academic work. This meant that whether academics were drug addicts, alcoholics, batterers, or sexual abusers, the only important aspect of our identity

was whether or not our minds functioned, whether we were able to do our jobs in the classroom.[24]

hooks finds that academia privileges educators who are "objective" in the classroom to ensure that their lived experiences would not interfere with their pedagogy. However, such pedagogy reproduces a hierarchy within the classroom that is not concerned with a liberatory education for their students nor for themselves that may reproduce harm and erasure of students of color lived experiences as a form of knowledge production. My Indigiqueer Zapotec feminist pedagogy aims to create a different form of teaching and learning to collectively heal from historical trauma is urgent and necessary. Also, I am reminded of the radical compassion that I have for my students means that I must also have radical compassion for myself. In my journey towards self-determination as an Indigenous queer woman I and others must continue to protect our own health and well-being as much as we aim to build theory and praxis that are healing and holistic As hooks affirms, as educators we "can be a witness, testifying that we can create a feminist theory, a feminist practice, a revolutionary feminist movement that can speak directly to the pain that is within folks, and offer them healing words, healing strategies, healing theory."[25] In other words, Black, Indigenous, women of color feminist and queer theory aims to foster pedagogies of care and mutuality. My Indigenous Zapotec feminist pedagogy aims to offer healing words, healing strategies, and healing theory that disrupt the binary of mind/body so that both educators and students inside and outside the classroom prioritize self-determination and collective liberation.

Conclusion

I model for my students how to challenge ourselves *inside* the classroom as much as we challenge systemic inequalities *outside* the classroom. I have offered my *tequio,* or community labor, to increase Indigenous visibility both on and off campus. I, like many Indigenous youth, experienced discrimination and racism by mestizo Latinx peers who used derogatory terms like *oaxaquita* to dehumanize us. bell hooks's liberatory pedagogical practices and tools have been a transformative experience for me as I initially struggled to teach a diverse student population on difficult topics. In my process of developing a pedagogy that is healing and transformative, I have made theory accessible to students who are invested in liberatory education. hooks engaged pedagogy made me use strategic storytelling to develop counternarratives so that students can be met with radical compassion rather than judgment in the classroom.

I also employ deep reciprocity that gives students agency in the classroom to analyze course materials, produce knowledge, and learn the various ways on how to be an effective ally on social justice issues outside of the classroom. A deep reciprocity that is grounded in my Guelaguetza values of collectivism and reciprocity makes it possible for me to develop meaningful relationships with students outside of the classroom. I had both the honor and privilege to work collaboratively with students through organizing on campus by co-founding a student campus organization and developed workshops on campus to disrupt monolithic narratives of diasporic Indigenous people.

As an Indigenous (Zapotec) feminist teacher, my pedagogical strategies further aim to challenge the logics of settler colonialism that erase Native and Indigenous people. As hooks reminds me that envisioning my wholeness takes courage, particularly as a first-generation Indigiqueer (Zapotec) feminist scholar that comes from a working-class background. My self-determination has allowed me to develop my own pedagogy to also recognize the wholeness of students and embracing their differences in the classroom. My pedagogy is concerned with healing from historical intergenerational trauma, particularly the erasure and Indigenous elimination of Indigiqueer people who have always existed within our communities. Theory and praxis are embodied by new generations of Indigenous people who aim to regenerate our knowledge systems, practices, and new traditions that do not reproduce gender colonial hierarchies or exclusion of Indigiqueer people in leadership positions. Thus my pedagogical praxis is rooted in healing to do social justice work within and outside the classroom., which is inspired by hooks, as well as Indigenous feminist educators, Chicana/Latina educators, Joteria-Muxerista educators, and queer migrant scholars who aim to build an effective learning environment to build theory and praxis rooted in healing. As a result, curriculum becomes relevant to students, including students' understanding of their privileges and oppression as systemic rather than individual.

Notes

1   Following Indigenous protocols, I introduce the setting and myself which is important for context and meaning. For more, see Timothy S. Pedro and Sweeney Windchief, *Applying Indigenous Research Methods: Storying with Peoples and Communities* (New York: Routledge, 2019).

2   In 2015, UC Santa Barbara was designated as a Hispanic-serving institution (HSI). A college or university is considered an HSI if at least 25 percent of its undergraduate students are Hispanic.

3   Anita Tijerna Revilla, Joana Nunez, Jose Manuel Santilla Blanco, and Sergio
    A. Gonzalez, "Brown Queer Feminist Strategies for Social Transformation," in
    Handbook of Latinos and Education : Theory, Research, and Practice, ed. Enrique G.
    Murillo, second edition (New York: Routledge, 2022), 22–34.

4   Juanita Tate, 66, "South L.A. Community Activist," *Los Angeles Times*, July 8, 2004,
    Retrieved August 18, 2023, https://www.latimes.com/archives/la-xpm-2004-jul-08-
    me-tate8-story.html.

5   The term *Guelaguetza* is more commonly used in the *Valles Centrales* region of
    Oaxaca while *Gowtzona* is more commonly used in the Sierra Juarez region.

6   bell hooks, "Language: Teaching New Worlds/New Words," in *Teaching to
    Transgress: Education as the Practice of Freedom* (New York: Routledge Taylor &
    Francis Group, 1994), 174.

7   Linda Prieto and Sofia A. Villenas, "Pedagogies from *Nepantla*: *Testimonio*,
    Chicana/Latina Feminisms and Teacher Education Classrooms," *Equity &
    Excellence in Education* 45, no. 3 (2012): 411–29.

8   Ibid., 424.

9   bell hooks, "Confronting Class in the Classroom," in *Teaching to Transgress:
    Education as the Practice of Freedom* (New York: Routledge, 1994), 181.

10 Ibid., 186.

11 Leanne Betamosake Simpson, "Land as Pedagogy and Rebellious Transformation,"
    Decolonization, Indigeneity, Education & Society 3, no. 3 (2014), https://jps.library.
    utoronto.ca/index.php/des/article/view/22170.

12 Ibid., 7.

13 Ibid., 13.

14 Jill Cowan, "Why Graduate Students at U.C. Santa Cruz Are Striking," *The New
    York Times*, February 11, 2020, https://www.nytimes.com/2020/02/11/us/ucsc-
    strike.html.

15 bell hooks, "Theory as Liberatory Practice," in *Teaching to Transgress: Education as
    the Practice of Freedom* (New York: Routledge, 1994), 59–75.

16 Ibid. 61.

17 Ibid. 70.

18 Revilla, et al., "Brown Queer Feminist Strategies for Social Transformation," 25.

19 Ibid., 26.

20 Ibid., 27.

21 Sandibel Borges, "Trickle-up Pedagogy and Queer Healing: Navigating Historical
    Trauma in the Neoliberal University," *Feminist Formations* 34, no. 2 (Summer
    2022): 197–213.

22 Ibid., 199.

23 Ibid., 207.

24 hooks, "Theory as Liberatory Practice," 16.

25 Ibid., 75.

Reading Circle as a Model of Cultivating Engaged Pedagogical Praxes

Savannah Geidel and Maia Butler

Institutional Context—Maia Butler

Since joining the faculty at University of North Carolina Wilmington as Assistant Professor of African American Literature in Fall 2017, I have been involved in numerous initiatives designed to build capacity for educators to better support an increasingly diverse student body. The demographics of our faculty and students are not representative of our surrounding community or our region. For instance, Black-identified faculty and students have remained steadily at about six percent of the total number of their counterparts. Though we occupy territory historically stewarded by numerous Indigenous peoples, we currently have two Indigenous faculty members on campus. In contrast, our staff, performing essential duties that keep the whole campus operational and also performing roles that are often overlooked, such as providing formal and informal support and encouragement to the students who share their racial or socioeconomic backgrounds, are overwhelmingly members of marginalized communities.

I am a queer Black woman whose research and teaching situates me in English as a departmental home, but also in the programs of Africana Studies, Women's and Gender Studies, and Interdisciplinary Studies as Affiliate Faculty. As is common for multiple marginalized faculty members, I have felt compelled to provide representation and advocacy in a number of various roles and efforts across campus. From 2017 to 2019, I served as Diversity and Inclusion Pedagogy Fellow in the university's Center for Teaching Excellence (CTE), developing initiatives and resources for faculty members. From 2020 to 2023, I served on the College of Arts and Sciences (now College of Humanities, Social Sciences and the Arts, as of July 1, 2023) Access, Equity, Diversity (AED) Committee and collaborated in research that led to co-authoring a report of recommendations to the college on priorities to improve campus climate for faculty, staff, and students. This report led me to steward a subgroup of the AED Committee through drafting strategic guidance for our college's administrators to implement policies and practices for each priority identified in the previous report. As of Fall 2024, the Office of Institutional Diversity and Inclusion at UNCW, which oversees all college-level diversity committees has been dismantled by our upper administration, so resource allocation and accountability to the objectives of the strategic guidance are unlikely.

My experiences as a faculty member participating in these efforts, compounded with those I undertook years ago as a graduate student at another institution, have informed my shifting understanding of the possibilities, pitfalls, and impacts of diversity work. I have come to believe that workshops and trainings designed to make one's syllabus inclusive via the redesign of instructional materials for improved accessibility and universal design accomplish two things: they allow for the university administration to attach resources to stated commitments, and for faculty members to demonstrate to administrators, colleagues, and students that they are making efforts toward providing an equitable education. However, the band aid of inclusive language in a syllabus does not mitigate or redress an approach to the subject matter that doesn't empower students to address the structures of oppression defining their field and impacting both their individual lives and the potential of their communities to construct freer and more just futures. In short, I am all the more convinced that fundamental principles of justice-centered pedagogy must be the grounding for: community building in the classroom; facilitation of content delivery, rather than banking models of education; ethics of care for the students' whole persons; and the connection of their class work to the impacts on students' families, communities, regions, and beyond.

Shortly after bell hooks's untimely passing in 2021, the UNCW Center for Teaching Excellence was preparing for Spring semester pedagogical reading circles; these groups are offered each semester and provide interested faculty with the opportunity to build community and to share and develop their pedagogical practices. I had also been invited to Co-Chair the Racial Justice Learning Community (RJLC) that semester was a position funded by CTE. The RJLC was formed the year prior in response to pressure on our university's Chancellor, Jose Sartarelli, who has since retired, to improve the campus climate around race and racism. Following the state-sanctioned murder of George Floyd in the summer of 2020, our students held demonstrations on campus and entered talks with our administrators. In one such talk, Chancellor Sartarelli proclaimed "All lives matter," to widespread dismay and demands for transparent reparative actions that would show the institution's commitment to valuing and affirming our Black students and their cultures. With this context in mind, I understood that the meaningful work to shift student experiences on our campus would likely come from those of us who have the most sustained contact with them and the most investment in their holistic development. I observed that the changes our students needed might be most impactful in the places and with whom they spent the most time, the classroom and their teachers.[1]

I envisioned the circle as involving faculty members across campus, staff members such as librarians and advisers, graduate students and tutors, as well as members of our community who hold teaching and facilitation responsibilities in a variety of public-facing and -serving organizations, and thus would hold valuable experiences and insights that would benefit us on campus. Ultimately, I saw an immersion in hooks's teaching trilogy as an opportunity for new and seasoned educators alike to revisit Black feminist pedagogical principles that could significantly shift the terrain on which we scaffold all our practices. I proposed the Teaching to Transgress Trilogy Reading circle and was given the green light.[2]

Framing the Reading Circle

My plan for the circle was to base our work around the three texts of hooks trilogy: *Teaching to Transgress: Education as the Practice of Freedom* (1994), *Teaching Community: A Pedagogy of Hope* (2003) and *Teaching Critical Thinking: Practical Wisdom* (2010). I envisioned the circle to be a space for thinking about how, almost thirty years after the publication of her first teaching text, hooks's engaged pedagogy not only remains prescient but also offers invaluable vision and guidance in the midst of the global Covid-19 pandemic and resulting shifts in education. Her initial collection of pedagogical strategies and reflections, *Teaching to Transgress*, seeks to counter the devaluation of teaching (in relation to producing scholarship), emphasizes the possibilities of both informing classroom praxis, and centers pleasure in communal learning as an act of resistance.[3] What can a reminder about the possibility, and even necessity, of pleasure in the classroom space (face to face, online, community) teach us in the pandemic era of social distance that has led to widespread feelings of loneliness and estrangement, anxiety, overwhelm, and apathy? Her second text, *Teaching Community,* shifts to include reflections on teaching outside of academia; hooks urges us to (re)commit to making revolutionary ideas accessible and "expand our communities of resistance."[4] She begins with the imperative to address public narratives that work to legitimize and proliferate claims that cultural studies programming promoting justice in education is neither rigorous nor constructive, all too familiar claims in our contemporary era of politically motivated and deliberate misreadings of critical race theory.[5] Building on the previous texts' examinations of the devaluation of the pleasures of teaching and learning in general and the value of justice-centered teaching in specific, *Teaching Critical Thinking* frames the exigent need for practical wisdom to address these problems in hooks's recollections of her foray into college education during the civil rights struggle, when even in that new age of equality in education, old hierarchies of race, class, and gender remained intact.[6] Of course, this paradox persists in the present as our own UNCW university administrators scramble to respond to student demands for access and equity in the #BLM era, at times facing resistance from increasingly hostile state legislatures (who control funding allocation—ours recently requested a full accounting of DEI activities, participants, and related expenses for the past three years), state university system (who make and enforce system-level policies such as our Compelled Speech Policy and are considering halting the tenure process), and our Board of Trustees (who participate in the tenure process and one of whom recently overreached and called for professors on our campus to be "punished" for protesting a compromised awards process). We know that we at UNCW are not alone in the broader national landscape of backlash against DEI and justice-centered pedagogy on campus and we do our work in solidarity with others in such locations as Texas, Florida, Indiana, Kansas, Kentucky, and others.[7] In these enduring contexts, hooks's work is evergreen; her recognition of teaching as a fundamentally political act and her call for the creation of transformative spaces of learning that are counterhegemonic and anticolonial continue to provide educators with the theory and praxis needed to co-create participatory spaces of self-recovery and collective liberation.[8]

Over the course of six weeks, our reading circle met bimonthly to discuss each of hooks's three collections of essays and teachings across two sessions each. In the spirit of hooks's own conception of a learning community, I envisioned the involvement of students, community members, and educators. However, scheduling issues challenged the availability of various learning community members, such as school teachers' daytime work hours, university faculty member's evening time childcare needs, and community members' time commitments to other organizing work. Over fifty folks initially expressed interest in participating, but the time slot we settled on only allowed for the inclusion of about half that number. In future iterations of the reading circle, broader impact and more inclusive discussion groups would be achieved by offering two sessions with different times concurrently or by offering the reading circle several times throughout the year on a rotating schedule.

In my bell hooks Teaching Trilogy Reading Circle proposal, I crafted the description of our activities and learning objectives as follows:

> In this pedagogical learning community, we will gather to read, discuss, and implement bell hooks's invaluable insights derived from a lifetime of teaching inside and outside the traditional classroom. Together, we will establish a supportive and generous space to tell the truth, to ask difficult questions, and develop transformational pedagogical praxis. The use of a longform or digital journal devoted to this pedagogical development journey is highly recommended. As engaged participants in our own learning, we will make use of these journals to take reflective notes and record questions that occur as we read. At each meeting, we will each offer our questions for the group's reflection and discussion. After each meeting, we will individually continue to reflect on our communally developed insights in the pages of our journals and begin to stretch our ideas toward implementation strategies. We'll open each session with an invitation to share our reflections before discussing the next readings and offering our questions about them.

After completing the readings, participating in collaborative learning sessions, and making use of their journal for reflection and ideation, participants will be familiar with and ready to practice implementing the following concepts:

- Co-created learning communities
- Engaged pedagogies
- Pedagogies of hope
- Pedagogies of care
- Anticolonial intersectional feminist pedagogies

In order to set the tone for the first meeting of the reading circle, and to familiarize folks with reflecting in their journals in advance of the circle discussions, I crafted Reflection Prompts I framed as "Preparing to Learn with Intention."[9]

- What brings you the most pleasure and joy about teaching and learning?
- What was a formative moment in your teaching and learning journey that informed where you are on your journey currently, or where you hope to be?

- When have you felt most empowered in your teaching and learning work and when have you felt most disempowered?
- What can your responses to the previous questions teach you about the spaces you are working to, or hoping to, co-create in the future?
- What difficulties or challenges have you experienced while teaching and learning during the pandemic? And in times of politically motivated challenges to teaching about race and social justice?
- What do you hope to learn from bell hooks about co-creating equitable, accessible, and engaged learning spaces?
- What do you hope to learn from bell hooks about educating for social justice?

Reflection Prompts for the text's introduction and first chapter, "Engaged Pedagogy" of *Teaching to Transgress*, were provided ahead of time so that folks could reflect in their journals while they read. Circle members were invited, but not required, to share their personal reflections. In that way, the journaling prompts were sometimes used as touchstones for discussion, but the discussion often developed organically from there.

Introduction:

- How does this introduction begin to define the following:
    - Active and engaged pedagogy
    - Resistance (on part of teachers and students) and fear
    - Flexibility and adaptability
- How does hooks's identity inform the development of her praxis? (Black, woman, Southern, rural, class?) How do our own identities inform our own respective developing praxes?

Chapter 1: "Engaged Pedagogy"

- What do I know already about engaged pedagogy? How do schools and educators use this phrase?
- How has reading this chapter shifted my understanding of engaged pedagogy?
- Many folks are familiar with hooks's work responding to and extending Friere's work, but how about Hanh? What does care for spirit and well-being add to our ideas about what is possible with critical pedagogy?

- Does the university encourage or make space and time for our own self-actualization? How or how not? Do we, or can we, make this space and time for ourselves and each other? How or how not?
- Practical Wisdom Questions:
  - ○ P. 15—Do we find this to be true, that students want to dwell in the personal in class discussions? If so, how do we bridge those contributions or confessions toward systems thinking?
  - ○ P. 17—What does it mean, or what can it look like, for educators to concede power and authority in the classroom?
  - ○ P. 18—How can teaching be a place to reinforce existing systems of domination? What do these look like in the classroom? Does educational administration promote or reinforce these systems?

Because I was teaching a graduate seminar in Africana Studies during the semester I facilitated the reading circle, and many of my graduate students were also working as Instructors of Record in our Department of English, I invited them to participate in the reading circle. Savannah Geidel accepted the invitation and became an important thought partner for me in the crafting of reflection questions and discussion facilitation. Further, we reflected together on the impact of the reading circle on our own pedagogies, as well as the stated impacts of the other participants. Savannah's observations about how the reading and the discussions with other participants expanded her conception of who are essential members of teaching communities. Her valuable insights have influenced my own sense of how to reconceptualize, revise, and revisit the reading circle in the future.

Reading Circle as Promotive of Transgressing Departmental and Disciplinary Borders—Savannah Geidel

I participated in the bell hooks's reading circle during my last semester as a graduate student in the English Department. Prior to joining the reading circle, I had been assigned essays by hooks in teacher preparation courses, both as an undergrad in Secondary Education and a master's student in English.[10] However, my opportunity to thoroughly discuss how to implement hooks's pedagogies was limited. Thus, I was excited to join the reading circle and develop my teaching practice further.

Though I initially anticipated the reading circle would help me enhance my teaching, I quickly came to realize it would also help me develop a commitment to establishing interdisciplinary connections with other educators. During the first meeting, I was struck by how few people I recognized; it was the first time I stopped to think about the multitude of people who occupy the university. While intimidating at first, the mix of disciplinary backgrounds introduced me to a collaborative possibility of teaching I had not previously experienced in traditional education courses.

Formal teacher training commonly frames teaching as occurring in designated spaces, such as the classrooms we teach in or the offices we grade in. Many education courses focus on research or theory, which is necessary content for future teachers, but it usually becomes a conversation on how to manage *your* classroom or how to teach *your* content-area. Yet, most K-12 teachers are expected to collaborate as interdisciplinary "teams," a task that can be daunting for beginning teachers, especially those who have little experience working with teachers outside of their content area.

In graduate programs, teaching is often seen as secondary. Thus, teaching assistants have limited opportunity to discuss ideas related to course materials or pedagogy. In my experience, we were required to take one teacher preparation course, which was asynchronous and focused primarily on pedagogical theory. We did have monthly check-in meetings, which allowed us to share ideas amongst each other, but given that there were few of us, these discussions did not allow for a larger picture of what was occurring on campus. Furthermore, there was little discussion about working with or alongside other disciplines or departments. As a composition instructor focused on Writing across the Disciplines, it was challenging to decipher what writing would be most meaningful for my students, as I had little to no insight into what was being assigned in their other courses. Though I believe my courses were effective in preparing students for college writing, I was often left wondering if they were able to make connections between our class and their larger educational goals.

A lack of collaborative focus in teacher training perpetuates a narrow understanding of institutions and reinforces the expectation that our work will be completed independently. For beginning teachers, the lack of collaborative work may lead to a feeling of isolation and make it more difficult to receive input from others. Seeking the support of others is made more difficult when barriers (both mental and physical) are in place; a department in which offices are separated by closed doors is less inviting and may reinforce the idea that one should be able to handle problems or concerns independently. Such barriers may lead to an increased feeling of imposter syndrome in which the individual may feel unprepared or unqualified for needing support in the first place, especially when compounded with anxiety, depression, and/or other life factors. For all members of a campus, the lack of collaboration limits the opportunities we have to develop our teaching practice and recognize our content-area as a piece of a larger puzzle. Though we can research new methods, it is primarily through discussion that we develop clearer understandings of how to implement new techniques and why such methods may be beneficial to ourselves and our students. When collaboration is present, teachers are able to workshop assignments or course materials, recognize different perspectives about their content area, and affirm their place within the campus community.

Meaningful collaboration is necessary to develop and enhance critical and engaged pedagogies that form connections between disciplines, ideas, and communities. In a conversational chapter "Ron Scapp," hooks notes that "to create a cultural climate where biases can be challenged and changed, all border crossings must be seen as valid and legitimate."[11] Though we often do not refer to our departmental divisions as "borders," departmental divisions, both physical and metaphorical, disallow us from easily working together. When we begin to come together despite these borders, we learn from and with each other, expanding our understanding of the work we do and the professional spaces we inhabit. Crossing departmental borders creates pathways to new methods of thinking and being, which are vital for pedagogies that challenge biases and lead to change.

Since teaching (and learning) can be mentally and emotionally taxing, establishing places on campus dedicated to an ethic of care can help mitigate the feeling of isolation and disconnection that often arise when working independently. Tending to our own and others' basic human needs positions education and the campus as a more holistic space that recognizes and welcomes each member of the community fully. Being familiar with others promotes an environment that is less stressful and more engaging as it challenges the prioritization of individuality. For teachers and students alike, this leads to education being a more joyful practice that is less about competing with others and more focused on the benefit of collaboration. Furthermore, connections across campus foster an appreciation of the work being done by our colleagues and promote a more supportive environment. Though our content areas may differ, cross-disciplinary conversation and collaboration emphasize the intersection of disciplines, promoting multiple perspectives and celebrating differences.

The bell hooks Teaching Trilogy Reading Circle created such space for cross-disciplinary collaboration. The reading circle was made up of faculty from multiple departments, including education, art, and nursing, as well as administrators, librarians, teaching assistants, and other university staff members. Though many of us had not met before the circle, we offered each other support, care, and love each week, helping each other work toward implementing engaged pedagogies. Bridging our separation and recognizing our commonalities despite differences in discipline, position, or experience allowed us to see teaching as a community practice, assist each other in implementing new and inclusive methods, and collaborate in challenging inequitable and oppressive campus policies.

The desire to revise our pedagogies and practice in a group setting highlighted a dedication to deepening our understanding of our students, ourselves, and the place(s) we occupied within the campus. In our meetings, we fused our personal experiences with hooks's work to grapple with challenges, share celebrations, and navigate confusion that we encountered within our classrooms, departments, and the university. As we discussed the text in relation to our professional experiences, our individual insights provided new ways of approaching our work, allowing us to implement engaged pedagogies in a meaningful way. As a beginning composition instructor, I found these discussions incredibly valuable; I focused my courses on interdisciplinary research and writing but was largely unfamiliar with the work being done in other departments on campus. Having the opportunity to familiarize myself with the work of other faculty members and the curriculums my students were involved in allowed me to alter my classes to better fit the larger context of the university.

Our participation in the circle also reflected our communal dedication to helping our students and each other grow, maintaining the care and love that hooks promotes. In *Teaching Critical Thinking*, hooks and Scapp write, "Collaborating with diverse thinkers to work toward a greater understanding of the dynamics of race, gender, and class is essential for those of us who want to move beyond one-dimensional ways of thinking, being, and writing."[12] Since each of us entered the space with different identities and backgrounds, we were able to approach the text and our classroom experiences from multiple perspectives, shifting away from the one-dimensional standpoint toward a more holistic, inclusive mindset. Our group discussions helped introduce us to new ways of thinking and being that altered the way we approached the classroom and our everyday lives.

During one of our meetings, we developed the saying "revise, don't cancel" in response to the harmful effects of Cancel Culture. We revisited this saying often while working through how to engage students in meaningful conversations and create more inclusive, welcoming spaces on campus without alienating or shaming others. Our mantra of "revise, don't cancel" spoke to the need for discourse that prioritizes learning and growth, rather than shy away from difficult conversations in a manner that dismisses or disregards harmful and/or hateful discourse, as ignoring the issue further perpetuates racism, sexism, ableism, and other forms of oppression. Reframing Cancel Culture as Revising Culture helped shift us away from a right/wrong mentality toward a mentality of growth and care that reinforces a dedication to change. Though this mantra may have developed from research, through sharing our experiences, concerns, and input, we were able to engage in an authentic discussion that led to tangible methods, all while underscoring that we were not alone in our efforts to work toward a more just community.

While our focus on "revise, don't cancel" was just one of our collective lessons, it emphasized our communal support of each other and our students. The ability to work through these conversations as a group not only helped us connect with each other but also spoke to the value of multiple perspectives in learning how to better support our students and create spaces for meaningful conversations. What grew from our weekly discussions was a dedication to challenge inequality and one-dimensional ways of thought with the goal of creating a truly inclusive and equitable space for our students and ourselves.

My participation in the bell hooks Teaching Trilogy Reading Circle continues to alter my view of teaching. After graduation, I taught English in a community college University Studies department where I worked closely with the other English faculty members as well as faculty and staff in other disciplines. The department's dedication to collaboration highlighted the importance of working as a team to support our students and each other. Currently, I am a writing lecturer in an agricultural institute where I work alongside faculty from different disciplines and students from various majors and backgrounds. Similar to my previous position, the close proximity of colleagues in other disciplines promotes frequent sharing of ideas and insights into motivating our students and ensuring their continued success.

Participating in the reading circle prepared me for working with others on a regular basis and continues to inform the way I interact with my colleagues and my students. I continue to use the ideas and lessons from our bell hooks Teaching Trilogy Reading Circle discussions to make connections across campus and engage in interdisciplinary conversations. I recognize that I have been incredibly fortunate to have colleagues who are invested in forming cross-disciplinary connections in both positions I have held after graduation. Though new faculty may not always have similar opportunities to engage in this work immediately, I believe that hooks's work, especially when shared in a group setting, can foster cross-disciplinary opportunities that are missing from many institutions.

Conclusion

For beginning teachers and seasoned faculty alike, hooks's work serves as a reminder that we are not alone in the classroom, and our departments are not the only spaces we can exist or think in; there is an entire university outside our office doors, and across that expanse, there are relationships waiting to bloom. An ethic of care and collaboration are the fertile soil that nourishes these relationships.

When we commit to learning and growing in collaboration, we create communities of care that hold us accountable to ourselves and to each other. These networks of support provide the solid grounding from which we can more effectively transgress traditional views of education and move toward intersectional ways of thinking and practicing, in which we see our students and ourselves as whole beings. We hope that the circles of care and collaboration that our bell hooks Teaching Trilogy Reading Circle inspires become nourishing ground on which to develop insurgent pedagogies that both support our students' whole beings and intervene in increasingly stifling or hostile educational environments in the era of conservative pushes for "anti-Woke" education.

The reading circle is a model of how to make room for ourselves—as diverse collectives of educators—to commit to developing and sustaining pedagogical practices that center pleasure, equity, and care. We came to the circle with intentions to prevent our discussions from perpetuating racist, sexist, and classist ways of thinking, as well as narrow definitions of who educators are and the myriad valuable ways we support our students. While in the circle, we pushed ourselves from making reflections to planning practices that would prevent oppressive or exclusive ways of thinking that impact our respective classrooms and departmental communities. When we see each other—faculty, staff, students, visitors—as partners, as members of the same space or overlapping spaces, we can work together to create a just environment in which everyone's voice is heard and in which education truly is the practice of freedom.

Teaching to Transgress Reading Circle Participants

Natalie Coe, Biology
Amanda Coyne, English
Regina R. Félix, Department of World Languages and Cultures
Courtney Johnson, Photography
Carolyn Kleman, School of Nursing
Jeanne M. Persuit, Communication Studies
Kati Sudnick, Communication Studies

Notes

1   Molly Wiant Cummins, "Locations of Possibility: Reengaging Embodied Pedagogy
     as an Act of Resistance," *Feminist Pedagogy* 3, no. 1 (2023): 1: article 5; Indeed,
     Wiant Cummins observes, "With no macro-level policy, teachers are, once again,
     the changemakers at the micro, where we have more control: Our own classrooms."

2   When I planned and facilitated the reading circle, I did not intend to produce
     research from the participants' collective conversations. For this reason, at the
     outset of our meetings, we did not discuss ethical use of the knowledge we
     produced together. Since the opportunity to write about our experience has
     come up, we have shared our draft with the participants at the circle and invited
     concerns, reflections, and suggestions for how to ethically represent our time and
     discussions together. I have also included at the close of this piece, the names of
     participants who wish to be credited as co-creators of the knowledge that informs
     this chapter.

3   bell hooks, *Teaching to Transgress: Education as the Practice of Freedom* (New York:
     Routledge, 1994), 10.

4   bell hooks, *Teaching in Community: A Pedagogy of Hope* (New York: Routledge,
     2003), xi–xii.

5   Ibid., xii–xiii.

6   bell hooks, *Teaching Critical Thinking: Practical Wisdom* (New York: Routledge,
     2010), 3.

7   Frances B. Henderson writes about her experiences as a Black Feminist educator
     at a liberal arts institution during this sort of political upheaval that results
     in increased labor, emotional and material for instructors doing the already
     challenging work of teaching students to transgress dominant power relations;
     Frances B. Henderson, "Black Feminist Pedagogy in White Southern Spaces,"
     Feminist Pedagogy 3, no. 1 (2023): 1–3: article 12.

8　hooks, *Teaching to Transgress*, "Introduction."

9　See Maria Guajardo's work on journaling as a valuable pathway for reflection and self-transformation for teachers committed to hooks's conception of engaged pedagogy; Maria Guajardo "Engaged Pedagogy and Journaling: A Pathway to Self-Transformation," *Feminist Pedagogy* 3, no. 1 (2023): 1–2: article 8.

10　Both the bachelor's and master's programs I completed were relatively small. I recognize that my experience will differ greatly from others and do not wish to insinuate that all teacher prep lacks cross-disciplinary collaboration. Furthermore, I do not wish to discredit the programs I completed or others like them.

11　hooks, *Teaching to Transgress*, 131.

12　hooks, *Teaching Critical Thinking*, 37.

19

Intersectional Latinidad as a Critical Praxis Connecting College to Classroom: Lessons, Lineages, and Legacies of Liberatory Pedagogy from *Teaching to Transgress*

Alyssa Garcia, Margarita Mojica and Glenview Middle School
Students of Latinx Workshop

Introduction

I always found it ironic during graduate school that all the focus was on research and the dissertation, with no discussion on training or pedagogy. Yet, if/when we become a professor a majority of our time is devoted toward teaching. And the learning curve is steep. As a newly minted Ph.D., *Teaching to Transgress* was my life vest. hooks's text became a step-by-step guide to my feminist pedagogy. I sought to implement Radical Engaged Pedagogy by modeling my classroom praxis according to three of her core tenants:

1) Communal learning as an act of resistance: "To hear each other, to listen to one another, is an exercise in recognition."[1]

hooks explains a central goal of transformative pedagogy: making the classroom a democratic setting where everyone contributes and takes responsibility for learning. Building community in the classroom by validating each individual voice generates excitement, creates a climate of openness, and fosters intellectual rigor.[2] As an educator, envisioning the classroom as a shared/ co-created participatory space from which to recognize one another's presence, I endeavored to increase student engagement by facilitating dialog, promoting active listening, and encouraging collaborative learning.

2) Creating alternatives to traditional systems of education that enforce dominance: "Systems of domination are already at work in the classroom to silence the voices of marginalized groups."[3]

hooks reminds us that education is not politically neutral. Traditional teaching styles reflect the notion of a single norm of thought and experience. These biases distort education while upholding and maintaining white supremacy, imperialism, sexism, and racism.[4] Unlike the top-down banking method of teaching, a liberatory classroom learning model is centered on a bottom-up counter hegemonic praxis that deconstructs old epistemologies, and validates nonconforming subjugated knowledge.

3) *Conscientization:*[5] "Critical thinking is the primary element allowing the possibility of change."[6]

hooks emphasizes how the critical process of theorizing enables and empowers. Self-defined identities that emerge from oppressed groups become an important standpoint from which to critique dominant structures.[7] As identity gives purpose to struggle, reflecting upon students' lived experiences makes education more meaningful for underserved communities. Allowing students to inhabit their positionalities supports different ways of knowing from which students develop their agency in the classroom.

This chapter examines the deployment of these tenets through a case study of how a *Latinx Feminisms* college course[8] inspired the creation of a parallel middle school *Latinx Workshop*. After providing an overview of the college course and origins of *Latinx Workshop*, we highlight four curricular modules: "Culture & Experience," "Body & Media," "Violence," and "Community & Action." For each we outline the course themes/objectives to the workshops' design and situate their pedagogical impact in relation to hooks.

College Course: *Latinx Feminisms*

In the spring of 2020, recognized as a top middle school educator in the state, I received the Illinois Golden Apple Fellowship. With this exciting opportunity to take a sabbatical and attend college-level courses at Northwestern University I enrolled in *Latinx Feminisms*. Profe Garcia organized the class according to three themes:

(1) *Politics, History, and Social Movements* explored identity politics via the creation, construction, and use of the term "Latinx." This section situated the terms used within past/current activism. As a class, we discussed historical contexts, structural forces, actors, and events that affect the Latinx experience. Additionally, this section highlighted the contributions of Chicana/Latina feminist thought in the United States. (2) *Identity, Voice, and Border Theory*

reflected on the ways in which Latinx identity is negotiated via alternative modes of expression. This section promoted self-representation and testimonio by exploring Gloria Anzaldua's (1985) concept of *mestiza consciousness*.[9] (3) *Intersectionality and Representation* provided an analysis of the role race, gender, sexuality, and class play in the Latinx experience. This section explored the diversity of Latinx communities, while interrogating power and privileges within them. Intersectionality, as a framework, was utilized to discuss how race, gender, sexuality, and class are mediated amidst institutional structures of systematic oppressions such as popular culture, education, health, labor/work, immigration, globalization, transnationalism, citizenship, and violence.

The class utilized a variety of sources of knowledge ranging from newspapers, archives, books, academic articles, poetry, art, theater, films, and literature to incorporate interdisciplinary perspectives. Delivering course materials in varied formats promoted multiple perspectives to encourage critical thinking across disciplines. All assignments, activities and presentations, centered on student voice, were communally shared to prompt collective discussion and dialog. Lastly, the final project was an open format from which the student selected their own topic, content, medium. It was from this final project assignment that I designed and created the *Latinx Workshop* for my students at Glenview Middle School.

Middle School: The *Latinx Workshop*

For thirty years, I have taught bilingual Spanish classes at East Moline Middle School in East Moline, a small northwestern town of 21,000 in Illinois,[10] where the Latinx student population remains steadily climbing. Out of the 1,100 middle school population, roughly 330 (approximately 30 percent) are Latinx students who are first-generation or recently arrived immigrants predominantly from Mexico, Honduras, and Guatemala. Yet despite the ongoing growth of the Latinx population in the area, the percentage of Latinx teachers in the district has never risen above 10 percent in the past twenty-seven years. As a first-generation daughter of Mexican immigrants, I have been vocal about the dire need to recruit teachers of color who better reflect our student population. Yet, my concerns were often ignored or met with resistance. The district has much work to do toward diversifying its staff and curriculum.

When I took *Latinx Feminisms* with Profe Garcia, it was only the second time in my educational trajectory that I had a teacher who looked like me. I found myself devouring the material since none of this information was available in our middle school curriculum. Previously, when integrating 15–20 minutes of Latinx content to my classes, I had to locate resources on my own. Now with this new-found information, I had essential materials to incorporate to the lessons. Thereby, I created a tailored workshop for the middle school Latinx students modeled on the original *Latinx Feminisms* course. The program would curate a much-needed space for Latinx students centering their voices, experiences, culture, and history. They wanted and needed a space where they could be unapologetically Latina. And so, the *Latinx Workshop: Self-Care, Tertulia, and Hermandxd* began to take shape[11]; it would be the first of its kind in our corner of Illinois. I targeted seventh- and eighth-grade students who identify as Latina/x and/or LGBTQ+, given that this age is a critical juncture about learning who they are and how they want to be seen. The year-long workshop met bimonthly for ninety minutes after school.[12] It consisted of eleven sessions modeled after the college course, only tailored for a middle school audience. Each session tendered research-informed, interactive project-based learning.

Module: Culture and Experience

This module emphasizes the importance of student expression and interrogating one's social location. As hooks reminds us, "The focus on difference has the potential to revolutionize the classroom."[13] Pedagogy needs to connect to the lives of students for them to be active participants rather than passive consumers.[14] Tapping into the authority of their experiences counters traditional education models that promote estrangement from one's language or culture. As such, naming one's identity and making it a central standpoint from which to critique dominant structures and disrupt cultural imperialism become political resistance.

College Course Themes and Learning Objectives

- Identity Politics, Essentialism, and the Construction/Negotiation of *Latinidad*: Discussing and connecting personal identities in relation to each other, students build affinities, invest in team building, and develop community.
- Intersectionality: Students engage in consciousness raising by exploring the diversity of the Latinx experience via issues of race, gender, sexuality, and class.

- Latina/Chicana Feminist Thought and History: A bottom-up engagement with Latinx histories counters the silences and stereotypes of traditional curriculums. This spotlights the intellectual interventions of Latinx scholars to recognize our contributions.
- Community Transformation: An engagement with Latinx history prompts students to unlearn false narratives, counter stereotypes, and undo the silences in traditional curriculums.

Workshop Design and Activities

Identifying development and exploring intersectionality are of key importance to the Latinx middle school students as they negotiate between two cultures/languages, encounter racialization, and navigate sexualities amidst their transition from childhood to adolescence. This session elicits an interrogation of one's social location to discuss the complexity of *Latinidad*. It allows for a process of self-discovery where students critique dominant stereotypes, as they learn that they "come from greatness," as a means of developing a greater sense of self-worth. For example, in an activity about the social construction of gender, participants reflect upon: What messages have you heard about how girls should act or dress? Are those messages different for boys? How? Do you agree or disagree with these messages? Here, students use sticky notes to post their personal thoughts to chart paper on the wall, followed by lively collective discussion and analysis of how gender shapes their day-to-day lives. When these chart papers were displayed on a shared classroom wall, it elicited strong reactions from other classmates, serving as an impetus for recruitment.

Pedagogical Impact: Identity and Voice

This module prompts introspection; students reflect on who they are as Latinas. A critical pedagogy of liberation responds to students' concerns and embraces their experience as relevant ways of knowing.[15] The exploration of our history and diversity becomes a prideful celebration of what makes us "unique and marvelous." The acknowledgment that we are not all the same enables students an opportunity to shape their own perceptions of belonging, alongside mutual respect for others. This module provided, "a learning community where differences could be acknowledged, where we could finally all understand, accept, and affirm our ways of knowing as forged into history and relations of power."[16] It provides a safe protective space for personal expression without fear of criticism or ridicule. Ultimately, students develop a strong sense of themselves individually, as well as solidarity in relation to communitas.

With a pedagogical emphasis of "coming to voice" and the "complex recognition of its uniqueness"[17] participants can "see themselves" and personally connect to course material. Assignments such as testimonios and reflective journaling enable students to develop self-awareness. Learning about their history that was absent from school books, this module recognizes the primacy of voices that are often silenced, censored, or marginalized.[18] Students empower themselves against hegemonic representations that suffocate their authentic selves. Now validated, participants critique the top-down whitewashed school curriculum they receive. Countering invisibility and stereotypes, students rescue and tap into their subjugated knowledge, developing pride in who they are. Their voices were violently muffled. Yet today, they are shouting and raising their voices. The *Latinx Workshop* is a forum of self-recovery and actualization, a liberatory space in which their voices are *finally* heard.

Module: Body and Media

This module invites students to be purposeful in acknowledging, discussing, and processing information about our bodies. As hooks emphasizes, "We must return ourselves to a state of embodiment in order to deconstruct the way power has been traditionally orchestrated."[19] hooks specifies that a liberatory pedagogy demands that one purposefully work with, through, and against the limits of the body so as to restore our mind-body connection. Western metaphysical dualism teaches as though only the mind is present, reinforcing well-learned distinctions between private and public which make us believe that love has no place in the classroom.[20] The erasure of the body, denial of emotion, and repression of pleasure inhibit our capacity to be whole. Developing positive awareness about our bodies and bringing the "private" into a shared public dialog are key components of integrating wellness into the classroom.

College Course Theme and Learning Objectives

- The Cartesian Mind-Body Dichotomy: Students dissect and dismantle traditional gender roles.

- Patriarchy, Power, and Sexism: Breaking down inequalities theoretically develops independent thinking amidst the deconstruction of mainstream narratives and societal pressures.
- Double Consciousness, Objectification and Commodification: Demystifying the process of cultural production inspires students to break away from the stigma and shame of body talk.
- *Blanqueamiento*[21] and colorism (historically and contemporarily): Formulating a race-based critical feminist analysis of popular culture enables students to critique hegemonic beauty standards with alternative self-representations.

Workshop Design and Activities

In this module students are prompted to become aware of and honor their bodies. We employ somatic activities such as yoga and breathing exercises as a means of reducing stress and anxiety often brought about by the school day. Students report they are inundated with distorted messages from social media 24/7. In the activity "selfie talk," participants analyze popular fashion print magazines and social media platforms. They examine and critique who is featured, who is not represented, what themes predominate, and what messages are relayed about beauty. This reflection prompts discussion of white supremacy and *blanqueamiento*. After a historical review of the Spanish colonial caste system in Latin America, students consider the contemporary legacies of colorism within *Latinidad* today. The session propels many "aha" moments as they share personal experiences of double consciousness. Like hooks (1997) they reflect on how hegemonic values of whiteness can result in self-hatred for Brown-Black Latinx skin color, especially for those with Indigenous/Afro hair textures and features.[22] Members now can contextualize their own experiences of conformity and racialized pressures.

Pedagogical Impact: Latinx Magic and Healing

This module prompts students to cultivate their own mind-body connections to improve their mental and physical health so as to advance a more holistic idea of wellness with practices that reduce anxiety and relieve stress. hooks inspires us to utilize theory as a location of healing; when we heal the splitting of the body and mind, we attempt to recover ourselves and our experience.[23] Here, physical exercises like meditation alongside creative activities/art therapy provide students a healthy outlet to express themselves, center their feelings, relax, and find joy.

Destigmatizing ideas about therapy, the workshop encourages healthy self-talk to strengthen emotional function and regulation. Emotional response does not diminish academic purpose or intellectual practice. Rather, it enhances the classroom by allowing students to be seen as more than their work.[24] Students can learn to their full potential when they feel healthy, supported, and comfortable in the classroom. Here they are provided a safe outlet to acknowledge, contemplate, and share their changing emotions and validated without judgment. Connecting personal reflections with a critical race feminist critique of media facilitates the development of an empowered body image. Students take agency in their own representation, one that instills confidence, combats low self-esteem, affirms racial pride, celebrates diversity, and collectively builds self-love. The workshop becomes a mechanism from which to prioritize wellness and re-emphasize the importance of holistically taking care of our hearts, bodies, and minds.

Module: Violence

This module strives to give students a "take home" message by prompting reflective critical thinking and engagement of the world around them. As hooks highlights, "A liberatory feminist pedagogy works to resolve the issues that are most pressing in a student's daily life by enabling transgressions-a movement against and beyond boundaries that makes education the practice of freedom."[25] hooks considers theory as a practice that helps us survive; it is a necessary life-saving tool that makes our experiences valid. When theory emerges from concrete efforts to make sense of our everyday lives, it is rooted in an attempt to critically understand both the nature of our predicament and the means by which we might collectively engage in resistance that would transform our current reality.[26] Thus, teaching theory is a political act integral to resistance and revolution. This process of "naming our pain," enables the classroom to become a space of productive dissent and radical confrontation.

College Course Themes and Learning Objectives

- Institutional Oppression: With a case study on sexual harassment students define, discuss, and process the effects of a social problem.

- Structure vs Agency: Upholding the feminist mantra "the personal is political" students juxtapose individual microaggressions amidst larger structural inequalities.
- Autonomy and Activism: Although agency exists within constraints, students can become empowered to develop strategies in response to " isms" and reclaim control of their bodies.

Workshop Design and Activities: *Rompiendo el Silencio* (Ending the Silence)

Students report that they are frequently targets of harassment both in and outside school on a daily basis. Students partake in an anonymous e-poll to quantify experiences such as: touching someone's private parts, bra snapping, drawing and publicly sharing sexually explicit pictures, rubbing up against someone in a provocative way, as well as sexual jokes, rumors, name calling, and text-messages. The survey exposes an eye-opening revelation: at such an early age, bodily violence is a serious epidemic in their lives. Galvanized by the confirmation that sexual harassment is not supposed to be part of growing up, students met with the principal to develop a bilingual prevention campaign. They created and posted educational flyers with the slogan #itsneverajoke, throughout the fifth- to eighth-grade areas including at restrooms, water fountains, and hallways. If/when a flier was missing or purposefully removed, members immediately replaced it. In addition, they attended a workshop to learn basic self-defense skills.

Pedagogical Impact: Liberatory Practices

In this module students relate their personal experience to a larger pervasive systemic social problem so as to define, name, and fight against sexual harassment. As hooks reminds us, "there is a particular knowledge that comes from suffering"[27] and "not all pain is harmful"[28] Rather, if we can allow for vulnerability, a culture of resistance can be formed that makes recovering from trauma possible.[29] By witnessing, naming, respecting, and speaking to our pain, we can theorize from that location.[30] In this light, theory is a liberatory practice that invokes a process of recovery from which students testify to validate their own truths and embrace their capacity for healing as healer.

This module fosters self-actualization, thereby prompting students to take agency over their own well-being. Students take back their power by claiming ownership of their bodies and investing in their school environment. They are empowered to make deliberate choices to take control, set firm boundaries about access/closeness, and actively resist-respond to transgressions against their bodies. This lays the groundwork for understanding consent and sexual relationships in the future, as well as endows practical self-defense skills.

Module: Community Engagement and Action

This module promotes social justice work that has an impact beyond the classroom. In her vision of an "education without limits," hooks describes that "[o]ne of the joys of education as a practice of freedom is that it allows students to assume responsibility for their choices."[31] Hands-on interactive learning provides a vehicle for students to work *with* local communities and collectively develop civic responsibility. As such, the classroom becomes a dynamic place where the transformation of social relations is concretely actualized. Here the false dichotomy between the outside world and the academy disappears.[32] This notion of public learning fosters the building of relationships that facilitates dialog and engagement so as to mutually expand our communities of resistance.

College Course Themes and Learning Objectives

- Human Rights and Global Citizenship: Students establish core principles of universal rights amidst civic responsibility.
- Activism and Social Justice: Students identify and analyze social problems that affect the Latinx community to then brainstorm strategies toward social change.
- Participatory Action Service Learning: Students discuss academic themes in relation to the world around them. Applying these tenets of ethical inclusive community-based activist/advocacy work, they collectively organize and execute a social justice project that impacts their local area.
- Testimonios and Networks: Grounded in historical national trajectories of Latinx protest, students build connections with community members and local activists.

Workshop Design and Assignments

After learning about Latinx-Chicanx social movements from 1960 to 2010, students hear first-hand testimonios of local activist leaders, as well as attend college campus visits to engage with first-generation Latinx college students. Social justice values are catalyzed into action as students collectively develop a community service project. The first project raised funds for personal hygiene items at a local women's shelter. In its second installment, the "Dignity Drive," aimed to protect an uninterrupted education for young women who are without resources when they unexpectedly menstruate at school. The successful campaign purchased and donated over 425 underwear and menstruation supplies of all sizes. Now each classroom has a dignity pouch with pads on hand.

Pedagogical Impact: Action-Praxis

Active and immersive classroom experiences disrupt power and promote justice. As hooks notes, when our lived experience is theorized and linked to the processes of collective liberation, no gap exists between theory and practice.[33] After students contextualize historical examples of *la lucha* with global human rights issues, they make connections between their local problems and other organized struggles against inequalities. Collectively they take this learning beyond the classroom setting as an expression of political activism.

This participatory service-learning model promotes a praxis that has a public impact. Upholding the notion of *Levantando,* rising up, students become actively invested in collaborative social change. Giving back on their own accord, students construct mutually beneficial relationships in and outside the workshop, with their school, families, and communities. In contrast to traditional top-down curriculum, the workshop is led and done for them, by them. As hooks suggests, "[W]hen students see themselves as mutually responsible for the development of a learning community, they [can] offer constructive input [and action]."[34] As participants develop organizational leadership skills with meaningful autonomy, the *Latinx Workshop* is building the next generation of inspirational civic leaders.

Conclusion

It is worth highlighting the ongoing college-middle school connection between the original *Latinx Feminism* course and the *Latinx Workshop*. Profe Garcia and Ms. Mojica have developed a mutual relationship of care, respect, and reciprocity. Teacher and student alike, we continue to inspire and motivate each other. The *Latinx Workshop* and its participants have been incorporated into ongoing collaborations with conference presentations, course guest lectures, college campus visits, and publications. As the *Latinx Workshop* recently wrapped up its second year, its success remains unprecedented. Participants expanded the workshop throughout the summer as well as actively recruited classmates and family. Alumni seek to continue engagement, requesting to remain active as they matriculate into high school. Mothers actively endorse the program; they want their daughters to learn the strength of being Latinx, so as to equip them with the tools necessary to confront a society that questions their worth and intelligence. In such a short time, the success of the *Latinx Workshop* has proven itself beyond measure. It is a win-win pedagogical model for its members, the teachers, the school, and local community; one that we hope will inspire an ongoing investment of district and federal funds for its future continuance.

The Latinx Feminisms college course and middle school Latinx Workshop are rooted in the principles of hooks's transformational engaged pedagogy. It confirms that the classroom can be a radical space of possibility and change from which we have the opportunity to labor for freedom.[35] This project fills a dire need for Latinx students that is not met in the traditional curriculum, yet does so by "teaching in a manner that respects and cares for their souls."[36] Here, students embark on an empowering journey of self-discovery that centers upon and celebrates their identities. The workshop builds a stable foundation of dignity, confidence, pride, and resilience that enables these Latinas to become more focused and invested in their education. As hooks outlines, this critical pedagogy seeks to transform consciousness so as to provide students with ways of knowing that enable them to know themselves better and enhance their capacity to live in the world more fully.[37] Together, the *Latinx Feminisms* college course and middle school Latinx workshop, honor and celebrate the legacy of bell hooks, serving as an example of the possibilities of praxis that she continues to inspire.

Appendix

Supplementary Figures

The following images provide examples of the sessions which comprise *Latinx Workshop*. These visuals illustrate particular sessions discussed in greater detail.

Culture/Experience

The image below shows testimonio poems written by student members of *Latinx Workshop* and displayed for their Women's HERstory event, March 2024.

Figure 1 Testimonios

Body media

The image below shows the Shine Bright Like a Diamond poem template for hermana poems to be written for the *Latinx Workshop* Women's HERstory event, March 2025.

<u>**Shine Bright Like a Diamond**</u>
by _____

Line 1 write your person's first name.

Line 2 write four (4) words to describe your person,

Line 3 write Sister (or Prima/Tia if your person is an only child) of and then list your person's sister's/s' name/s, (it's okay to limit the number of cousins/nieces/nephews to 3 or 4),

Line 4 write Lover of and then three (3) things your person loves,

Line 5 write Who has and then three (3) details of their beauty,

Line 6 write Who needs and then three (3) things your person needs,

Line 7 write Who gives and then three (3) things your person gives others,

Line 8 write Who dreams and then three (3) things that your person dreams of,

Line 9 write Who would like to see and three (3) things your person wants to see,

Line 10 write Member of Latinx Workshop,

Line 11 write your person's last name.

Figure 2 Shine Bright Like a Diamond poem example for hermana poems to be written for the *Latinx Workshop* Women's HERstory event, March 2025.

The images below show the Shine Bright Like a Diamond poem example for hermana poems to be written for the *Latinx Workshop* Women's HERstory event, March 2025.

EXAMPLE   EXAMPLE   EXAMPLE

Shine Bright Like a Diamond
By Mrs. Mojica

Maria Guadalupe.

Loving, Hard-working, Orgullosa, Resilient,

Hermana de Carmen, Maria, Miguel, Manuel, y Jose Luis,

Lover of laughing with amigas, beautiful summer flowers, and pajaritos que cantan,

Who has thick curly dark hair, gorgeous bronzed skin, and a cute round nose,

Who needs care, amor, and respect,

Who gives friendly smiles, kind words, and a shoulder to cry on,

Who dreams of going away to college, traveling, y ser mujer independiente,

Who would like to see the ocean, the Northern Lights, and a sunset in Paris,

A member of Latinx Workshop,

Gallardo.

Figure 3 Shine Bright Like a Diamond poem example for hermana poems to be written for the *Latinx Workshop* Women's HERstory event, March 2025.

Violence

The images below show flyers *Latinx Workshop* made and put up at our middle school to call out sexual harassment. The flyers were written in English and Spanish with QR codes explaining the difference between flirting and sexual harassment.

Figure 4 A flyer made by *Latinx Workshop* and put up at our middle school to call out sexual harassment. Each flyer was written in English and Spanish with QR codes explaining the difference between flirting and sexual harassment.

Figure 5 A flyer made by *Latinx Workshop* and put up at our middle school to call out sexual harassment. Each flyer was written in English and Spanish with QR codes explaining the difference between flirting and sexual harassment.

Notes

1   bell hooks, *Teaching to Transgress: Education as the Practice of Freedom* (New York: Routledge, 1994), 40.
2   Ibid., 39–40.
3   Ibid., 81.
4   Ibid., 35.
5   Freire describes conscientization as the process of moving away from passively received understandings of self toward developing a critical awareness of one's social reality through reflection and action; Paulo Freire, *Pedagogy of the Oppressed* (New York: Continuum, 2010).
6   hooks, *Teaching to Transgress,* 202.
7   Ibid., 70, 88.
8   This class, cross-listed with the Latina/o Studies and Gender-Sexuality Studies Programs, was a combined upper-level undergraduate-graduate course.
9   Gloria Anzaldua, *Borderlands La Frontera, the New Mestiza* (San Francisco, CA: Aunt Lute Books, 1985).
10 While foreign-born persons comprise 11.9 percent of the city's population, the Latinx population comprises 18.6 percent of East Moline (2020 Census). For the past forty years, meat processing plants such as Tyson and Farmland located in nearby Joslin and Monmouth, Illinois have attracted immigrants to the area.
11 Ms. Mojica secured funding from the school's Diversity Office and the "Lights on for Learning" federal grant.
12 In its second installment the program met bimonthly.
13 hooks, *Teaching to Transgress,* 144–5.
14 Ibid., 15, 20.
15 Ibid., 89.
16 Ibid., 30.
17 Ibid., 185–6.
18 Ibid., 173.
19 Ibid., 139.
20 Ibid., 138, 198.
21 The concept of *blanqueamiento* refers to the ideology and practice of ethnic, cultural, and racial "whitening" in Latin America and the Caribbean. It is a system of beliefs that places socioeconomic advancement and success in relation to racial "development," such that "whitening" as an adaptive strategy, physically or culturally, is emphasized as a precursor for upward mobility; Alyssa Garcia, "Blanqueamiento," in *The Oxford Encyclopedia of Latinos and Latinas in the United States,* eds. Suzanne Oboler and Deena J. González (Oxford: Oxford University Press, 2005), 143.

22 "Tell me that I am lucky to be lighter skinned, not black black, not dark brown, lucky to have hair that is almost straight, otherwise I might not be in the wedding at all." In her childhood memoir hooks discusses her experiences with colorism and the ways in which light-skinned Black women are societally favored in comparison to those with dark-skin; bell hooks, *Bone Black: Memories of Girlhood* (New York: Henry Holt, 1997), 9.

23 hooks, *Teaching to Transgress*, 59, 175.

24 Ibid., 155.

25 Ibid., 12.

26 Ibid., 67–9.

27 Ibid., 91.

28 Ibid., 154.

29 Ibid., 21, 170.

30 Ibid., 43, 74–5.

31 Ibid., 19.

32 Ibid., 195.

33 Ibid., 61.

34 Ibid., 206.

35 Ibid., 207.

36 Ibid., 13.

37 Ibid., 194.

20

Community Writing Programs as Communities of Resistance

Charles McMartin, Nicole Crevar, Maxwell Irving, and Charisse Iglesias

For me this space of radical openness is a margin—a profound edge. Locating oneself there is difficult yet necessary. It is not a "safe" place. One is always at risk. One needs a community of resistance.[1]

—bell hooks

While working together in a community writing program in Tucson, Arizona, we—Charlie, Nicole, Maxwell, and Charisse—have drawn inspiration from bell hooks's conception of communities of resistance. Our program, Wildcat Writers, is a community of high school and college writing teachers and students dedicated to cultivating creative and critical literacies through impactful community-based writing projects. We collaborate with low-income and predominantly Latinx high schools in Tucson and build relationships across educational divides to create social-justice-oriented collaborative projects[2] related to pressing social issues facing our students and their communities. Despite our community-focused mission, we are funded through the University of Arizona's English Department and constantly have to balance articulating the value of our work to the university while staying true to our mission as a social justice-focused program.

hooks's conception of communities of resistance has helped us navigate existing on the margins of two educational contexts that are motivated by corporatized measures of success—standardized test scores for high schools and national rankings for the university. While we engage our students and ourselves in the cultural and linguistic lifeways that help us feel connected and hopeful and build on the assets we already possess to address the intersecting issues facing us and our communities, our institutions reinscribe white supremacist capitalist patriarchy.

Our schools in Arizona are at the center of the expansive legislative attacks on critical race theory (CRT) and diversity, equity, and inclusion (DEI) programs. Our superintendent of schools, Tom Horne, who famously used fear-mongering tactics to ban ethnic studies in Arizona in 2010,[3] was reelected in 2022 by promising to ban CRT in public schools. He also promised to investigate any Arizona educators suspected of teaching CRT concepts saying he would set up a "hotline" where any teacher, parent, administrator, or student could call the Arizona Department of Education and report the use of what they perceived as CRT.[4] These scare tactics have left teachers in a similar situation as election officials who have been abused and assaulted for working in democratic institutions. Like those election officials, many teachers in Arizona are leaving their jobs.[5]

For those of us who see education as a practice of liberation, the current demonization of teachers and curricula that redress the intersection of oppressive systems facing us and our students is not new. Our institutions have always been instruments of "estrangement, alienation, and worse assimilation."[6] Indeed, our work has always been and will continue to be pushed to the margins. However, hooks reminds us that our "marginality is much more than a site of deprivation [...] it is also the site of radical possibility, a space of resistance."[7]

We follow hooks's lead by making a "distinction between that marginality which is imposed by oppressive structures and that marginality one chooses as a site of resistance—as a location of radical openness and possibility."[8] Rather than conceiving of our space based on our lack of resources and support, we see it as a space where "we are transformed, individually, collectively, as we make radical creative space which affirms and sustains our subjectivity, which gives us a new location from which to articulate our sense of the world."[9] According to hooks, communities of resistance create a space where marginalized people can claim their agency in the margin, join with others who share in their suffering, and work in community to transform the contexts that oppress them. For example, as high school teachers and Ph.D. students collaborating in community spaces at the margins of our institutions, we have claimed these spaces as sites of collective empowerment and radical possibility, developing measures of success rooted in community needs rather than neoliberal markers like test scores or enrollment numbers.

We embrace the margins as a space to maintain the agency and openness necessary to build a community of resistance committed to social justice and liberatory education. In cultivating this community, we established our own networks and influence,[10] operating independently from the university and public school district. While integrating into these institutions might provide greater credibility and funding, it would also risk complicity with white supremacist, capitalist, patriarchal policies and values. Instead, we remain on the margins, defining success through our community's needs. This commitment is exemplified by our advisory board, which includes experienced high school teachers, graduate students, and non-tenure-track faculty who have helped cultivate the Wildcat Writers program. Together, we focus on centering our values of liberatory education as we build curricula, lead service learning projects, and evaluate our community writing program.

In order to represent each of our intersectional experiences and the ways we grew together as a community, we have adopted a polyvocal narrative approach.[11] Polyvocal strategies provided us with a "creative alternative strategy of textual production" that has helped us organize our voices so that they can be "analyzed simultaneously or separately."[12] Specifically, we emphasize the ways that our polyvocal reflections complicate our positionalities as we moved between our educational contexts and developed personal relationships. We hope our narratives show how sharing experiences across contexts helps not only build stronger support systems for liberatory educators, but also creates powerful coalitions that critically reflect on lived experiences, theorize the systemic problems facing educators, and provide hope for collective liberation.

Charlie's Sense of Belonging

After teaching high school English for four years in a district obsessed with test scores and unwilling to adopt curricula that reflected the experiences of its predominantly working-class Mexican American students, I returned to graduate school. Wildcat Writers was the first place where people understood my values as a critical educator working to connect my curriculum to the lived realities of students. Charisse and Nicole were the graduate coordinators of the program at the time, and we immediately connected over our shared commitment to enacting social justice with our teaching. During our walks along the Rillito River and dozens of conversations at coffee shops, I felt known and loved. hooks explains that we come to spaces on the margin through shared suffering and that we collectively claim those spaces for ourselves as a place of radical creativity and belonging. For me, these spaces begin with feeling known and loved. Known in that we share all of ourselves—the difficult, complicated, contradictory, as well as the passionate and put-together—and try to understand all that we can about others in our community. Loved in that we care for each other in transformative ways that help us become more self-actualized versions of ourselves. That is what I have experienced building relationships with Charisse, Nicole, and Maxwell in Wildcat Writers.

Nicole, Maxwell, and Charisse's stories and their teaching illustrate the vital role of liberatory pedagogies and reciprocal learning for those of us aiming to work beyond our institutional constraints. Nicole's story about the impact of collaborative teaching among educators committed to social justice has acted as a model for my collaborations in Wildcat Writers. Maxwell's commitment to prioritizing the development of student identity over placating the neoliberal measures of success used in our schools inspires me to continually reevaluate how I measure the success of my teaching. Charisse's dedication to centering the voices of community stakeholders in her research has helped me redefine what success should look like in the academy. These stories have sustained me by offering models of courage, creativity, and care that remind me to hold onto my liberatory values, even in the face of institutional pressures, and by showing me that transformative change is possible when we prioritize relationships, community, and justice. Our community of resistance has cultivated my hope that dominant ideologies can be dismantled and that our curriculums can center the experiences and histories of our students and their communities.

Nicole's Sense of Growth

When I joined Wildcat Writers in 2018, I was a new educator and hoped to learn as much as possible from an experienced high school teacher partner. Although I aspired to inform my pedagogy with a social justice framework, I lacked classroom experience and, quite frankly, confidence. Wildcat Writers became one of the most transformational experiences of my educational career due to its inherent emphasis on reciprocal learning for both teachers and students. This core aspect of reciprocity, I believe, is what helps many of us achieve a sense of community and belonging, as Charlie details in his narrative, which then empowers us to *resist* the institutional structures that limit our students' learning and engagement with the world.

Reciprocal learning, at its core, is a form of what bell hooks terms *engaged pedagogy*—or, a form of pedagogy that emphasizes well-being, self-actualization, active student participation, and consciousness-raising. In Wildcat Writers, reciprocal learning entails educators co-creating curricula and student activities (see Appendix A), meeting to debrief and reflect on how those activities went, and, most importantly, involving students in the process of their own learning!

That first year, my partner and I navigated our respective institution's course requirements to co-design our courses. Because of Wildcat Writers, we felt we had the support to push back against standard curriculum frameworks, including the expected adherence to AP Exam preparation for my colleague's AP English Literature class and the University's expectation to teach an Annotated Bibliography as part of my college writing course. While we strongly believed in the importance of preparing students for college-level writing and research, we wanted to engage them in more holistic learning that combined lived experience with critical thinking. This approach stands in stark contrast to our institutions' current emphasis on quantitative learning outcomes, which Maxwell critically challenges in his narrative. Therefore, we employed the type of culturally responsive practices that Charisse outlines to design a project that prompted students to make connections between the social issues in an AP-required reading, Shakespeare's *Othello,* and real-world social issues in our local community (see Appendix A). Working collaboratively, the student partners found immigration, citizenship, and racism to be the core social issues present in both Shakespeare's play and our contemporary social context. This project engaged students in active participation and reciprocal learning, as each student brought knowledge to the table—the college students shared their research findings while the high school students shared their community's lived experiences relating to the social issue.

To foster a successful partnership for our students, my partner and I emulated a positive partnership experience—one based on respect and openness to collaboration—by sharing with our students the benefits and challenges that we faced as educators while designing the project. Being open and honest with students and bringing our whole selves into the classroom resulted in our students feeling more empowered and excited to learn from each other, which strengthened my confidence in the classroom.

Maxwell's Sense of Agency

Where Nicole explains her growth through her first partnership, I discuss my growth over many years working with my university partner, Charisse.

Although Charisse and I have worked with thousands of students, it has largely gone unnoticed in our community. A focus on quantitative goals and data, as if academics were the same as economics, has entrenched an increasingly neoliberal political ideology in the spaces we work in. We experience further angst as we risk not complying with these ideologies because we prioritize cultural relevance and responsiveness in our classrooms, building common identity, community, and dialog.

Charisse and I crafted courses focused on the facilitation of students' identity formation. Charisse used concepts in visual rhetoric to teach students about composing narrative comics that reflected their progress as writers. Part and parcel to this was the creation of iconographies, pictorial representations of identity, and subjective experience that were cartooned to communicate and appeal to a near-universal audience. Charisse's approach to teaching comics changed how I taught literacy narratives in my Mythology course. Instead of essays about their experiences as readers and writers, I asked students to craft multimodal narratives about any part of their identity. Engaging students in a manner that activates, excites, and endeavors toward helping them realize a positive self-concept in their critical period of identity formation is to transgress the political and institutional boundaries that typically govern and depersonalize academic spaces.

Charisse's Sense of Responsibility

I am a community-engaged researcher who left academia because of the lack of professional and compensated support to build programs like Wildcat Writers, programs that bridge the gap between intensive research institutions and their neighboring communities. As Charlie noted in his narrative, community writing has always lived on the margins. One of my academic colleague's department chair considered publications co-written with community partners as only half a publication, even though emotional and intellectual labor and cultural humility are required for meaningful community partnerships. Community-based research is devalued by the capitalist, white, supremacist university system that operates to suppress research that goes against the status quo, to control the flow of knowledge, gatekeep information, and devalue the contributions of nonacademic practitioners.

Despite this perception and ongoing systemic struggles, I continue to pursue these partnerships because community-based research results in culturally responsive research design, data, and interventions—the creative process that aligns with Nicole's narrative on reciprocal co-learning. Working alongside community partners allows me to understand their lived experiences and unique expertise on what goes on in their communities so I can better frame how I conduct research. I do not want to become a researcher who works with marginalized communities but does not protect the lived experiences, traditions, and (un)intentional data misinterpretation of those communities. Black, Latinx, and Indigenous communities, for example, have faced unrelenting racism from researchers and institutions that have caused the historical mistrust toward life-saving interventions. Valuing and authentically interpreting data that communities consensually provide to researchers should be honored to maintain trust within the community-academic relationship. Trust building is an ongoing process—a process that I still practice with my Wildcat Writers partner, Maxwell—that attempts to ensure collected data are accurate so that researchers can conduct studies that authentically speak to the needs of those community contributors.

Inspiring Communities of Resistance
(Charlie, Nicole, Maxwell, Charisse)

Many people who work with Wildcat Writers move on from the program, but they still carry its heart and values with them to their new contexts. As they shift, our space on the margin shifts with them. Wildcat Writers continues to provide a sense of belonging for our community within and beyond Tucson. Some former participants have sought to recreate Wildcat Writers in their new contexts. For example, Kate Street and Barb McDonald used their experiences with Wildcat Writers to create the Parallel Learners Program at Sunnyside High School in Tucson, a program that partners students with disabilities and students without disabilities. Rachael Shah used her leadership practices as graduate coordinator of Wildcat Writers to begin Husker Writers at the University of Nebraska. Rosanne Carlo took her transformative experience with Wildcat Writers and replicated its mission and values with SI Writes, a community writing partnership at The College of Staten Island CUNY. Brad Jacobsen continues to build relationships with high school teachers in El Paso to establish a community writing program at the University of Texas at El Paso. Adele Leon has furthered her leadership expertise and commitment to community writing by founding the SoFlo Writing Project at Nova Southeastern University, which supports southern

Florida educators by providing professional development opportunities and pedagogical resources. In this way, our community of resistance has inspired other communities of resistance. After experiencing the sense of freedom, openness, and possibility that come from creating these action-oriented and grassroots communities, we can continue to combat the white supremacist, capitalist, patriarchal forces that govern our educational institutions.

Appendix A: Crevar's Examples of Co-Created Curricula and Student Activities

English 102 (Wildcat Writers): Assignment Arc

Class Theme: Othello, Elizabethan to Contemporary Arizona Issues (Critical Thinking, Collaboration, and Community Building)

Assignment 1: Historical Analysis Essay, due Week 4

This first assignment will be a historical analysis essay pertaining to social and political issues that occurred during the Elizabethan Era. This essay will be in response to guided readings and class discussions surrounding this topic, with an underlying lens for students to grasp if any of these issues are still relevant today. The paper will be short, about 2–3 pages in length.

Assignment 2: Contemporary Issues Research Paper, due Week 12

This second, larger assignment will be a 6–8 page research paper in which students will select one of the sociopolitical issues raised in *Othello* and apply it to contemporary, local (Arizona) issues. The research will include articles and scientific reports or data published within the last five years relating to their chosen issue (e.g., citizenship). The students will be partnered with one or two WW high school students and they will select the same issue to report on. This assignment will be research-heavy and will engage students to think critically about how issues that occurred in Elizabethan England are still relevant today (and therefore, how Shakespeare is still a relevant text to study).

Assignment 3: WW Multimedia Project and Presentation, due Week 15

This final assignment will be a collaborative multimedia project between the UA student and high school student. Both students will have selected the same issue to research (although their findings, arguments, and research may differ).

Students will meet together (f2f) and collaborate digitally to create a multimedia presentation of their findings. Their presentations will involve deeper critical thinking in that they will be expected to propose potential solutions to these issues in contemporary times.

Assignment 3: WW Multimedia Project & Presentation

100 points

(25% of Course Grade)

Theme

Reflecting on A1 and A2 Essays and WW Partnership

Assignment Prompt

Task Description

Through this assignment, you will work with your WW partner to create a multimodal (multimedia) presentation that reflects on the findings of your Assignments 1 and 2, Historical Analysis Essay and Contemporary Issues Research Paper. Through your presentation, you must (a) review the topic and findings of your papers, (b) explain how your contemporary issue and findings relate to Elizabethan England and *Othello*, (c) propose a potential solution to your researched issue, and (d) reflect on your experience with the Wildcat Writers Program. The goal is to engage in critical thinking and to form connections between historical issues (relating to our conversation of Elizabethan England and *Othello*) and contemporary issues. This project will allow you to engage with different modes of "writing" and creating content through a variety of technologies. CREATIVITY is highly encouraged!

Requirements

Your project should

- have a creative title
- clearly articulate your contemporary issue and research findings
- include a minimum of three images or graphics (unless doing a video)
- include a References (APA) or Works Cited (MLA) page listing all sources cited in your presentation

Possible Technology Options

- PowerPoint
- Prezi
- YouTube
- Google Slides
- iMovie (can upload to YouTube)

Course Objectives

After completing this project, and its associated course module, you will have made progress toward the following student learning outcomes (SLOs) for ENGL 102:

1 E. respond to a variety of writing contexts calling for purposeful shifts in structure, medium, design, level of formality, tone, and/or voice.
2 A. employ a variety of research methods, including primary and/or secondary research, for purposes of inquiry.
3 2B. evaluate the quality, appropriateness, and credibility of sources.
4 D. synthesize research findings in development of an argument.
5 D. identify the collaborative and social aspects of writing processes.
6 F. reflect on their progress as academic writers.
7 B. reflect on why genre conventions for structure, paragraphing, tone, and mechanics vary.
8 4C. identify and effectively use variations in genre conventions, including formats or design features.
9 4D. demonstrate familiarity with the concepts of intellectual property (such as fair use and copyright) that motivate documentation conventions.

Student Activity: Wildcat Writers Bios

Prompt

Write a detailed personal bio for us to best match you with a Wildcat Writers partner. Please upload your bio as an MS Word document OR as a shared Google Docs link to the course assignment dropbox titled "Wildcat Writers Bios."

Please include the following in your bios:

1   Introduce yourself. Be very detailed. You want your partner to understand your background and culture. Include information about where you were born and where you grew up. Is your family from here? If not, where do they come from? What is your cultural heritage?

2   What are your qualities as a student? Think about what makes you unique from others.

3   What are your interests and hobbies? Be detailed and specific.

4   What are your goals for the future? Why are those your goals? How will you attain them?

5   Last, what do you expect to get out of this program? Why?

Notes

1   bell hooks, "Choosing the Margin as a Space of Radical Openness," *Framework* 36, no. 36 (1989): 19.

2   See Charisse Iglesias and Maxwell Irving, "Composing Reciprocity with Comics: Composing the Labor in Community-University Partnerships," *The Journal of Multimodal Rhetorics* 5, no. 1 (2021): 3–17; Jacqueline Gale, Charles McMartin, Blake Karpan, Aryaman Mehra, Sebastian Loera, and Jade Lopez, "Reimagining Student and Teacher Engagement through Community Writing," *Arizona English Journal* 54, no. 1 (2024): 3–17; and Rachael Shah, *Rewriting Partnerships: Community Perspective on Community-based Learning* (Denver, CO: University Press of Colorado, 2020).

3   Jeff Muskus, "Arizona Ethnic Studies Classes Banned, Teachers with Accents Can No Longer Teach English," *Huffington Post*, 2010, https://www.huffpost.com/entry/arizona-ethnic-studies-cl_n_558731.

4   Eddie Sun, "Arizona Launches Hotline for Public to Report 'Inappropriate' School Lessons," CNN, 2023, https://www.cnn.com/2023/03/11/politics/arizona-critical-race-theory-department-of-education-tom-horne/index.html.

5   Justin Wing and Suan Lugo, "Arizona's Severe Teacher Shortage Continues, ASPAA Survey Shows," *AZEDNews*, February 28, 2022, https://azednews.com/arizonas-severe-teacher-shortage-continues-aspaa-survey-shows/.

6   hooks, "Choosing the Margin," 21.

7   Ibid., 20.

8   Ibid., 23.

9   Ibid., 23.

10 On the importance of community advisory boards, see Brad Jacobson and Rachael
    Shah, "Building Our Ideals into Program Structures: Democratic Design in
    Program Administration," *Composition Studies* 51, no. 2 (2023): 86–194.

11 Viola Thimm, Mayurakshi Chaudhuri and Sarah J. Mahler, "Enhancing
    Intersectional Analyses with Polyvocality: Making and Illustrating the Model,"
    Social Sciences (Basel) 6, no. 2 (2017): 37.

12 Ibid., 7.

Index

www.ingramcontent.com/pod-product-compliance
Lightning Source LLC
Chambersburg PA
CBHW061718270326
41928CB00011B/2030